THE ART OF ENCHANTMENT
A LIFE IS A JOURNEY NOVEL

MARYANN CLARKE

ALL RIGHTS RESERVED. No part of this publication may be reproduced, distributed, or transmitted in any form or by any means, including photocopying, recording, or other electronic or mechanical methods, without the prior permission of the publisher.

Copyright © 2017 by: Mary Ann F Clarke Scott

ISBN: 978-0-9949507-7-2

This is a work of fiction. Any resemblance of characters to actual persons, living or dead, is purely coincidental. MaryAnn Clarke Scott holds exclusive rights to this work. Unauthorized duplication is prohibited.

WANT TO READ THE FIRST BOOK IN THE HAVING IT ALL SERIES?
BUY ON AMAZON ASIN: B01KP7IMUC
WANT TO CONNECT WITH ME?
www.maryannclarkescott.com
maryann@maryannclarkescott.com

If you enjoy reading this book, please rate it and leave a review on Amazon HERE. Your opinion can make or break an author's success, and it means the world to me. Click here to leave a review: https://www.amazon.com/review/create-review/ref= cm_cr_dp_d_wr_but_top?ie=UTF8&channel=glance-detail&asin=B06XFX4B7C

For John,

My romantic hero, also an architect, though not exactly a swashbuckling, motorcycle-riding one like Guillermo.
Thank you for your steadfast love and support, for believing in me the writer, and for indulging my desire for travel, especially to Italy, where we both can get our fill of art and architecture.

"Follow your bliss and the universe will open doors where there were only walls."

Joseph Campbell

"Now a soft kiss - Aye, by that kiss, I vow an endless bliss."

John Keats

CHAPTER 1

R eligion. Rebellion. Sex. It had the makings of a best-seller. Clio hummed and danced her fingers on the steering wheel of her new Fiat 500 as she zoomed along *Strada Provinciale* 88. Everything in her dreary, fettered life was about to change.

A line of twisted cypress trees stood at attention along the crest of a nearby ridge. Like the statues of her beloved Italian saints, they kept watch over the neatly mown fields that rolled down the slope toward her. Maybe they were watching over her, too.

Clio was tortured by doubts that her ideas would gel in time for the critical meeting tonight, at which she must, she *must*, persuade Dr. Jovi that she was ready. If she failed, he would refuse to extend her deadline in the morning - again. If he did that, she would find herself cut loose, without an advisor, without an office or a sponsor, without a Ph.D., and forever without the approval of her patient but demanding academic parents.

Some people would be critical of Clio's need, at twenty-seven years of age, to please her mother and father. Those people had never met her parents.

She was out of time.

Until she'd seen the little statue of Saint Clare of the Cross at the Franciscan Monastery this afternoon, Clio despaired of ever having the clarity of vision to complete her thesis. Oh - she'd come up with a half-baked theory that had sustained her research for the past three years. But Saint Clare had convinced her that she really was onto something, and that would give her the passion and drive to write her final dissertation. Passion. Ecstasy. Bliss.

She laughed out loud. How ironic. She needed passion to complete her thesis about passion.

Long shadows snaked across the green hillside as the early evening sun dipped lower in the Tuscan sky. She would be back in the city within the hour, and still have time to freshen up and go over her notes and sketches before her eight o'clock dinner appointment with Dr. Jovi.

Nevertheless, Clio pressed a little harder on the gas pedal, and leaned into a long curve in the road, thrilled at how smooth and responsive her new car was to her command. The gift from Father was clearly meant as an incentive, and she would make sure he received her long overdue thanks - in the form of graduation, at long last.

Then, free from his prescriptions for her education and her career, she could finally decide how she wanted to live her life.

A pair of headlights flashed over the rise in the dimming light up ahead, and Clio slowed a little, prepared to pass another vehicle on the narrow winding road. The other car took shape suddenly in the gloom, larger than hers. Waves of loud music rolled toward her, punctuated by sharp shouts and laughter. Her pulse kicked. They weren't slowing or pulling to the side, the maniacs. Some young idiots, probably drinking.

Clio gripped the steering wheel tighter, and seconds later they were upon her, hogging the centre of the road. There was no room.

She veered sharply to the right as the car hurtled past with inches to spare. Violent grinding and metallic screeching ripped the air as her wheels slammed into the low barrier at the side of the road. The steering wheel tore from her grip. Her car was hurled up like a stone from a catapult.

Everything blurred. Light and dark flashed. The seatbelt jerked her hard against the seat. Air whooshed from her lungs. Squeals. Crunches. Thuds. The world quaked. Sharp pain shot through her head. Dark and silence enveloped her. Music and shouts echoed in her head, a sickening counterpoint to the terrible drumbeat of her heart.

∼

Guillermo didn't mind riding out to Pia's farm for the weekend, though he was certain he'd have more fun if he'd stayed in Florence and taken Teresa or Patrizia out for wining and dining, followed by a little after-dark gymnastics. Or Teresa *and* Patrizia. Now there was a thought that warmed him. He shimmied on his seat to adjust his suddenly tight bike leathers, the powerful engine of his Ducati Multistrada vibrating between his legs.

A dark car whizzed past him on the empty road, nearly knocking him over with the sheer turbulence of its draft, loud music blaring. *Faccia di merda.*

He was positive he'd have more fun if he were at liberty to ride for the sheer joy of it, with no destination. There was nothing he loved more than a fast ride on his bike through the rolling Tuscan countryside, or failing that, in his Alpha Romeo convertible, the wind in his face, his blood thrumming. Nothing made him feel more free and alive.

But duty called. Bianca was uncharacteristically hysterical when she'd called this afternoon, and he was genuinely concerned about his little sister. She was also nearly incoherent, sobbing and ranting something about their eldest brother Jacopo. His calls to Jacopo went unanswered, not surprisingly, since his big-shot politician of a brother was always in a meeting or press conference.

A phone call to his older sister Pia for answers resulted only in an invitation to join her and Paulo for the weekend. She'd been evasive, and said she'd explain when he arrived. And so he'd dropped everything and raced out of the city after work.

For as much as he loved freedom and speed and good times, he loved his family more. And though the knowledge often felt like a heavy yoke around his neck, he knew he'd do anything for them, even if it killed him.

CHAPTER 2

Clio awoke to her own moaning. Her head throbbed with pain. She cracked opened her eyes. Slowly her surroundings took shape. She swiveled her head around, and it swayed on her neck. *Oh, so dizzy.* Dark green light outside, as though she were in a dense jungle. Her head was so heavy. Above her, the collapsing air bags hung from the steering wheel and dash, her hands flopped over her head. What? Why–?

She was upside down, still strapped into her seat, hanging at an awkward angle. The whole car was flipped over. She must have blacked out. It was murky dark. Her head hurt like hell, but that was all she could feel at the moment. Panic surged through her. *I have to get out.*

The front windshield was cracked, glinting blue shards. She groped for her seatbelt, grabbed it like a sling, and popped the latch.

Flailing, she collapsed in a twisted pile on the canvas roof. It bowed like a hammock under her. Sharp pain. Cold water soaked through her clothing. She shuddered. Ominously, displaced water seeped through the smashed windshield.

She scrambled upright and shouldered one door, then the

other. Crumpled and wedged tightly against the edges of the ditch, they wouldn't budge. She was trapped. Her pulse tripled. Out, she had to get out.

Beyond the cracked windshield, dense thick-bladed grasses pressed against the car. Or rushes.

Think, think. She sat back and swallowed thickly. She'd have to go down to get out. A small tear gave her a start. She jabbed two fingers through, gripped the loose flap. Pulled. *Rrriippp.* A larger fistful of canvas. She yanked again. *Rrriippp.* And again. More water, and mud, and rushes poked up and bent over, dense as a rug beneath her. Icy water seeped over the edges of the hole. The blades were thick and sharp as knives. *I have to get through there.*

When there was a hole big enough to fit through, she lowered one foot into the tangled wet mess, shivering. Below the roof, her foot sunk knee deep into water and mud. It sucked at her sandal. She crouched down, lay on her stomach, shivering, and poked her head outside, under the car roof. *Oh, my God!* It was tight. And dark. She'd drown in a foot of water. If she lay flat, she could pull herself out on the surface of the rushes, and avoid sinking. Not far. Just past the trunk. *Please, please, please let me get through without getting stuck.*

She gripped handfuls of rushes and pulled herself forward, inch by inch, pressing her face against her sleeve, praying she didn't sink. The rushes sliced her hands, but she gritted her teeth against the pain. *Keep going.* Hand over hand. She squeezed under the car, just barely, on the flattened bed of rushes and mud. The roof scraped her back. Rushes scratched at her arms and legs, and the cold water soaked through to her skin. She had to go on.

~

Guillermo was getting close now. No more than another kilometer to Villa Cittadini. *I wonder what Pia and Anna have conjured for dinner?*

As he crested a rise, a dark shape loomed in the shadows of the drainage ditch up ahead. A flash of red. And something moving. What the hell?

What is that?

He pulled back on the gas as he neared. *Stronzo!* A Fiat was overturned in the ditch, having rolled over the low metal barrier and wedged in against an earth berm, bridging the gap. Someone crawled among waist high rushes in the ditch, then stood and flagged him down.

He decelerated and pulled to the side of the road to see if he could help.

Her pulse raced every inch of the way, but in moments she felt the space open up, and the rounded edge of the metal car frame curve away above her head and shoulders. Lifting her head, she opened her eyes, and sucked in a lung full of air. *I made it.* Slipping back, water and mud rushed into her mouth. "Agh!" Gasping, spitting, coughing, she yanked once more and pushed up, free of the dense rushes. Parting the blades with her hands, she shimmied out and placed her feet down, awkwardly tottering to a standing position on the rough squishy surface.

Her feet sank into the mud and water between the rushes, but she was free. She was alive and free. Her chest swelled with relief.

Just then she saw a light flash and arc overhead. She glanced up. It was nearly dark now. A headlight up ahead, approaching. Clio waved her arms over her head and shouted. "Stop! Oh please stop!" Whoever it was, was already slowing. Thank God. She was saved.

A motorcycle roared to the margin of the road and stopped. The engine quit and the headlight went out. Then it came back on again. Beyond the bright, blinding light, the dark silhouette of the rider strode toward her.

"*Stai bene?*" A deep rumble as he cleared his throat, and spoke with a deep voice.

"Em. I...um." A man in motorcycle leathers stood on the edge of the pavement, his helmet held casually in one hand. Her heart kicked against her ribs. *Thank God someone's here.*

"*Scusami? Signiora? Sei tu ferita?*" His face was shadowed.

She took a mental inventory of her body. "N-no. I don't think so. Nothing serious."

A tremor shook her from head to toe, as much from shock as from the cold wet that had begun to seep into her flesh. It was a miracle she had got out alive. Her heart kicked again, an echo of the terror she felt those first few terrible seconds when time stopped and she flew through the air.

"Ah. You are English-a? You are okay?" He spoke in strongly accented English.

Clio stared at him. "I understood. I speak Italian," she answered in Italian. He stood aggressively, feet apart, and she cringed inwardly. He wasn't exactly the rescuer she had imagined. But at least he was someone who could help her. If she didn't get out of here soon she'd get hypothermia standing here all night in wet clothes. She moved to climb out of the ditch, but her feet wouldn't budge. She'd sunk into the soupy mud like wet cement.

"Ah, *bene*. What happened here? You lose control?"

She shook her head. "Some bastards drove me off the road. I swerved to avoid a head-on and flipped over the barrier. As you see." She gazed at what remained of her new car. Father would kill her. Shit.

"*Si.* Drunks?" He nodded.

"Maybe. Probably. They were shouting and driving very fast. With loud music."

Again she tugged on one leg, and then the other with more force. But they wouldn't move. She tried to wiggle her ankles, but more of the icy water and muck seeped in between the soles of her bare feet and her sandals. Even if she could inch her legs out, the sandals were never coming.

Now what?

"Tsk." He scraped a hand over his shadowed jaw, mumbling curses. *"Figli di puttana."*

"Yes. That's exactly what I thought."

What a disaster. Her field trip to the little chapel at the Franciscan Monastery seemed like ages ago, rather than just the couple of traumatic hours that had passed, the blissful expression on the face of the statue of Saint Clare of the Cross a fading memory. Saint Clare! Panic rose within her as the setting sun flared. Dr. Jovi would be so angry— he would give up on her. She had to call him right away. But her phone was…gone.

"Have you got a cell phone?"

~

Oh, *merda*. He forgot she could understand him. She spoke very good Italian, for an Englishwoman. No, not English. Wrong accent. American, perhaps.

Guillermo gazed at the wrecked Fiat. No way that was going anywhere. He pulled out his cellular and dialed the emergency number.

"Can I use your cell phone? *Per favor?*" She gazed at him, two large bright eyes peering out from her muddy face.

"I've got it." He held up a hand while he waited to be put through and looked her over. A wet lump. Her hair hung like a brown, mud-caked club down her back. Her face was mud-splattered. Not an attractive sight. But her wet summer clothing clung to her, making it perfectly clear she *was* female, though she seemed oblivious to the transparency of her shirt, or she would be screening the sight from his curious eyes instead of clasping herself across the middle, trembling. Hardened nipples pressed against wet cotton. His groin tightened in reflex. *Stupido. Pazzo.* Turn it off once in a while! Only the failing light saved her from indecency. Not the time to be noticing. Instead, he saw that she shivered, from shock or cold, or both.

"*Emergenza.*"

"No, no," she protested.

What? Was she crazy?

"*C'è un'auto in un fosso sulla Strada Provinciale 88.*"

At last. Guillermo gave their approximate location and explained what happened, requesting assistance.

"*It will be an hour, minimum, to send a car. The tow truck will take even longer.*"

Guillermo ground his teeth. An hour! He didn't have time for this, but he couldn't very well leave the poor woman stranded. She hunched, shivering and wringing her hands. "A tow truck won't do it. It'll need a flatbed with a crane," he said.

"Never mind the car," she moaned, and Guillermo scowled at her in confusion.

"*Oh. Like that,*" the dispatcher continued. "*Hmm. Perhaps it could stay until tomorrow? The driver, eh...could you help...?*"

Guillermo sucked air, pushing back his sleeve to check the time. He was late already. Pia would hold dinner, but she'd fret whether he called or not. "I will take her with me and keep her comfortable. The car is totaled, I'm certain. I'll be nearby, at a farm, at Villa Cittadini, if you want to call for details."

The dispatcher agreed, and he left his cellular number. Wonderful. Wonderful. The wet, dirty woman was now Guillermo's responsibility, convenient or not.

"*Bene.* Let's go. I'll take you somewhere warm."

"That's very kind, but I can't damned well move!"

"What?"

"I'm stuck... in the mud."

He groaned. This misadventure would ruin his bike leathers and his evening, but she was helpless. "Give me your hands."

She lifted her filthy hands, and he cringed inwardly, reaching for them. Her fingers were long and thin, but sturdy. He gripped tightly and pulled, and she promptly fell to her knees with a wail of despair.

"Eh. Sorry. You really are stuck."

"You think I'm joking?" Her cross voice was muffled, face down as she was. He felt a surge of angry irritation flame through him. Then he realized she had, in fact, crawled out of the wreck through the ditch after a terrible trauma. Not so passive. In fact he felt a flash of admiration that she was still standing.

He stepped tentatively down the side of the ditch, careful to stand on the solid banks to avoid sinking into the mud. He shrugged off his leather jacket and, wincing, draped it over her shivering shoulders. Hooking one arm under hers and wrapping it around her ribs, he hauled up. She hardly budged.

Stronzo! He slipped further down the slope with a splash, and icy cold swamp water trickled into his boot. He jerked his leg forward, straddling the ditch in a wider stance, bracing himself like an iron bridge.

"Okay, I'm going to grab you from behind and pull." He did just that as he took hold of her torso, his arms nestling around her ribcage. She was both firm and soft, lean around the middle, and quite tall, he realized, once she was pressed up against him. His body responded to the sensation, though his mind reminded him that he couldn't even see her under the covering of mud, in the gathering dusk. Focus!

He tugged against the resistance of her planted feet. And heaved. And hauled, applying steady pressure. He grunted with the effort. Little by little he released her from the grasping mud, until her bare muddy feet flew up and out, and they both tumbled against the side of the embankment, crushing the reeds. "Ungh!" She drove the air from his lungs as she landed on top of his chest. Cold water filled his boots. *Cazzo!*

"My shoes!" she cried, though her feet were bare.

CHAPTER 3

Despite her protests, the biker would not leave her, and he wouldn't agree to wait for the emergency vehicle to arrive. Neither would he lend her his cell phone. He seemed tense and jumpy, as though he couldn't stand still for a moment. He was convinced they might not come at all so late on a Saturday night in this remote area, since there were no major injuries.

"Come. Let's get going."

She hesitated. Clio was so very, very cold. Rigid with her shivering.

She needed to get home to Florence for her meeting. And also to download her photos and write up her thoughts about the little statue at the Monastery before the impressions faded. Time was short.

"What time is it? I have an appointment in Firenze."

He ignored her, moving toward his bike. "We must get you clean and warm first."

"But I need..." She looked down. Of course she would have to get cleaned up first.

He rummaged in his pannier and handed her a t-shirt, and she considered changing into it, even in front of a stranger. Instead she used it to wipe her hands and face, and mop her sopping head. He handed her his helmet.

"Wait!" Reality slammed her hard as she remembered her precious things. "I can't leave my car!"

"It will be towed to Montecchiello tomorrow. They will contact me and you can sort it out later."

"But I..."

"There is no point in staying here. You can get cleaned up and I will drive you there, or back to Florence if you prefer."

Oh, thank goodness. Hopefully she would get back in time for her appointment. "But my research..."

"Research?"

"I can't leave my research things. My laptop. Camera. Sketchbook. They're in the trunk. I need them, and I'm not leaving without them. My future literally depends on them."

"Hah. *Bene.*" He went to his bike, opened another compartment and pulled out a tool. A small crowbar of some kind, and marched back into the ditch, straddling it once more, and poised the tool above the inverted trunk hatch. His bike leathers stretching across his very handsome lean legs and taut backside distracted her, until he lifted the tool to her trunk.

"What are you doing? You'll break it!"

He looked at her in such a way that clearly spoke of her poor Fiat's fate. Her heart sank. Her beautiful little car. Ruined. Finished. "Signorina. Relax. All I am doing is tickling her fanny a little." His white teeth flashed in the weak moonlight. "She will open for me in just a moment."

As if to prove him right, one jerk and the hatch popped and swung open like a flower blooming.

"They can't get wet!" she cautioned, lunging forward, hands outstretched.

He deftly caught her bags as they tumbled out.

Once they had stowed her belongings in his saddlebag, he mounted his bike. "Hurry, Signorina..."

"Clio. Clio Sinclair McBeal."

"Clio. I'm Guillermo. Hop on and hold tight." He held his helmet out toward her. A deep rumble ripped the quiet night air as he started it up, and the warm, fuel-tinged air reached her nostrils.

"I...oh. I couldn't get on that."

He sighed. "Clio. You have no choice." He swept a hand in an arc around the empty landscape as evidence.

She rubbed her cold arms, hugging herself. He was right. It wouldn't be safe to stay alone in the dark on the side of the road. Reluctantly, she donned the helmet and flung a leg over the seat behind him. He reached behind and grabbed her cold arms, planting them firmly at his sides.

He grasped the handlebars and gunned the engine, then pulled out. "You are going the wrong way," she shouted over the noise. "Montecchiello is back there!"

"Later, later. I told you first we must go to Pia's."

She had no idea who Pia was, and barely the strength to pound her fist on his leather clad back as they picked up speed. "Firenze!"

She couldn't make out his shouted answer, but his shoulder-length dark hair swept back and forth as he shook his head, no. It was too late to argue so she hung on tight.

Then they were flying through the night air at an alarming speed. If she weren't so miserable, it might have been thrilling. But Clio was so cold and numb, she hardly noticed the ride. She couldn't say how far they rode, but it seemed both an eternity and an instant before they turned into a long gravel drive between stone gateposts and climbed a hill through an allée of pine and cypress trees.

It was full dark. She couldn't see clearly through the helmet's visor. She simply became aware that they were no longer moving, the steady vibration and dull roar between her legs had finally ceased. He sat upright, slid off the bike, hopping on one leg. He stood looking at her, then reached forward and pulled the helmet from her head with a slow, steady tug. She daren't even think about the horror of her muddy hair. His dark curls were a wild tangle from the wind.

"Where are we?" Her teeth chattered.

"Come. You are cold." He turned and led the way toward a dark edifice with a dimly glowing entry portico and warm light streaming from several tall windows onto the courtyard. She hobbled after him, the gravel of the drive biting into the bare soles of her feet.

The moment they approached the door, it flew open, and a flood of golden light, raised voices and barking dogs spilled out into the night.

"Memmo! Memmo! There you are. Why didn't you call?"

They were swept into a large rectangular hall with a high, coffered ceiling. A beautiful, curvaceous dark-haired woman was embracing and kissing the biker– Guillermo– with exclamations of delight and distress. A tall, quiet, neatly groomed man hovered in the background, closing the door against the cool night. Clio stood rigidly. Sconces on the smooth plastered walls flickered, shadows dancing. A large dog, no two, scrambled around them, bumping against her legs.

The tall man spoke a quiet word and the dogs followed him out of the room, leaving behind a somewhat calmer atmosphere.

"Pia, this is Signora... Clio, eh... Mc-a...*scuzi*, but I have forgotten your name already," said Guillermo, hunching slightly in a deprecating fashion, peering closely at her.

"Oh! Clio. Clio Sinclair McBeal." Clio gathered her wits and her manners, and wiping her hand on her trousers, which did nothing to rid her of dirt, thrust it toward the woman.

"Pia Cittadini. It is my pleasure to make your acquaintance, Signora Sinclair." She shook Clio's hand, ignoring the dirt and damp, smiling. She exuded warmth and comfort, and Clio felt the cold stiffness of their wet ride draining away.

"I apologize for my... my appearance. I'm afraid–"

"Pia. Pia, *cara*. I found this lady in a ditch. Her car was upside down. It's a wonder she is alive."

"My dear, how terrible. Are you not hurt at all? It is a blessing. How uncomfortable you must be. Right away we will take care of this." Pia clasped Clio into her motherly embrace and swept her toward a staircase, propelling her upward. "Memo, make yourself at home, *caro*. We will wait with dinner until you are cleaned up. Tell Paulo. I will help Signora Sinclair. *Si?*"

"I'm so sorry to intrude. He... um, Guillermo, he said he would give me a ride back to Florence, or Montecchiello, to see about my car."

"*Si, si.* Of course. But not like this. First you must be clean and warm and fed. Come."

And she was carried away in a gust of warm wind like *Il Maestrale*.

CHAPTER 4

Left alone in a beautiful guest suite, Clio finally let go of the tension that had held her together for the last couple of hours. Her body was stiff and achy. She couldn't remember the last time she'd been comfortable, and desperately wanted to be clean and dry. An attentive Pia led her to the ensuite bathroom and helped her strip off wet and filthy clothing, then whisked them away with the promise of prompt laundering.

A hot shower beckoned. She had never been so chilled. They were right of course. She couldn't head back to town in this condition. She prayed Dr. Jovi would understand, though of course she must try to call him right away. *He will be waiting for me.*

Once under the hot stream of water, she stood, numb, for a long time, allowing the heat to penetrate until her skin tingled, allowing the reality of her situation sink in. Eventually, she thawed both physically and emotionally, and the shock she'd been holding at bay ripped through her in waves. She began to shake, and as heat suffused her cold limbs, the hot tears rose up and escaped. She cried and cried and cried until she was simply standing in the stream of water hiccuping and gasping for breath.

It was nothing. A stupid accident. It had been her misfortune to be in the wrong place at the wrong time. She knew it was shock. But still. She *had* nearly died. And her car was totaled. And her parents would be... she didn't know what. Furious, though it could not be her fault that any of this had happened, they would find words to make her feel responsible. She felt guilty already, as though she could hear the disapproval in their voices. See their stern faces.

What a contrast to her warm welcome here. She gathered that the woman, Pia, was Guillermo's sister. The tall quiet man, her husband. Guillermo had been heading here for dinner, she supposed.

How fortunate for her that he had happened by, and so late, when most people likely had arrived at their Saturday evening destinations. Already sitting down to dinner. He seemed a pleasant man, helpful and generous, certainly well-loved, though perhaps a bit domineering and impatient. That was typical, she had observed, of Latin men. Not an especially endearing trait.

A melancholy wave rippled through her. Regret? How did she ever end up in her own family, always feeling like a misfit? How lovely it would be to come home to such a warm welcome. To know that you were loved, and even if you arrived late, wet, and dirty with a stranger in tow, that you would be accepted with warm and loving arms. That your trials would be fretted over and accommodated instead of criticized.

She helped herself to lavender scented shampoo and soap, and gingerly cleaned the mud from her hair and scraped skin. "Ow." She winced as her fingers slid over a huge bump on her forehead.

A familiar hunger ate at her, a desire to feel loved and accepted, to feather a nest and build a loving family of her own. She wondered for the millionth time whether she would ever find her "one great love." She laughed silently at the literary pleonasm. But the years marched on, she was twenty-seven, and still nothing much about her life had changed. She sighed. Perhaps once she'd finally completed her Ph.D. and settled into a secure teaching position somewhere, Father and Mother would be content to let her live her own quiet life. Perhaps then she would meet someone special.

Her nostrils filled with the calming scent of lavender. Eventually, Clio became calm and relaxed and warm through and through, and despite the lovely sensual heat that embraced her tired body, began to feel self-conscious about the amount of hot water that she was consuming. She stepped out of the shower to find a pile of soft, fluffy blue towels awaiting her. She dried off, wringing out her long, tangled hair. The oval beveled mirror over the vanity was fogged, and she wiped a small window in the veil to see how she had faired from her ordeal.

She already knew there were scrapes, bruises and scratches all over her body. Wounds she didn't feel in the aftermath of her accident, either because of shock, or because she was numb from the cold water, had been stinging and aching as she thawed in the hot water.

Even in this, Pia had anticipated her needs, and left some antibiotic ointment and bandages on the vanity. Perhaps she had noticed some of Clio's scratches when she undressed. Clio's forehead had an angry red goose egg over one brow, slightly abraded. Her hands and elbows were scraped and bruised. Her shins were covered with long fine lashes, the result, she presumed, of crawling and wading through the rough reeds in the drainage ditch. What a mess.

She carefully applied ointment and bandages to the worst of her wounds, painstakingly untangled her hair, and then peeked out of the bathroom door. The room was still and quiet, and seemed empty, so she wrapped a towel around her torso and ventured out, her bare feet warm against the cool, smooth floor. It was a beautiful room, with a timber ceiling. She brushed a palm over the lovely silky smooth pale yellow Venetian plaster on the walls. An iron four poster bed with a deep burgundy spread had lovely satin trimmed yellow brocade cushions arranged artfully at the headboard. Ochre-toned shutters covered a pair of tall narrow windows. This room, together with the entry foyer and stair she had seen, gave the impression of stately age, and she inhaled the perfume-scented musk of the ancient building. Clearly this was an older farmhouse, or villa with some pedigree, that had been lovingly restored.

Glancing around, she at last noticed some clothing draped over a floral fabric chair, and a handwritten note sitting nearby on a wooden dresser.

"I hope these fit. I think we are a similar size. Please come downstairs when you're ready. Pia."

Clio looked at Pia's clothes. A long flowing skirt in a subtle green and tan paisley pattern. She touched the soft silk, her fingers tingling. Very pretty. Not the kind of thing she usually allowed herself to wear, but the fabric was deliciously beautiful and feminine. There were undergarments, too, clean and fresh. She tried on the pretty ecru lace bra. A tiny bit large, but flattering just the same. Then she donned a shear chiffon blouse in an exquisite pale sienna color with a floppy layered collar and low neckline, worrying that the layers of sheer lace and chiffon actually could be seen through.

Clio appraised her image in the mirror over the antique dresser. She saw a person she hardly recognized, curvy and womanly. She swallowed, feeling a strange sensation in her stomach that matched the sensual sweep of the delicate fabrics on her clean skin. Rather fancy clothes for a dinner at home, but... well, what choice did she have? Hopefully her own sensible clothes would be clean for the ride home after dinner.

The sound of footsteps echoed in the hall beyond the closed door. *Oh, the phone. I must hurry.*

She combed her fingers through her thick wet hair, twisting it loosely and tying it with a self-knot. She had no tie, but it would stay, more or less in place, as it dried, because of its thickness and curl. It seemed incongruous, anyway, to braid it tightly when her clothing was so soft and pretty. But if she didn't restrain it, her hateful hair would expand into a giant ugly red cloud.

She stood and reviewed the effect in the dresser mirror. Strangely feminine, a result she habitually tried to avoid. At least she was clean and dry. She smoothed down her uncomfortably girlish clothes and ludicrously tumescent hair and ventured downstairs.

～

No sooner had Guillermo entered the salon than his brother-in-law, Paulo, approached him with an indecipherable expression on his face and handed him a glass of vivid garnet-hued wine.

Guillermo lifted the glass to his nose. "Eh? What's up, Paulo?" They had insisted he come for dinner this weekend, and after Bianca's oddly distressed phone call, he was anxious to know what was going on.

Paulo sipped his wine, dipping his long aristocratic nose into his glass, and peering at Guillermo over the rim with a twinkle in his dark eyes. "First tell me what you think. Then tell me what you're up to, *fratello*."

Guillermo shrugged and sipped. The intense flavors of wild dried cherry, plums, and forest fruit rolled over his tongue. Hints of spice, tobacco and warm earth. He swallowed and took a breath, letting the powerful tannins grab his palate. "Nice. Brunello?"

"*Si*. I'm playing with the oak, and the aging. This is just out of oak. It's a little experiment of mine."

Guillermo nodded and took another sip, swishing and letting the bright ripe fruit flavors explode in his mouth. Paulo had real talent. He really would succeed in rebuilding the Cittadini Brunello di Montalcino family winery. Guillermo wished his own elder brother showed some interest in restoring the home farm and vineyard, but his political career precluded all of that.

"*Bene.* Good work, *fratello.*" This was a little joke between them, brothers by marriage. There had been a little rough patch, at the beginning, when Paulo and Pia first married. They were very different in temperament, Paulo staid and quiet to Guillermo's reckless and adventurous spirit. But now, they understood each other very well. They were two sides of the same coin, and tolerated... no, loved each other. Pia had chosen well. Guillermo was more comfortable with Paulo than with his own elder brother, Jacopo, who was more like Father, and not in a good way. Guillermo moved into the comfortable green salon and chose an arm chair, easing back.

"Well?" said Paulo.

"Well, what?"

"Tell me the truth about this woman you brought. It's a spectacular ruse to bring a friend for the weekend, but you know it's not necessary. Your, eh, *inamorata* are always welcome, despite Pia's..." Paulo gestured vaguely, and they both understood what this meant. Pia's pinched faces, rolling eyes, earnest lectures about his love life, his choice of women, his future.

Guillermo choked on a swallow, coughing. "Did you see her? You have to be kidding me."

Paulo waited, eyebrows lifted, clearly convinced there was more to the story.

"No, no. This is really just as I told you. I don't even know this woman. Besides she's too old, I think, and priggish. I'm not sure what she is, but certainly no *inamorata* of mine." He laughed softly. "You should know better, Paulo. I have high standards."

Although none were known to stick around very long, Guillermo always had a glamorous, beautiful woman at his side. Women seemed to like him very much, so that had never been a challenge.

Paulo laughed, "I do know, but seriously. You just rescued her? This doesn't seem like you."

"Certainly it does, *caro.*" Pia entered the room with a plate of antipasti in her hand, bending to offer it to Guillermo. He helped himself to some prosciutto and olives. She met his eye with a smile. "My little brother is most selfless and benevolent. A *buon Samaritano.*" She brushed his long hair from his forehead as she had when he was small, carried the tray to her husband, and bent to kiss his mouth. Then she set it on a small table and left the room. "You don't know him if you think he would leave a stranded lady on the roadside."

"Were you listening in?" Paulo asked, but she didn't reply, tossing a smile over her shoulder.

Both men burst into laughter as she walked away.

"It's true," said Guillermo, lifting his brows and giving his head a little shake, "I'm a saint," and they laughed again.

Just then the object of their conversation entered the room, and their laughter died in their throats. Guillermo glanced up into the most astonishing wide-set blue-green eyes, the color of the Ligurian sea, set in a lovely oval face, surrounded by a thick mane of stunning auburn hair loosely tied back. A Pre-Raphaelite painting. Such a plump mouth, wide and ripe for kissing. She was so much younger than he had thought.

He shot to his feet, nearly upsetting his wine. He set it down and strode toward her.

"Signorina! *Bella.* How well you look." He would have thought she was an entirely different person, but he knew there was no one else here but the housekeeper-cook. Clio had made a dramatic transformation into an exquisitely beautiful woman.

A pink flush rose into her alabaster cheeks. Delightful. "Thank you." Her gaze dropped shyly to the rug. "I…uh. Your sister was kind enough to lend me some clothes until mine are laundered."

Ochre freckles dusted her nose. An angry red lump swelled on her forehead. Her forearms were patched with bandages. He reached out to take her hand, bringing it quickly to his lips, so soft, she smelled like lavender and ointment. "They suit you very well."

The sound of Paulo clearing his throat brought him to his

senses. He stepped back. "Ah. How rude of me. My sister's husband, Paulo Cittadini. Please meet Signorina Clio...em. '*Scusi.* I have forgotten again." His eyes met Paulo's, in which he saw the suppressed laughter and teasing that he kept from his face.

"Clio Sinclair McBeal." She narrowed her eyes and snatched her hand away from Guillermo, reaching for Paulo's, now standing beside them.

"You are not badly injured, I hope?"

"Not at all, *grazie.*"

They shook hands, and Guillermo ruefully reviewed their playful conversation from a moment ago. This beautiful young woman he would gladly take to his bed. It seems his body knew better than his mind, even in the dark.

"*La ringrazio molto per avermi fatto benvenuto nella vostra casa,* Signor Cittadini," she thanked him. "I find I am at your mercy this evening."

Again Guillermo marveled at her excellent Italian. But for a slight accent, she could have been a native. Paulo said, "You are American, Signorina?"

"Please, call me Clio. Yes American and Canadian, both."

While her attention was focused on Paulo, Guillermo let his eyes roam over her. She was tall, as he had already observed. But in the dark, under the mud and wet shapeless clothing, the rest had escaped his notice completely–except for her breasts, of course. His body betrayed him with a hot spasm in the groin. Not only young, but beautiful. Pale and soft, with vivid eyes and hair, long limbs and luscious curves that had been hidden under her utilitarian trousers and shirt, and were now only hinted at under her sister's long silky skirt and sheer, flounced blouse. Guillermo felt himself flood with warmth and stir in his trousers. What a surprise.

"A glass of wine, Clio?" Paulo offered, and she consented.

When Paulo had stepped out of the room, Guillermo recovered his manners and turned to her with a welcoming smile. "I am so happy to see you dry and comfortable, Clio. I hope you will not mind recovering here for the weekend. I am very happy to have the opportunity to get to know such a beautiful woman much better."

"For the weekend?" she squeaked. "Are we not returning to Florence tonight?"

Guillermo froze. *Eh?* "Tonight? Of course not. It will be much too late after dinner. And I came for the weekend. My visit here is long overdue, and my sister is expecting me to stay."

"That was before–"

"Not at all. You are as welcome as I am. You must stay also."

"But I have–"

Paulo returned with her wine. "Yes, I insist also. It is no imposition, I assure you. We have plenty of room."

"Oh no." She bit her lip, drawing Guillermo's attention to it's fullness and rich ruby color once again. "I don't mean to be ungrateful, but I have an appointment. It's very important."

"In Firenze? Tonight?" Paulo asked.

"Yes. I must–"

"It's much too late now, Clio. It would take us more than two hours in the dark," Guillermo said.

"But... did the police call about my car?"

"*Si.* They called. I'm afraid your car will not be transported to Montecchiello until tomorrow. And that's only if they can find the fellow with the truck on a Sunday. I told them you would contact them on Monday, and I can take you there on the way back to Firenze, as long as we leave early. I have a meeting in the city."

She seemed to deflate, and her aquatic eyes swam with tears. A long-fingered delicate hand rose to her brow. She had a red welt above her eye, and she flinched as she inadvertently touched it. "I'll be kicked out now. I have to call him. I have to..." She turned to Paulo. "May I use your telephone, please?"

Kicked out? Of where?

"Of course," Paulo said.

"Here. Use my cellular," said Guillermo, handing it to her. His chest squeezed with compassion. She was so overcome with some inexplicable grief. He felt a powerful urge to comfort her and protect her from whatever dire consequences seemed to await her late return to the city.

She took his phone and excused herself, retreating to the far side of the room, and slipped into an armchair facing the dark windows. He watched her anxious reflection in the glass as she dialed. He was quite overcome by her beauty and frailty, all the more so because it took him by surprise. He sensed a kind of stubborn strength in her, despite her having been overwhelmed by her traumatic experience.

"Hello? Dr. Jovi? It's me Clio."

Guillermo tried not to eavesdrop, but he was compelled by his curiosity. A doctor's appointment on Saturday night? He glanced up to find Paulo silently observing him, an expression of amused pity animating his face.

"...and so he brought me here, to a country estate. I won't be able to..."

"Uh. What's for dinner?" Guillermo asked half-heartedly, trying to tear his attention away from Clio. Whatever Pia served would be delicious, he knew.

"You'll find out." Paulo laughed, picked up the weekend newspaper and shook it out. He obviously knew Guillermo wasn't really listening.

"...so sorry, Dr. Jovi. I know I'm behind. I know I promised. I couldn't help..."

Surely no one could blame her for the accident. Guillermo stood up. He could help.

"'*Scusi*, Clio. Please allow me, to vouch for, uh..."

Clio looked up at him, her distress apparent. She said nothing as he gently took the phone from her hand. "*Buonasera*, Dr. Jovi?"

The nasal, gravelly voice of an old man replied, "What? Who is this?"

"This is Guillermo Gabriel d'Aldobrandin."

"D'Aldobrandin...of the uh, *il Ministro dei MIT?*"

"*Si.* My brother Jacopo. It is I who came upon Signorina Sinclair this evening, after the automobile crash. It is very lucky for her that I arrived on the scene."

"Indeed?"

"*Si.* I believe she would have suffered hypothermia if she had stayed out any longer, although her injuries, thankfully, are not serious. I assure you the young lady was not to blame in any way. It was a terrible accident caused by some delinquents. She is very distressed that she cannot keep her appointment this evening. She has tried to persuade me in every way that it is essential, however, I cannot return her to *la citte* until Monday, perhaps midday. Once we have investigated the condition of her wrecked vehicle in Montecchiello."

"Oh? Is that so?"

"*Si.* It is. I trust you will be able to reschedule this important engagement with Signorina Sinclair? I would feel personally responsible if she were penalized on my account."

A gruff noise emanated from the phone. Guillermo did not know what to make of this taciturn old man. "Please put Clio on the phone, *Signor.*"

"Of course. *Buonasera Dottore.*" Guillermo handed the phone back to Clio with a reassuring smile, though he was no further enlightened as to the nature of Clio's emergency, or the identity of the old man, and could by no means assure her that disaster had been averted.

Clio listened as the old man apparently found plenty of words for her ears, and Guillermo backed away, returning to his chair and his glass of wine. Again he met Paulo's eye, and between them they silently agreed the whole business was strange. "Way to name-drop, *fratello.*" Paulo's newspaper came up again, and Guillermo sighed.

"But I have." Clio exclaimed. "Everything became clear today, Dr. Jovi. I was going to write it up before our meeting. I see it now."

Guillermo's ears pricked up again.

"Yes, of course, I have photographed it and made sketches. Mm-hmm."

Her voice had altered, growing impassioned and musical. "The painting of Saint Clare of the Cross at the Franciscan Monastery was a revelation. It was so like Bernini's Saint Theresa, and yet not. The situation was different, not so public. There was a unique quality to her ecstatic state.The artist is unknown, but yet very talented. Her swoon is most exquisite. One can only assume the artist knew his subject very intimately. And it pre-dates Bernini. Yes. And if you have not seen the blissful expression on the upturned face of the little saint, Dr. Jovi, then you must make the pilgrimage one day to see it in person."

Guillermo leaned forward and peered at the glowing reflection of Clio in the window glass. Her posture had changed. She sat upright, and her face was open and animated. Instead of folded inward and contained, her body moved energetically and expressively, her hands drawing languid arcs in the air. The scene caused a stirring in his loins, yes; how could it not given the subject matter and the messenger, but also a pressure in his chest. An acute tension. Her passion for her subject moved him, as it transformed her. And if he thought she was beautiful before, now he could see that there was much more to this enigmatic woman who had fallen into his lap.

"Dinner is ready, everyone," announced Pia as she strode into the salon. "Please come to the table. Oh. I'm sorry, Clio, I didn't realize you were on the phone."

"No. I'm finished. It's alright." Clio stood up, once again reserved and polite, but a rosy flush remained on her cheeks, and her eyes were dark and bright with remembered excitement. Guillermo was smitten.

CHAPTER 5

As they took their places around the dining table, Guillermo realized that not only had he not gotten any information from his sister and Paulo about Bianca's upset, in his fascination with Clio, he'd forgotten all about it. He let it go for the moment, thinking that he would find an opportunity later, as the food was served and everyone was fully engaged with the delicious meal that Pia and her long-time housekeeper Anna had prepared. One of his favorite meals- a rich flavourful pork rib slowly cooked into a relaxed sauce that melted on the tongue, served with creamy polenta. As the meal was winding down, and Paulo sat back to savour his wine, Guillermo broached the subject.

"So. Bianca called me today," he tossed out tentatively.

"*Si?*" Pia's voice was deceptively light, as though they hadn't already discussed this, but he detected a note of frisson. "And how is she?"

"She did not seem well, in fact."

"Oh. Is she ill? Or broken-hearted again. Or does she need money?" The titter of laughter that Pia and Paulo shared was patently false. Okay. So they definitely knew what Bianca's phone call was about. Somehow.

Guillermo gauged Pia's coyness, wondering what this was leading to. "No. I don't know. She doesn't...didn't call me with her problems. But she was agitated about Jacopo." He watched Pia's eyes dart to Clio, then meet Paulo's steady gaze with a frown. Something was definitely up. "She was incoherent, if you ask me. She was going on and on about the villa being in jeopardy of some kind."

"Oh? How so?" Pia lifted a fork to her mouth.

"Pia. Cut the crap. I came here to find out what's going on with Jacopo. I want to know."

"Memmo. We have a guest," Pia murmured quietly, almost a moan of despair.

"I realize that, *sorella*. But..." Guillermo's heart squeezed, constricting his breathing. He glanced at Clio. "Is it *so* bad?"

"*Non voglio parlare.*" Pia's face crumpled, and she buried it behind her serviette with a squeak.

Of course she didn't want to discuss it with a stranger at the table. Clio leaned toward Pia. "I'm so sorry to intrude. Should I go upstairs?"

Paulo took a deep breath and visibly squared his shoulders. "No, of course not. It all will be in the news anyway."

Guillermo's pulse kicked up. He turned to Paulo. "What are you keeping from me?"

"Well. On the one hand, it's not so bad as we thought it might be. Jacopo has negotiated a settlement, and he can keep his office." His gaze jumped to Clio again, making her eyes widen with alarm and discomfort. "The press is not good, but his people are handling it. He will be cleared of all charges."

A settlement! But that was good. At least their family name would not be besmirched while a long, unpleasant court case got dragged out in the press, or worse, that Jacopo would have to abandon his political career. "What kind of settlement?"

"It's terribly complicated, Memmo. He has sworn an affidavit to the effect that there was no intentional nepotism, that he did not know the companies awarded the contracts were subsidiaries of those in which he had invested. And he of course has to pay penalties, and divest himself of his interests."

"Ah. So," Guillermo paused. That was bad for Jacopo. But there was more. Everyone else was too much on edge. "And?"

"That is where it gets complicated. Apparently Jacopo borrowed heavily to invest in these ventures. He borrowed from friends and colleagues, and he... he mortgaged the estate, Memmo. Heavily."

Guillermo frowned. "So, if he sells his interests, he can repay the loans, no?"

Paulo shook his head. "No. The value is not there. He must cut his ties clean, but he will come away with almost nothing. And still he must repay the debts."

"There will be nothing for Villa Cielo, Memmo," moaned Pia. "The estate *essere rovinato,* ruined!"

"He's going to sell it, Memmo. We are losing it." Pia's tears flowed freely now.

Clio sat very still, trying desperately to become invisible, watching Guillermo pull on his lip, scowling furiously as he absorbed the news about his brother. All through dinner, she had been quietly scheming, hoping to persuade him to change his plans and take her back to Florence tonight. She didn't care how late it was, and she didn't think he was the kind of man who kept early hours. She needed to get to work. She needed to work around the clock to meet her deadline.

Dr. Jovi was strangely impressed by Guillermo's involvement in her predicament, and had consented to defer her doomsday deadline to Tuesday at the latest, but she could tell he was unhappy about it. He was a stern man, her father's agent, and not one to go back on his word. And his word had been: Clio you're out of time. After three years, her research was at an end. She was required to submit a final, final, final summary of her thesis statement and a firm plan for the execution of the final thesis document over the next month or two. And then deliver on it. Or else she would lose her status as a doctoral candidate, she would lose the support of Dr. Jovi, she would lose her funding and she would bring down the wrath of the all-powerful Dr. Donald McBeal. Her father.

It made the loss of her Fiat500 seem trivial by comparison.

But now, the extraordinary troubles of this mysteriously prestigious d'Aldobrandin family overshadowed her own. How could she impose any further on them for help?

Guillermo scraped his hands over his stubbled cheeks, his frustration simmering, flaring. "And you? You cannot help?"

Pia, wiping her eyes, said, "You know I pooled my inheritance with Paulo's when we married, *caro*. And now we have poured every Euro into the restoration of the vineyard and winery. We have nothing."

"*Stronzo!*" Guillermo's fists came down hard onto the table, rattling the china coffee cups and saucers and cutlery that lay scattered about on the linen after desert. "Why did Jacopo not come to me?"

"What could you have done, *fratello*? What can anyone do? This is bigger than any of us can fix."

"That's not the point." Guillermo was shouting now, his face dark with anger. "He should have consulted me. I'm his brother. Technically it is *my* estate, too. And Pia's. Jacopo had no right to borrow against the family property. You know I am also the *Conte*. All the d'Aldobrandins are entitled."

"It's true, Memmo. But what is done is done."

Clio's heart raced. These Italians were so volatile, and she hated conflict and such feverish excitement. It was oppressive. Guillermo's pale blue eyes flashed angry sparks. Clio felt that he was burning up all the oxygen in the room, stealing the breath from her lungs.

Then, without warning, Guillermo rose from his chair and stormed from the room. The door slammed, his motorcycle roared to life and screeched out of the driveway, a spray of gravel clattering against the windows and walls of the house as he tore away.

CHAPTER 6

"He'll be back," Pia murmured into the uncomfortable silence. Clio looked up, still speechless. She raised her brows at Paulo.

He cleared his throat. "Yes. Sure. Of course." His eyes wavered. "Give him a little time."

Clio wasn't so sure. At the rate he was going, Guillermo could be halfway to Florence by now. If he didn't drive off the road in the dark.

She had begun to form an impression of Guillermo that wasn't particularly favorable. Despite his gallantly having come to her rescue, he had seemed to her arrogant, domineering, too smooth–a typical chauvinistic Italian man. Then once she came downstairs, things did not improve. He epitomized those qualities that she had learned to be wary of–his smooth, confident exterior, the way he looked at her, with that sense of privilege, as though he just knew any woman he desired would fall at his feet. He lay on the charm altogether too thickly, and clearly was accustomed to impressing people and getting his own way, especially women.

She frowned at the way he way he sidled up to her and slathered on the compliments. The way he flirted when he saw her with the mud washed off. The manner in which he imposed on her telephone call with Dr. Jovi and dropped the family name, expecting results. Even though his gestures were kind, she could not like or trust a man like that. He was patently insincere.

She swallowed and released the breath she had been holding. *All I want is to get away from here.*

The housekeeper Anna slipped discretely into the room to collect the remaining dishes.

Pia stood and approached Clio, resting her hands on Clio's shoulders. "Come, I'm exhausted. Let's go up and get ready for bed. I'll find you a nightgown and a toothbrush, and whatever else you need."

Clio thought she couldn't possibly sleep after all the excitement, though she was relieved to escape this strange family's evening of turmoil. Yet at the suggestion, she registered a bone-deep fatigue settle into her bruised and battered body. The stress of the accident, the physical abuse she'd endured, and everything since, had left her drained. She nodded slowly. "Yes. I think I am tired enough to sleep, thank you."

Upstairs in the yellow guest room, Pia gave her a silky nightgown and a few, necessary toiletries to get through the night and the morning.

"That blouse and skirt look better on you than on me. The greens go so well with your beautiful eyes and hair."

Clio refrained from saying how uncomfortable she'd felt in Pia's borrowed clothes. "Ha. My hair is not beautiful. But thank you for saying so."

"Why would you say such a thing? It is spectacular."

"It's a spectacle, all right. I can hardly control it." She smoothed her hands over her crown, pulling her knotted hair forward.

"Well, why would you want to? You can stop traffic with it."

"That I can believe." She laughed.

Pia stepped closer and reached for Clio's thick twisted knot, pulling it apart with her fingers. "Let me see it." She worked the strands apart and combed it with her gentle hands, and Clio's face heated as she felt it getting larger and wilder. "Oh, Madonna. Clio it's lovely. And the color. It's positively Titian." She fluffed it out, achieving precisely the effect Clio worked so hard to avoid.

Clio laughed, self-conscious. "I suppose that's true enough, but I think I've got double the amount of Venus or Violante."

Pia sat on the bed and gazed at her. "Tell me about yourself, Clio. You seem well-educated. What do you do?"

Clio chose the floral padded chair by the dresser. "Education is about the only thing I have done. I'm an art history student, working on my Ph.D. here in Italy. On the Renaissance. Both my parents are academics. Mother is a linguist, Father a professor of Classical Studies. I've spent my entire life on campuses, in classrooms, museums and galleries, or with my nose in a book. It's my world. It's all I know."

"Amazing. So much culture."

"In theory only. It sounds like your family have lived it."

Pia nodded ruefully. "Yes." She paused thoughtfully. "I feel I should explain a few things. You've been thrown into the middle of a very difficult time for our family. You see, we are a very old family, Clio. Our ancestors were the hereditary Contes d' Aldobrandin, dating back to the sixteenth century."

Clio gasped. "So old. I had no idea."

"*Si*. The first *Conte* was a military general alongside Giovanni dalla Bande Nero. He was ennobled at the same time. Our home, the Villa Cielo Incantato, has been our country seat since around then. Later, there were *palazzo*, but over the years, they were lost. Only the villa remains as part of our family heritage. Of course these titles are defunct now. But still…you can imagine. We are very proud of our heritage. Of our history."

"Yes, of course. And so you should be. I've never… I mean it's wonderful. To have such a personal, intimate connection with the Renaissance. I'm in awe, truthfully."

Pia smiled. "Well, as a student of Renaissance art, you are

perhaps particularly attuned to it's value. But of course we are, for the most part, sensitive to our obligations. The villa and gardens are not the most grand, but they are very special. And there are notable decorations and collections within it still. The thought of losing it..." Pia broke off, her voice cracking, and fresh tears welled in her eyes. She pressed a hand to her mouth.

Clio shifted to the bed beside her and embraced her. "Surely something can be done to save it. I know many old families have difficulty maintaining large estates. It is very expensive. But there are ways."

Pia took a moment to contain her emotions. She sighed. "But now it is too late." She paused, her gaze drifting to the middle distance. "Our eldest brother, Jacopo, has chosen to pursue a career in politics, as the elder d' Aldobrandin have done for many generations, as I'm sure you have deduced. He has become very successful. Very prominent. But now, these efforts of his to raise funds... well. His strength lies in governance, not in business, I'm afraid. His devotion to his career has led him to neglect the home farms and vineyards, and repairs to the villa. Our father had other business interests, of course. But he too, was frustrated. Instead of growing, the family assets have declined. Jacopo has been trying desperately to lift the estate out of debt for years. I suppose that is why he took such risks. I don't know." She stroked her brow and shook her head, and Clio gave her shoulders a sympathetic squeeze.

"It's more than the history," Pia continued, her voice quavering. "It is our home, too. The place where we all grew up."

"Your parents are..."

Pia shook her head. "Both our parents died too young, Clio. Our mother in her forties, when she was still beautiful and vibrant. And Papa not many years later, of a broken heart, I would say. He was so devoted to Mama, so in love with her, he was like a shadow without her. The villa, well... it is all we have left of them."

As Clio listened, her eyes moistened with tears.

Once Pia had left her, Clio climbed into bed and reflected upon the mercurial man who had rescued her tonight, and then abandoned her here among his loving family. She could not like him.

And yet, her body betrayed her. Whenever she stole a glance at him, a long-forgotten heat uncoiled within her. She felt a self-conscious tremor of shyness and exhilaration. In the dark, she had not registered his appearance beyond the facts of his tangled hair, and bearded face, not surprising on a biker. In the light, his physical beauty stole her breath, and she could not help but admire him, if reluctantly.

In some ways he captured the same classical Latin beauty that had drawn her to Hektor in her youth. He seemed to be made for love, with well-formed lips in a tanned, stubbled face with a strong jaw and chin, prominent laugh lines bracketing his mouth and eyes. Heavy dark brows that drew attention to his shockingly bright blue eyes, framed by a fringe of black lashes, that had the audacity to wink and sparkle and flirt and laugh at her. Her! Clio. His flashing white smile. And a head of unruly too-long raven black hair that made her fingers twitch.

And now, to add fuel to the fire, a volatile temper. The violence promised by his flashing, boiling mood made manifest in ridiculous, embarrassing, childish conduct. However justified it might be. Where had he gone? Was he coming back? He may be terrifying, but he was her ride home.

~

All Guillermo could feel was the cool night air beating against his face, and whipping the thin fabric of his shirt like a flag in a gale force wind. The exhilarating pounding of his heart behind his ribs. His hands, tight on the handlebars of his motorbike, were numb from the pressure and the cold. He rode and rode and rode. He gave no thought to where. Without conscious thought, one could follow the same country road for a very long time. He passed through more than one tiny hamlet, where the dark shapes of stone buildings closed in on both sides, its inhabitants sleeping, and then disappeared in a flash, but mostly he rode through farmers' fields and vineyards, over hills and through valleys, the silhouette of trees barely visible in the remote areas where the only light was shed by a silver sliver of moon.

He didn't care. He only wanted to escape, to get as far away from Pia's and that conversation as he could.

Perhaps if he rode fast enough, and far enough, he could escape the ugly truth. But as the countless kilometers passed, and the hours of the night unfolded one after another, he knew there was no escape. Already he could detect a lightening of the sky at the eastern horizon. He was tired, so tired.

As his mind became calmer, he started to feel the cold. He hadn't stopped to grab his leathers or his helmet, simply leaping on his bike and tearing out of Pia's driveway as if pursued by demons. Now, leagues away from anywhere he had occasion to regret it. And likely he would soon run short of fuel. *Stronzo*.

He'd gone crazy. His mind was incapable of processing what Pia had said, incapable of accepting it. And yet, given Jacopo's circumstances, and knowing his brother as he did, how could he be surprised? If anyone in the family in four hundred years was stupid enough to lose the estate, it was Jacopo.

His eyes burned hot, and his stomach roiled with upheaval, rejecting the very notion. His muscles were stiff, not only from his long wild ride, but from the tension that had held him in its grip for hours.

He pulled to the side of the road and came to a stop, killing the engine. The echo of the engine's roar flew away into the fading darkness, leaving Guillermo in utter silence, his ears ringing, his hands frozen to the bike. He flexed his fingers slowly, prying them free, and then wrapped his arms around his torso, shivering.

Oh, he knew how to ride. Often he had hopped on his bike and taken off, riding without purpose or destination in mind, just for the thrill of feeling free. Carefree.

He supposed he had on occasion ridden off to escape some unpleasantness. A breakup with a girlfriend. A tense client meeting. A throbbing head and sickly stomach the morning after enjoying himself a bit too heartily. But never had he ridden so desperate to get away, to escape, to be free from the reality of his life.

A terrible pressure pushed up from somewhere deep inside of him. A surge of fear and self-pity. He was sure he would explode with it, until at last he tilted back his head and let loose a monstrous bellow of pain and frustration and rage.

A flock of starlings exploded out of the field and took to wing, the tattoo of their hundred thousand wings knocking against the imminent daybreak like drums of war. As if it heard them, or him, the sun broke the surface of the horizon, throwing darts of brilliant hot vermillion light racing toward him across the earth.

He flinched and raised his arm to shield his eyes from the blinding light. Then he turned his head to follow the rays of sunlight as they awoke the sleeping landscape, electrifying dewdrops that clung to each head of grass and grain. His land. His people's land. His connection to this place was a powerful part of him. It defined him. His love of the buildings, the land, the history of Tuscany and Umbria were a large part of why he had chosen to become an architect, weren't they?

But did he need to own a villa to keep that connection alive? It was not a question he ever thought to ask. Villa Cielo Incantato had always been there. He supposed it always would be. But the time had finally come for his family to let it go.

It left an intense, unbearable aching hole in his chest.

Jacopo always put his trust in the wrong people. *If he had come to me, I could have helped... somehow. I would have found a way.* Maybe. Now it was too late. Jacopo was broke, more than broke, desperate. Pia's life was with Paulo, and he had his own family estate to care for. Their resources, though not insubstantial, were completely tied up. Bianca had nothing but her trust fund. She couldn't even manage her own affairs. Even if they pooled their funds, this was too big. There was nothing that could be done.

Guillermo was not poor. He had significant funds saved and invested, and he financed a very comfortable life with his own trust fund, investments, professional income and company dividends. But this was beyond his power. There was nothing he could do, even if Jacopo had respected him and trusted him enough to ask for help.

Disheartened, Guillermo started up his bike and pulled out. Pale country greens and golds and blues emerged from the murk of night. He'd find out where he was, get some gas, and take the shortest route home.

Ah, hell. No, he couldn't even do that. He was obliged to return to Pia's. There was a certain fiery-headed beauty that he was obligated to take care of. There would be no escape for Guillermo today.

CHAPTER 7

In the morning, Clio's own clothes were cleaned and pressed. She dressed carefully, minding her abrasions and stiffness, braided her hair tightly, and ventured downstairs, wondering if Paulo or Pia might drive her at least as far as Montecchiello where she could check on her wrecked car. Or perhaps she should ask them to drive her to Chiusi, so she could take a train back to Florence as soon as possible. It was an enormous imposition, though. A dart of sharp pain pierced her temples, and she realized she was grinding her teeth from worry. Why did she have to crash so far from anywhere?

But of course, it was her visit to the little saint that allowed everything to click into place. Now she could begin to write. So it seemed everything happened for a reason.

The d' Aldobrandin family's circumstances were very sad, but this was nothing to do with her, and the best thing she could do to help was get out of their way and let them deal with it. Besides, she had her own problems. She was a hair's breadth from losing three years' work and having nothing…absolutely nothing to hold onto. No degree, no career, no future. She didn't want to think about her parents' disapproval. They would disown her if she failed them.

"*Buongiorno*, Clio!" Pia's cheerful voice echoes through the house the moment her bare foot touched down in the foyer.

Clio turned to face her. "*Buongiorno.*"

"Join us in the breakfast room, this way." Pia turned and disappeared through a doorway. Resigned, Clio followed, padding barefoot along the cool marble floor tiles. Pia had left her a pair of flats, but they were too small for her giant Scots-German feet. She'd have to do without shoes. She might as well have breakfast and coffee before attempting to leave.

Passing through a doorway toward the rear of the hall, she was surprised to find a second dining room with a wall of tall arched windows opening onto a lovely limestone terrace. Sunlight flooded the tiled red and gold breakfast room, diluting its sharply contrasting contours. The smell of coffee and delicious food wafted to greet her.

As her eyes adjusted, she made out three occupants sitting at a long table. Paulo and two children.

So. Guillermo had not returned last night. Disappointment snaked through her intestines. *Ridiculous.* What did it matter? It was better this way. She did not really expect him to be here. This was entirely in keeping with his type. Selfish and unreliable, he would escape from anything that smacked of an obligation or responsibility. She would rather have as little to do with him as possible.

Clio sat in the chair indicated as Pia introduced her children, Gabriel, nine, a shocking miniature version of Guillermo complete with too-long wild dark locks and startling blue eyes, and Gemma, a sweet, brown-haired girl of seven. "*Buongiorno*, Clio," said Paulo, pausing his quizzing of the children about some music practicing to accommodate the introductions. They were lively and well-mannered as they acknowledged her.

"What instruments do you play?" Clio asked them.

Cutting off Gabriel's sullen, eye-rolling reply of "*violino!*"

Gemma bounced in her chair and began to chatter about her new, half-size cello. Charming.

"It is a very beautiful shiny red, just like *Zio* Memmo's motorcycle. And I am just big enough to– Eee! Memmo." she screamed and flew out of her chair. The two large dogs, previously dozing at Paulo's feet, leapt up, woofing, and Gabriel was close behind them, a little too cool to squeal, but obviously just as excited. "Memmo! Memmo! Mama said you left already before we could see you." The group of them, children and dogs, swarmed around the table like locusts and converged behind Clio's chair.

"When did you slink in, *fratello*?" Paulo asked, laughing.

Her stomach fell and twisted into a tight knot. *Oh, no. He came back.*

"*Si, si, bambini.* I could not leave without visiting my favorite niece and nephew, could I?"

Clio refused to turn and take notice of the interruption. He was obviously too accustomed to being the centre of attention. She rubbed the back of her neck, where an involuntary shiver prickled her skin at the sound of his warm, soothing voice.

Guillermo circled the table, children hanging on him like monkeys in a tree, dogs circling adoringly around his legs. Clio tried not to stare. He wore a silky blue football jersey that stretched across his well-developed chest and shoulders as he deposited the children back into their chairs. It brought out the color of his eyes. His hair was wet from the shower, draped in curling black tendrils pushed back from his forehead and behind his ears. A coil of molten arousal spiraled up through her core as the fresh, soapy scent of his body wafted into the room. *Stop it.* She pushed the sensation back down.

This physical attraction was stupid. It was only her body remembering Hektor, and how he had awakened her young womanhood. She was a little susceptible, perhaps, to his type of dark Latin beauty. But then, she'd been young, innocent and careless. How could any girl, her sexuality budding, have resisted beautiful Hektor? Dark hair, long, lithe limbs, flashing smile. Her young blood stirred when he was near, and when he whispered words of love in her willing ear.

But seriously. She wasn't fifteen anymore. *Some self-control, Clio.*

Not only did she dislike and mistrust Guillermo's smooth sexy demeanor, she knew better than to surrender to his charm. She didn't buy it. He was superficial. And dangerous for someone like her. Furthermore, she had no business even thinking like this. She had her priorities straight, and completing her thesis took precedence over *all* distractions now. Even if she were looking for love, this would be the wrong place to begin her search.

Patience Clio. Once you have your Ph.D. and a good job, you can relax and begin to think about your future life. Then you can contemplate the kind of partner you want and need. But not yet. She tried to soothe her inner yearnings, the unfulfilled hunger that ate at her more and more. She mustn't let her deprivation lead her to do anything foolish.

But, my God, he was gorgeous. She stared hard into her coffee cup, taking a long draught.

"Signorina Clio. *Buongiorno.* I see you are restored to your... usual, virtuous self."

Clio looked up and locked gazes with his. It was not her imagination that he was laughing at her. His eyes crinkled at the corners, and sparkled blue, blue, blue and mocking. No, his face had softened, the corner of his mouth tilting almost imperceptibly. He was... he was *admiring* her. A flush of hot embarrassment erupted into her face, her pulse quickened, and she dropped her eyes again. It felt as though he were undressing her with his gaze. How could he do that? She shook her head at such nonsense. It was only that he caught her in the midst of her own heated thoughts.

"Good morning. I also understood that you had left."

His head bobbed from side to side. "Well. Yes, clearly I left. But I could not abandon my *charge*, could I, after all the trouble I went through last night? I must see through this heroic gesture and keep my word to you. I returned a couple of hours ago."

Words and notions flitted through her head. *Charge*, he'd called her, placing a peculiar emphasis on the word, making her think of all its possible meanings. Responsibility, yes. But also *attack*. Accusation. Demand. Electricity. Thrill.

Clio tried to calm her too-rapid breathing, concentrating on her breakfast.

"I apologize, Signorina, for my behavior last evening. I was merely shocked by the news, and decided to take a ride to clear my head." With his eyelids drooping, his lower lip protruded thoughtfully, dismissing his passing tempest, though Clio thought it was another pose. *I wonder how he really feels today?* There were blue smudges of fatigue under his eyes. And an air of melancholy under his charming surface.

Anna brought his coffee and plate, and he tucked into it with gusto. Everyone else resumed eating, and soon the children were squirming.

"Come outside with us, Memmo," begged Gemma. She pulled at his sleeve. "I want to show you something."

"Ha. I've heard that one before, young seductress."

"Leave Memmo to eat, *cara*," Pia said.

"I'm finished eating," Clio said. "Would you let me come outside with you? I'd love for you to show me around the gardens."

Gemma eyed her shyly. But Gabriel sat up straighter. "I will give you a tour of the estate, *signorina*," he offered gallantly.

Clio rose, glad to escape those penetrating blue eyes.

∾

Once Clio and the children had excused themselves, Guillermo was able to grill Pia and Paulo for a few more pertinent details about Jacopo's situation. From them he learned that the property was not publicly listed, but that Jacopo was working discretely with a very high-end estate agent, who was personally bringing eligible candidates forward for Jacopo to meet.

He determined to hunt down Jacopo and talk to him the minute he returned to Florence. Even if there was no hope, he felt the need to confront his brother. Maybe there was something he had overlooked.

But for now, there was nothing to be done and no point in dwelling on it. Outside in the garden roamed a beautiful red-headed stranger who needed more than a little of his personal attention.

He rose and excused himself, strolling out the glass doors in search of her.

When he saw her this morning, he was surprised and amused yet again by her appearance. Gone was the feminine, Pre-Raphaelite in flowing garments from last night, with unruly, freshly washed curling hair. In her place, he supposed, was the persona she presented to the world. Buttoned down and restrained and so very serious. Her beautiful wild auburn hair was ruthlessly smoothed and braided to keep it under control. And she was wearing the clean and pressed version of the clothing he'd found her in— a pale pink oxford shirt tucked into ill-fitting ecru chinos that almost succeeded in concealing her long luscious figure.

He laughed to himself as he rounded the side of the farmhouse, imagining how much fun it would be to melt her icy facade. No one with that hair, and those eyes and full, ripe lips could be insensate, or as uptight as she pretended to be. He only needed to find the key to her heart. Well, if not her heart, her libido.

He came upon them on the far side of the rose garden, overlooking the swimming pool terrace, with the vineyards stretching out beyond.

"The farm has been in Paulo's family for many generations," he said as he approached. Clio and the children turned when they heard him. He gave Gabriel the evil eye and head jerk, and the boy, good sport that he was, took the hint, suggesting that his sister go with him to the barn to see a foal.

Guillermo gestured for her to walk with him under a grape arbor that arced along the side of the hill lined with lavender and chamomile shrubs, their scent rising as the morning warmed. "But the family, they have been city dwellers for years, leasing out the land to tenant farmers, and it was in ruin. It is Paulo's wish, and his mission to restore it. He is a talented winemaker, so that is his principal passion."

"I suppose that is what you would like to see happen at your own estate?"

Guillermo paused, closing his eyes for a brief moment, swallowing the bile that rose in his gullet. How had she managed to turn the conversation to his own property? "I am no farmer," was all he said. "That was my brother's responsibility. I am an architect, however, and it pains me to see our lovely villa go into the hands of some stranger who may not value it as we have done." He cleared his throat. "Paulo and Pia have done a wonderful job restoring the farm house."

She smiled. "I agree. The parts I've seen are lovely. I'm very fond of Umbrian limestone."

"Perhaps you would like to see the *cantini*...?" He noticed then that she wore no shoes, and indicated her bare feet. "Are you alright walking?"

"Oh, yes. I'm fine, and I would. Thank you."

He led her along a path and down to the entrance of the caves. "Tell me about yourself, Clio. What brings you to Italy?"

She seemed to ponder his question for an inordinately long time. He had expected a simple answer.

"My father, I suppose. Although he was Canadian, and Mother American, between the two of them, their careers have taken us abroad more than we have ever been home."

"And home is...?"

"Oh, well. Technically it's Princeton University, in Cambridge,

Massachusetts. Both my parents teach there, and we have a house. But I was born in a French hospital, and have spent much of my life in Europe. I was often at boarding schools in England and Switzerland. And touring Greece and Italy, especially, because of Father's research and teaching."

What an extraordinary life. It was like she was a high-class nomad. "Which is…?"

"Classical studies."

"I see. And your mother?"

"Linguistics."

They approached the entrance to the caves. The large wooden doors were ajar, and a dim light shone from within, though no one would be working here on a Sunday. They paused at the threshold.

"Have you never had a home of your own, then?"

She blinked. "Yes. Many. Oh, nothing like yours of course, nothing with such history and significance." *Again with the villa, like a virus, she would not let it go.* "Usually I am studying somewhere completely different from my parents."

She was not at all like other American girls he had known. "But you are always studying?" He led the way into the darkened interior.

"Hmm. Oh, lovely vaults. So far. I'm very close to completing my Ph.D. I have only to write my thesis, the research is complete. More than complete. I've changed my mind too many times, gone shooting off in too many different directions. I'm totally out of time, actually."

"Thus the urgency. And Dr. Jovi?"

"My advisor, at the Accademia di Belle Arti in Florence. He's also a close friend and colleague of my Father."

They strolled through stacks of crates and wooden barrels. It was too early to offer her a taste of wine, but the space itself was private and peaceful and had a certain rustic architectural charm to it. "What will you do? Afterwards."

"I'll do what my parents do. Get a teaching post somewhere, and continue to do research in my field. I'll publish."

"Is this what you want to do?"

She looked at him, tilting her head in a most charming way, blinking. He noted that her eyelashes, rather than being auburn like her hair, were thick fans of deep chestnut brown that framed those lovely aquamarine eyes of hers. "I don't understand."

He looked back at her, equally nonplussed. What had he asked her again? Oh, right. Career - her key. What was so complicated about his question? "To be an academic. To spend your life teaching and doing research. Is this your passion?"

She rolled her shoulders and her gaze darted around aimlessly. She swallowed. "It's... it's what we Sinclair McBeal's do. We use our brains. That's always been stressed as the pinnacle of achievement."

Hmm. "I notice you also take photographs and sketch."

"Yes, I enjoy the research and record-keeping. As an art history student must do. More than the writing, actually."

"But it is not your passion. The art."

"Oh, I love art. All art. I think I've spent more time in galleries and museums than anywhere else in the world. It makes me very happy. But I also love teaching. Although I suppose..." she trailed off.

"You suppose...?"

She shook her head. "Oh, nothing, really. I just think I'd be better at teaching young children than university students. I'm not very good with...people." A rosy blush flooded her cheeks, and he smiled.

Guillermo saw his opening. He stopped walking and turned to face her. The dim lighting of the cantina cast deep shadows across her face. "*Bella*, Clio." He lifted a hand to her cheek, stroking his thumb across her exquisitely contoured jaw. She shivered minutely, and he pulled her closer with a gentle hand on her arm, bending his face close to hers. "You are so beautiful. I know simply by looking at you that there is so much more to you than meets the eye. You are a passionate woman. You stir my blood. Already I am devoted to you. I wish to show you–"

"I'll just bet you do!" She shoved roughly against his chest. He stumbled back.

"Eh–?" He touched his chest where the imprint of her hands still tingled.

"Get over yourself." She whirled around and strode toward the entry archway. Stopping and turning back, silhouetted against the bright sunlit day beyond, she let him have it. "How dare you? Do you honestly think you can impress me with those disingenuous, stale lines? I'm very sorry to offend you. I am most grateful to you for rescuing me and to your family for taking me in under duress, but you insult my intelligence if you think you can wrap me around your finger and have your way with me." She paused while he wondered at her shadowed expression, and the red halo that limned her hair. "Pah!" she spat and stormed away.

Guillermo blinked and stared after her. Stale? He frowned and scratched a hand over his jaw. Ho. So that's the way it was going to be.

CHAPTER 8

Guillermo chose to give Clio a lot of space for the remainder of their stay at Pia and Paulo's. He was polite and friendly, but gave equal attention to his sister, his brother-in-law and their children as he did to the stubborn, uptight redhead that had rejected him so decisively in the *cantini*.

He told himself he was really not interested in her anyway. He was not in the habit of working for the affections of the females in his life. He told himself that withdrawing his attention would cause her to regret her words, and bring her round of her own will. But that did not in fact occur. She seemed perfectly content when he kept his distance. In fact he was a little put out, and a little confused, and not a little frustrated by her.

From his sister, and from snippets of overheard conversations between them, Guillermo learned that, ironically, the infuriating woman was writing her thesis on the portrayal of religious ecstasy in Renaissance art. Ha. What would an iceberg like that know about ecstasy, religious or otherwise?

When she spoke of it, however, there was no evidence of ice in her veins, but rather fire. Her eyes sparkled and her face flushed with excitement as she described the various paintings and sculptures she had discovered for her research. In his mind's eye, those flashing teal eyes and blushing cheeks were for him, and he could imagine her amazing flaming hair spread out across his bed.

When she explained the way this particular phenomenon in Renaissance art was a manifestation of the Italian Counter Reformation, she came alive. He was utterly persuaded by her thesis that the portrayal of ecstasy in all its exquisite and earthly familiarity was the culmination of a mingling of spiritual and physical passion that epitomized the brilliant, opulent, theatrical and sensual nature of the Italian Baroque period. Caught up in her excitement, his own face felt hot and his loins bothered.

Stronzo. He nearly came in his jeans.

Thankfully he survived the rest of Sunday and Monday's civil drive to Montecchiello, where she confirmed that her car was not salvageable, the frame having been twisted beyond repair. She filled out a few forms at the local police station and then they continued on their way to Florence, where he dropped her off at the Accademia di Belle Arti in via Ricasoli where she assured him her advisor would be working and expecting to see her. So he left without discovering where she lived.

So. Just as well. He was rid of her at last.

After that, he dived back into his everyday existence with a vengeance. He worked hard, and played even harder. He parked his Ducati, pulled out his new Alpha Romeo 4C, and packed his agenda with client meetings, sumptuous dinner parties and hot dates. If Clio's face intruded into his thoughts at all, it was only with a remembered flash of annoyance. And he refused to think at all about Jacopo and the villa. Soon, he would forget these disturbances and settle into the life to which he was accustomed.

He awoke in the mornings *sfatto*, with an excruciating headache, a mouth that tasted *merdoso*, another beautiful rumpled blond in his bed whose name he couldn't remember, and a *topa* that burned like hot coals to remind him what he'd been doing with her. He began to recognize the patterns of his life with contempt.

Io sono un fessacchione. A complete idiot. He was filled with self-loathing.

He tried to assuage his feelings of shame and disgust more than once with shopping sprees for new shoes and new shirts and beautiful leather driving gloves, but when he'd been driven to snap viciously at a client for compromising the perfection of his design with frivolous excuses about budget and regulations, he finally admitted that he was a wreck. He had to stop denying his rage and confront Jacopo.

The next day, he gathered enough steam to drive to the center city and find Jacopo at his constituency office, surrounded by his lackeys. Apparently they were still in the thick of putting a fresh new spin on his indiscretions, or as they would have the citizens believe, his *tradimento*. Betrayal.

When Guillermo saw Jacopo, he was flanked by a smartly dressed man and woman in the midst of draping him with various shirts and ties, while he scanned papers on his desk and consulted with another aide. He made instant and meaningful eye contact. "Memmo!" He broke away from his assistants to embrace Guillermo, ties falling off of him like confetti.

"Hey! Guillermo, how are you?" came a flutter of greetings from Jacopo's familiar staff, as they pulled him back and surrounded him again. Guillermo's chest tightened and he narrowed his eyes at his brother, taking a slow breath. *Stay calm.*

"*Ciao*, Guillermo."

"So what brings you here?"

"Can you get out for a quick espresso? We need to talk." Guillermo raised a brow.

"Sorry, you can't have him."

"Not right now," Jacopo gestured at the bustle around him.

"We've got to get him ready for a press conference at two."

"Angela?"

A moment later, a striking young woman brought Guillermo an espresso, handing it to him with a broad, admiring smile.

"*Grazie*, Angela." Guillermo flashed a smile and a wink, and she returned his look coyly. Too easy.

"Seriously, Jacopo, we need to talk. Privately."

"I know, I know. But we can talk here. I have no secrets from my people."

It felt wrong to him, this openness with family business. "Maybe you should have a few more secrets, eh? Isn't that your problem?"

Jacopo grunted. "I didn't plan for this to happen."

"Maybe a little more planning, then. You do have *people*."

"We're dealing with it. What do you need?"

Don't dismiss me. "I had dinner with Pia and Paulo last weekend."

"Aha."

"It was Bianca who sent me out there. She was hysterical when she called me."

Now it was Jacopo's turn to be silent, his jaw working.

Guillermo ground his teeth. It was too hot in the office; he was sweating. Jacopo was being a jerk. What was the point in playing dumb?

"Is this how you confront your accusers in the house? With dumb silence?" *Why didn't you call me?*

"Memmo–"

"Memmo, Memmo. What? You expect me to say nothing? Do nothing?" Guillermo flexed his fist, cracking his knuckles.

Jacopo said, "In some ways I feel the most regret on behalf of Bibi. She was so young when Mama and Papa died. I think for her the villa is a kind of security blanket."

"*Stronzo*! Security blanket? Villa Cielo Incantato is not some asset you can liquidate when it is convenient, *fratello*. You seem to be in denial about what you are doing here. This is not your personal property to dispose of."

Jacopo's eyes widened, his lips thinning. "You speak of convenience, little brother?" he hissed.

Guillermo tossed his espresso back and handed the cup to

Angela, hovering nearby. Jacopo's eyes followed him, annoyingly calm.

"Yes, I do. You are taking this action with no thought to others. No consideration for the rest of us, no respect for the past, or for future d' Aldobrandins. You leave your own children no legacy, nothing! It is all about you and your political career."

"You are a great one to give speeches, Memmo. What have you done for the family? Where have you been when there are repairs to make, staff to let go, or bills to pay? *Pfft*. No one knows more about self-interest than you."

Guillermo snorted. His chest was tight, squeezing his throat, preventing words from forming. As if he knew he would regret what he would say next. He fought the impulse to say something viciously hurtful, or worse yet, to curl his hand into a fist and punch his brother's lights out. *If only you had called me! No, no. What's the point?*

"Why didn't you call me?" he blurted.

Jacopo stilled, assessing Guillermo. "What would be the point, Memmo? What could you or anyone do now?"

Guillermo worked his jaw. "Something. Something, surely. It can't be too late." He stood, staring at his brother. He flipped one hand out, in a gesture of appeal. "We could have talked it over. Problem solved together. I could have helped."

"It is too late for me, Memmo. I have no choice." Jacopo shrugged dismissively. Guillermo saw himself fling vile words in Jacopo's face, or slam his fist into that dogged expression, but would not do anything to damage his relationship with his brother. He'd had enough of his condescension and disregard, though. Why he always should be the one who made concessions and kept the peace, he didn't know.

Rubbing the back of his neck, he asked, between clenched teeth, "What is the status now? Paulo said you listed with Andreas Fitucci of Imobiliare Patria."

"Yes. He will call me if an interested party comes forward."

"So that's it? You will lie back and wait passively to give up?"

Jacopo scrubbed his hands over his face. "I am tired, Memmo. I've been trying to solve this problem for years. And look where it has gotten me. Worse than when I started. Now I am barely hanging on to my career, my livelihood. I have a family to support, eh? I've had to make tough choices."

"It's not good enough, Jacopo." Guillermo shook his head. "There must be something you've overlooked. Some other way to avoid this disaster."

Jacopo's eyebrows rose up cynically. "You are the clever architect, little brother, why don't you find a way?"

Guillermo hesitated, supressing the urge to storm out. He nodded. "Maybe I will." He turned and strode out, quietly closing the office door behind him.

But what *could* he do? Nothing. Nothing. Nothing. Maybe Jacopo was right to let it go. He had to give it up. Let it go. He clenched his teeth so tightly his jaw ached, and his head began to throb. He raised his hands to his hair, tugging on fistfuls of it, and scrubbed down his face with his hands. Already he felt the stress. It would kill him, just like it killed Papa. *Stronzo! Allora, e chi se ne frega?* Who gives a damn?

Guillermo knew what he was good for. He knew what he was good at. He was a good architect. Award-winning, in demand, well paid for his specialty: adding sleek modern glass structures to the ancient and crumbling stone facades of Florence. Making the old new again, able to support the fast and free and ever-changing demands of modern Italy. He lived a good life. Fast and fun. He wanted for nothing. Why go looking for problems?

A heaviness pulled at his limbs, weighing him down, like the limestone walls of the villa, hundreds of years old. He preferred the lightness and freedom of his modern designs. Why would he choose to threaten his comfort and pleasure and freedom for an old dilapidated house and farm that could bring him no profit or joy?

It was foolish to agonize over what could not be changed. To be haunted by ghosts. Guillermo, like his brother and sisters, must look forward and not back. His head pounded, and he paced restlessly along the polished empty corridor of the constituency office building. He felt the need to escape the city, to retreat to a quiet place to think.

An image of a smart, stubborn, aloof, secretly passionate redhead returned to his mind's eye. He recalled how aroused she became when she spoke of the Renaissance art of her thesis research. Perhaps she would enjoy seeing his family home, and its modest collection of sculpture and frescos. Its beauty might warm her reserve. If he could do nothing for the Villa Cielo Incantato, then perhaps the villa, in all its obsolete glory, could do something for him yet, before it was too late.

~

Clio felt relief more than joy.

She was suffused with warmth and a sense of satisfaction at her progress, at last, though the pressure to perform continued unabated. Dr. Jovi had approved her final thesis premise and outline. She was even feeling generous towards Guillermo d' Aldobrandin for rescuing her, and keeping her stranded at his sister's home all weekend. Despite her panic, all had turned out well. Even though she'd lost her lovely new car, the insurance would cover the cost of a replacement, so even Father could not be too angry.

Her little adventure had relaxed her and seemed to fuel her enthusiasm for her thesis. Now she was hard at work at her cluttered desk in her little corner of her shared office space at the Accademia di Belle Arti without threat of eviction–for now.

"*Scusi. Potete dirmi dove trovare Signorina Sinclair McBeal?*"

Clio glanced up at the sound of her name.

Before she had a moment to react, Guillermo appeared in her open doorway. Clio sat upright and stared.

"Ah. Clio. *Ci si sono*. I have found-a you." Why was he speaking heavily accented English when he knew she spoke Italian? Just to prove he could?

"Uh...hello?" Her lunch seemed to roll over in her belly. What was he doing here? She stood up nervously.

Guillermo was wearing his biking leathers again, and had tucked his helmet under his arm. His long, wavy dark hair was tumbled around his handsome face. He raked it back with one hand, and held it there, regarding the wall behind her, his mouth ajar.

She spun around, checking behind her. What? There was nothing there but her research. Photographs and sketches pinned up on the wall.

At last he spoke. "You are surrounded by your...ah, saints-a. You do not find them distracting?" His face was flushed, and he blinked rapidly.

She frowned. "How could they be...?" Then it occurred to her what he meant. For some people, the close-up shots and detailed drawings of all that ecstasy was disconcerting. Confusing. "Oh. No, well. I...no."

He laughed. "If it were me, I'm afraid I could not think clearly. Always I would be-a...imagining other activities."

Now it was Clio's turn to blush. She dropped her gaze. "What brings you here?"

He switched to Italian. "I wanted to see that you were alright. That you got home safely, and that your advisor is not giving you any difficulties about the weekend."

Her officemate Jonathan appeared, wide inquiring eyes peering over Guillermo's shoulder.

She scowled at him, and he passed on. Responding to

Guillermo, she said, "No. No, everything is fine. I'm steaming ahead actually." She patted the papers on her desk and shuffled them around pointlessly.

For several moments, they stared awkwardly at each other, saying nothing. Clio's heart hammered against her ribs.

"And you?" she said. "Any news about your villa? Any changes?"

His brow darkened as his blue gaze searched the floor for an answer. "No. I..." He sniffed. "I had a conversation with my brother, *naturalmente*." He shrugged, then forced a smile, his white teeth flashing. "But now you mention it, I am planning to drive out to the villa this coming weekend. To have some quiet, and to pick up a few personal items. I thought you might like to see it. You come, no?"

Clio's pulse sped up. Oh, would she. But no. Bad idea. She had to work, and spending more time with him was dangerous. She nibbled her lip. Why would he invite her along? What could he want? It couldn't be good.

"I can't help admitting curiosity. But..." She shook her head, waving her hand at the same time. "I don't think that would be appropriate. We hardly know each other."

He recoiled. "Oh, no, no, Clio. Please don't think that of me. I realize my actions were inappropriate. I was overcome with your beauty, but I have control over myself now. I promise you, that I have only honorable intentions. At Villa Cielo Incantato there are staff," –he turned his palms upward, reasoning– "the old house-keeper and gardener." He thought a moment. "We would not be alone even. My younger sister Bibi will join us. You will be perfectly safe with me. I promise to be a gentleman."

Clio was intrigued to be sure, by the villa and its history, but she felt unaccountably disturbed by his presence, even here in her small office. How would she feel spending another two days in his company. She caught another glimpse of Jonathan passing by behind Guillermo's back. It was best that she not get involved.

"I'm sorry, Guillermo. It is kind of you to think of me, but I really must work very hard to meet my deadline now. I shouldn't be taking the weekends off for any more touring or recreation."

"You could work." He stood upright, brightening. "I would give you the time you need, but you would see the villa, too. And the gardens. I think you would like the gardens very much."

"I'm sorry, no." She smiled sadly. She would never get her thesis written if she continued to be distracted by new sites. She was such a history junkie.

Guillermo slumped against the door jamb with a heavy sigh. He stared at her, frowning, no, pouting, until she felt uncomfortable, and a little sorry for him. He really didn't have much experience with rejection, that was clear.

"Perhaps then you will allow me to take you to dinner sometime?"

She felt her throat tighten in pity. How could she reject him again? "Well, maybe, yes. I could do that. Sometime."

Guillermo's face broke into a wry, self-satisfied smile with a twinkle of satisfaction in his blue eyes, and dipped his head in a tiny, old-fashioned bow of acknowledgement. He stepped forward and scrawled his phone number on the corner of a paper on her desk. "*A vostro piacimento.*"

She laughed, shaking her head, as he turned on his heel and left. At my pleasure, indeed. What does he know about what gives me pleasure?

The moment he was gone, Jonathan popped into the office and dropped into his seat, swiveling to face her. "*Well*, darling? Do tell."

CHAPTER 9

"None of your business," Clio hissed at Jonathan and stepped to the doorway to watch Guillermo as he swaggered down the corridor. How could she give in to him, the spoiled brat? How could she not?

Still laughing, she turned back to find Dr. Jovi standing behind her. She yelped. Then she laughed. "Oh, my goodness. I didn't know you were there, Dr. Jovi."

"Who was that?"

She was well aware that Jonathan was listening in as well. "Oh, you know. Guillermo d'Aldobrandin. You spoke with him on the phone, remember? He's the man who rescued me on the road Saturday night."

"Ah. He's that sort, is he?"

"What sort?"

"A ruffian." He waved a hand dismissively. "A rogue."

"No."

"He is riding a motorcycle? Just look at him."

The sound of Jonathan's stifled laughter made her frown. He covered it with a cough, and she shook her head.

Clio half agreed with Dr. Jovi, but although she didn't entirely trust Guillermo, she felt compelled to rise to his defense. "I am looking. He's from a very good, respectable family. They were very kind to me."

Dr. Jovi snorted. "Yes, I've read a few things about his family in the news lately."

"Oh." She winced, and her face and ears tingled with heat. "I get the impression his brother is not bad at all. He has made some error of judgment, I understand."

"Oh, so you are privy to the family's secrets now, are you?" His tone was mocking.

"Not at all." She recoiled, stiffening.

"Be very wary, Clio." Dr. Jovi lifted a scolding finger, and wagged it altogether too close to Clio's face for comfort or dignity. "It would not be wise to get involved in a frivolous romantic entanglement right now. Especially with the wrong sort of person. Your father and mother would not approve, you know. You must stay focused on your thesis, my dear. Time is of the essence. You don't want to be a disappointment to your family."

Shut up, already! Clio rubbed her temples. *What am I, fifteen years old?*

"You know it would be such a waste of your talents if you were to get sidetracked by a man like that. You have a promising academic career ahead of you. There is no future for you there." He droned on, his balding head shaking. "I can't keep covering for you, Clio. Soon I will have to have a frank discussion with *Dottore* Donald."

Clio stood speechless. Was he threatening her? She brushed a hand to the back of her neck, slick with perspiration.

Heat suffused her face. "Yes, of course, Dr. Jovi," she said through clenched teeth. "Excuse me, please. I have to get back to work." She strode into her office and closed the door, stopping just short of slamming it in the pompous old fart's face.

She stood and breathed, just breathed, until she was a little calmer. She'd never felt so insulted in her life. How dare he lecture her that way?

She was vaguely aware of Jonathan gaping at her.

"What are you looking at?"

She lifted her hands to her face, pressing her hot eyes. Then she moved to her desk and stared down at the number scrawled on the corner of her notepaper. She picked up her phone and dialed.

"You go, girl."

"Oh, shut up, Jonathan."

~

Clio's phone call had shocked him, just minutes after he had left her office at the Accademia di Belle Arti on via Ricasoli. He had only just mounted his Ducati at the curb by the arcade, licking his wounds, but also looking forward to the promised dinner, and the opportunities it presented for furthering his cause.

"What inspired you to change your mind, *Bella*?"

"Merely that I'm very intrigued by your historic family villa, and under the circumstances..." she hesitated, "I knew this would be my only chance to see it. It is not often we academics have the doors of private villas thrown open to us."

Sure. Purely academic interest. He didn't believe it for a moment. But that was cool, he could play to that.

It had been a long shot, admittedly. Her rebuff in Paulo's *cantini* had been decisive, and yet, he sensed a hidden passion in the woman that intrigued him, and spurred him on to pursue her.

He dialed his little sister's cellular. Now he had to convince Bibi to go as well. He prayed she had no commitments for the upcoming weekend.

"Bibi, *cara*."

"Who is this?"

"*Bi*-bi."

"Oh. *Buongiorno*, Memmo." Her voice was sing-song and falsetto, so he cut to the chase.

"Right." He snorted. "I want something."

"What else is new, Memmo?"

"Hey. I went to Pia's because of you and your *piagnucolio*."

"Hmph. I wasn't whining."

He made a face. "So. What are you doing this weekend?"

Bianca was silent for a moment, and he could hear the hiss of her drag on her cigarette. "I'm not saying yes. What do you want? And what's in it for me?"

"I thought you might like a weekend at the villa. I'm going. I'll... introduce you to Carlo." Bibi had been nagging him for an intro to his colleague.

"Hmm. You want me to be there at the same time as you? Since when, *fratello*?"

Admittedly, it was far fetched. "Since now. I need a... uh, a chaperone."

The *tintinnio* of Bianca's hysterical laughter filled his ears for several moments. "You want me to interfere between you and a woman. I understand correctly?"

He sighed. "*Si*."

More hysterical laughter. "What's the matter with you?"

"It's a long story. I'm motivated."

"Hmm. So now I'm curious. I was going to go to a concert. But it was going to be boring anyway. Are you driving?"

Guillermo thought about that. "*Si*. But you have to make your own way there."

"Wha-at?"

Guillermo shrugged, though she couldn't see him. "I don't want you to stink up the car with your smoking."

"Yeah, right. Fabio."

"What's wrong with Carlo? You always ask about Carlo."

"Carlo *and* Fabio."

"*Yeesh*! Deal."

"See you there."

This weekend away would be pure pleasure. Guillermo was determined to show Clio a good time, whatever it took. Escaping the confines of the city was a brilliant stroke of genius. He needed to get away again, and he always enjoyed the pampering he received at the hands of Marcella and Martino when he went home to Cielo Incantato. The old couple, husband and wife caretakers of the villa since before Guillermo was born, were the closest thing to parents he and his siblings had left since the death of their own parents.

Except for *Nonno*, who was more child than parent.

Even though it had been accidental, Clio's last adventure in the *campagna* had been good for her, and had given him the chance to get to know her. The villa was the perfect bait to lure the lovely Clio Sinclair McBeal away from her single-minded industrious focus on her school work and the watchful eye of her over-bearing advisor.

And it would give Guillermo another much-needed chance to win her over. He was always up to a challenge. When it came to smart beautiful women, there were too few challenges, and his recent exploits in the city had definitely begun to pale.

He drove south on the SR2 through Poggibonsi and Sienna. It would take a little longer than the A1 Autostrada. Depending on how the weekend went, they could get home faster through Stazione Montepulchiano. The scenery was better this way, and the longer he was in the car with Clio before rewarding her with a destination, the longer they could be alone, the better they could get to know each other. That was the theory, anyway.

For him, the smaller roads were a pleasure in his Alpha Romeo. It wasn't that he no longer enjoyed the rolling green and gold patchwork hills, and rows of cypress trees flanking the country roads, but the drive itself was the thing. Hopefully her recent accident did not make Clio unduly nervous. His C4 handled the narrow, winding roads beautifully. He prided himself on his skill, and he did love to drive.

He glanced sideways at his passenger. An enigma – Clio was as frumpily and conservatively dressed as before, no encouragement there. She seemed to adjust her wardrobe neither up nor down for the country weekend. Her wild hair was pulled back into a disciplined plait, just like her character. And yet, as he surreptitiously studied her pleasing profile, her strong jaw was set stubbornly, and her gaze trained determinedly on the horizon ahead. She was on some kind of a mission. Although he did notice one white-knuckled hand gripping the side handle, and the other the edge of her seat.

"*Bene*. I look forward to showing you around, *allora*. I could not imagine a more beautiful or desirable companion for a country retreat."

She sat back and shot him a wary glance. "I can't see what possible relevance my appearance has on your visit, *signor*. You did promise me to be a gentleman, did you not?"

He swallowed. "*Certamento*. I remember my words and will keep my promise. But, *Bella, mi sento attratto*. It does me a great benefit to look upon you and admire you, though I cannot gratify my desire with actions. Please allow me to dream." He flashed his most charming smile, with a wink for good luck, and had the satisfaction of seeing a pink flush bloom on her cheeks as she pursed her lips and turned her gaze out the side window.

"Please call me by my name. You are too familiar with your terms of endearment."

"*Scusi. Sono abbagliato da te.*" I am dazzled by you. "You have an exquisite fire that enflames me...Clio." He whispered her name like a caress, as though he could taste it.

"You Italian men are all the same. Liars. Arrogant liars." She spoke sternly, but the corners of her mouth had begun to twitch. She would not give him the gratification of making her smile with his efforts. Fine. Enough for now.

He laughed and left her in peace to enjoy the sublime blue hazed vista. Perhaps it would work to help him soften her shell.

"Tell me, where is the villa?"

"Not very far from the Cittadini estate. A little west of there. It is south of San Quirico d'Orcia. That is why we drive through Sienna. But you can go the other way, also."

"Did Pia and Paulo go to school together? Is that how they met?"

"Not exactly. Our parents knew Paulo's. They moved in similar circles."

"Aristocratic, you mean?"

He wet his lips, thinking. "There has been no aristocracy since the sixties, you know. But yes, in some respects people keep the same habits. The same friends, from one generation to the next."

"And... Pia mentioned that your parents passed away."

Of course she would ask. Americans had no subtlety. He pushed through a heaviness and forced himself to reply in a matter-of-fact tone. "Yes. Nine and five years ago."

"So Jacopo has been trying to..."

He shrugged. "Trying, yes. I suppose. But really his interests are in politics."

"But I heard you say..." She stopped herself, her eyes darting away uncertainly. "I'm sorry. I thought you said something about you also being the *Conte*?"

Guillermo's stomach hardened and heat raced over his neck and ears. Why did I say that? *Pazzo.* "Er...it was nothing. I...well, technically we four all inherit the estate, and the archaic title. But it is unimportant now." He waved it away with a sweep of his hand. "I was angry with my brother. It is past."

Her lips pursed, but she said nothing.

They drove in silence for several minutes, each with their own thoughts.

"Have you thought of ways to save the villa from bankruptcy yourself? Could you pay the debts?"

He forced a smile. "It's not my job."

"But you care. Don't you? Maybe there is something you can do. I know of several estates that have been saved by some very creative funding schemes. I could dig around for you."

"Ah. I'm sure you could, with your research skills. But no, thank you." His stomach twisted uncomfortably. "Are you hungry? We could stop somewhere for a snack." He scanned the horizon for a turn off or a sign. He didn't want to get caught in Sienna traffic, so he had just taken the ring road. Perhaps on the other side.

"You're trying to change the subject. Why don't you want to try?"

He snorted. "I have a busy life, Clio. I have a comfortable apartment in Firenze. I don't need the villa. I'm not sentimental about it."

"I don't believe you."

"You don't know me very well, *Bella*." He took a deep breath and calmed himself, but his jaw was tight, his shoulders stiff. A strategic change of subject was called for.

"Tell me more about your thesis. I confess I was not listening well when you told my sister. But now I have seen these intriguing images you collect on your wall, I have a desire to know more."

She huffed out a breath, her eyes narrowed at him. The lovely arcs of her auburn brows lifted. "Are you sure you want to know? Once I get started…"

"*Si, si.* I really want to know."

"Well. If you insist." She studied the landscape and the sweeping

Tuscan sky, choosing her words carefully. "As I'm sure you know, the Baroque period was a period of aesthetic excess."

"That is perhaps how it appears to northerners." It seemed he was going to get a dry academic lecture for his pains.

Instead her face bloomed into a broad, glorious smile such as he had never seen before, like the sun breaking above the horizon at dawn, and he was so stricken that he nearly swerved off the road. His heart slammed into his throat, and he quickly corrected course.

She didn't seem to notice.

"You've got it exactly. How insightful you are." Her face had become flushed, and her eyes wide and bright. Her natural beauty was enhanced by her enthusiasm.

"Uh..." What had he said? He scratched his beard. "Am I?"

"Yes, that is the crux of it." She leaned toward him, releasing her warm floral scent. "There are differences of opinion, of course. There always are. But my research is attempting to thoroughly document, particularly through new or lesser known examples, how the portrayal of religious ecstasy was consciously or unconsciously a rebellion against the imposition of a new morality by the advance of Protestantism."

"*Si...*" *Is that what I said?* Her perfume wafted over to him. *What is that? Gardenia?* He shifted on his seat.

"But more than that, the examples I have found confirm, or well, I suppose support the premise that the response emerged spontaneously and simultaneously, not just as the spread of influence from say, Bernini or a handful of better known artists, but as a grassroots response. I have examples that demonstrate that regional artists, young, unknown, inexperienced ones even, were using the religious theme of ecstasy, whatever you want to call it, as illustrated through visions, visitations, epiphanies, and what-have-you, to portray physical bliss. And I am arguing that this evolution was an indigenous and sensuous response to the elaborate, magnificent, brilliant aesthetic environment of the early Baroque period."

She waved her hands, inscribing arcs in the air. Unconsciously, she had pulled at her hair, and now strands of luscious curling Titian red escaped from their bonds. He had to force himself to keep his eyes on the road.

"By indigenous, you mean, uh..."

"Yes. Italian."

"Hm." He swallowed. *Well, being Italian, I can see that.* Like now, for example. There was no mistaking the fact that he had a whopping *erezione*.

She frowned. "You don't believe it?"

"On the contrary. I do believe it." He was undoubtedly *tiro*, hard, from watching her excited, bright countenance, and listening to her suggestive words. She seemed on the one hand oblivious to the innuendo, and on the other, quite affected by the whole notion herself. At least in the abstract. If one could have an abstract heartbeat.

"So you see, it is as if the natural cultural disposition is expressed or... or unable to be repressed, in the context of such delights of sensuous experience. Like... like Shakespeare holding up a mirror to nature, in all its beautiful, emotional, bawdy truth, the sumptuousness and sensuality of the Baroque environment led to an unconscious and conscious release of the guilty pleasures that even earlier Christianity, and certainly the encroaching threat of Protestantism, did not permit. You see?" She gestured with her hands, to emphasize her point, now that she was getting to the climax of her explanation.

He groaned. His head was spinning.

"Now, in the context of Baroque extravagance and indulgence it was not only alright, but it was a point of pride to take this notion of sensuality to its logical and perfect peak of expression - the orgasm - disguised, of course–"

"So let me get this straight. You're arguing that the excessive emotion and overt sensuality inherent in the art of the period caused people...well Italians anyway, to walk around in a state of perpetual arousal."

"Yes, more or less. It was visceral."

Stronzo. Unbelievable. How could she talk about such things as if they were a dry academic subject? "You are very persuasive...Clio."

She smiled, assuming, he supposed, that he was as excited about her thesis as she was.

Per amor del cielo! For the love of heaven! What was he doing?

CHAPTER 10

"He grinned. "But tell me Clio. Do you actually *like* Italian men? I think you secretly do."

Clio felt her smile falter, as an unwelcome flash of desire shot through her. He could never know how he affected her. He was impossible. Why did she come? She jerked back in her seat, her bag toppling to the floor, its contents spilling. She fumbled to catch them and stuff them back in, tucking her purse between her feet. Heat tingled in her cheeks.

She flinched as he reached across and stroked her under the chin with one warm finger, lifting her face up to meet his eyes. He glanced at her, turning his gaze back to the road, but his sensuous mouth pulled taut in a small amused smile, his head shaking slightly, as though he was contemplating a puzzling surprise, but something delightful and intriguing.

"Um. I understand your villa was built in the sixteenth century?"

"Eh?" His grin slipped.

He had pulled off the main motorway some time ago, after they had passed through a small town with a tumble of small rectangular buildings in soft brown limestone, their roofs stacked up like a house of cards, that she assumed was San Quirico d'Orcia. They were winding along a narrow, twisting road of a similar scale to the one where she had her accident, but more roughly paved. She shifted to look out the window, her breathing constricting as the memory of her car veering and flipping shot through her body. As they continued to climb, the vista opened out, and she could see more rolling green hills and golden fields. He was going a little fast for her comfort. She clutched the seat and side handle as Guillermo steered the car around curve after curve, gravel crunching under the tires.

"C-can you tell me about its history? Do you know much about it?"

"Of course. We were all told the family history growing up. We could not study the history of Italy without understanding our role in it."

"Was it significant?"

"Well, you will not find so many references to our family in the history books. But we were important supporting players, you might say."

Oh, she loved this. History first hand. She focused on his face, and not on the steep drop off to her side of the road, slowing her breathing. This is what she was hoping for. "Oh, tell me, please."

He smiled again, his eyes crinkling at the corners. Such a vivid blue, matching the sky beyond his window. "Our family goes back a very long way, but it became notable with Francesco d'Aldobrandin who was a military captain during the Italian Wars, and assisted Cosimo I, in particular, with the defeat of the Sienese at the Battle of Marciano in 1554. After Cosimo became Grand Duke of Tuscany in 1569, Francesco was made a Conte. It was afterwards that the villa was constructed, on land he was gifted by the Duke."

Guillermo was turning out to be a better storyteller than she'd expected. Somehow, his smooth manner and cavalier attitude led her to suspect that he was not very attentive or interested, or for that matter academically inclined.

The narrow road was climbing higher and higher now, and they were winding their way back and forth along a series of small switchbacks. Tall cypress trees punctuated both sides of the road, and sloping, rolling golden fields stretched out in both directions, between tumbling groves of green trees, with the occasional stretch of wild-looking grapevines in undulating rows.

"Oh, this is amazing. So, so beautiful." The villa was so much a part of the history of this land, and even better, built during the later Renaissance period. "I've been curious…Cielo Incantato doesn't sound like the kind of name given to a villa of that period."

He laughed. "No. It wasn't. It was always known as Villa d' Aldobrandin della Monte. Very descriptive. Very dull. Or so my mother… so my mother used to say. It was she who renamed it–Enchanted Sky. She was…" he hesitated, "…well, she was fanciful. An extraordinary woman. Very romantic."

The way he said romantic, one would think this was a disability. How curious. Just a moment before, she saw a fierce spark of devotion in his eye. Perhaps it was only his sadness at having lost her so young.

"Tell me about her."

After a silence, Guillermo cleared his throat. "Perhaps another time. We will arrive soon."

"The villa then. Prepare me a little."

"Ah. The villa. Well, you will soon see. It is a little run down, as there have not been funds recently for all the maintenance that is needed. But it is still a very beautiful house. There is a simple rectangle–the original building from about 1575, almost monastic, strongly influenced by Antonio da Sangallo the Elder–with a grand arcaded first floor, and graceful *piano nobile* under the tile roof. It has very lovely classical proportions. " His voice was wistful, full of admiration.

Clio said nothing to interrupt his narrative, awed by his obvious passion for the topic.

"It is built of a soft butter-coloured smooth limestone, with subtle beige columns, cornerstones and rustication. There is also a later addition, a ballroom built in 1665, of a single story, that stretches off to the west, with a stone baluster, and a large terrace on the roof. I believe this to be designed by a student of Flaminio del Turco out of Siena. My favorite piece, though, is the rectangular tower that rises up another three stories. This you can see from far away, and a group of very old cypresses stretch up beside it into the sky. I think that's why..."

He stopped talking as they approached a rough wall beside the road. He slowed the car, and they turned and maneuvered through a pair of tall stone gateposts. Low stone walls, lined with cypresses on one side, and a tumble of greenery and bright red geraniums on the other, flanked the crushed rock driveway. Some rustic stone outbuildings blocked their view for a moment, and then they rounded a corner, and there it was. Villa Cielo Incantato.

Clio drew in a breath, and brought her hands to her mouth. Oh. It was perfection. So beautiful. So grand. She leaned forward, craning her head back to take in the tower and the trees he had described. Vivid green vines scaled the walls on one side, and the drive opened out into a gravel forecourt framed by trimmed boxwood hedges, and neat rows of conical boxwoods in terra cotta pots. More red geraniums welcomed them from pots on terraces.

Guillermo stopped the car and cut the engine, and for a moment they sat in silence, admiring the lovely villa. Clio looked over at Guillermo, grinning, unable to find words to express her joy. She wanted to share her euphoria with him, to tell him how happy she was to be here, to see this place. She was so grateful to be here now, with no regrets. She placed a hand on his arm, and he jerked. When he turned his head to face her, his eyes were bright with tears.

"Come." His voice cracked, and he quickly cleared his throat, swallowing. "Let's stretch our legs. I'll show you the gardens first." He opened the car door and leapt out, pacing around to her side. He swept her door opened and stepped back.

"Martino," he hollered over his shoulder.

Clio climbed out and stood, gazing at the villa. Sure, it was a little weathered, but this added to its charm. The window frames looked like they needed some serious care. The planting, now she could see it more clearly, was a little rough. "Let's go."

They walked side by side, and she gave him a moment to recover himself. She supposed coming here made the realization that he was going to lose it hit home in a way it had not before. Perhaps he was remembering his time here as a child, or with his parents.

He led the way around a corner and onto an ashlar terrace, again lined with planted pots of geranium in splashes of vermillion. A modest iron table and chairs sat at the far end. They stepped to the edge, and Clio's heart seemed to trip, and stutter.

Below, down a wide, shallow arcing series of steps, gardens stepped down the slope in a series of limestone terraces, interspersed with wild mounds of lavender, chamomile, rosemary and vigorous oleander bushes with blooms of red and pink. The first large terrace was paved in a spacious flagstone rectangle, with trimmed lawns all around. Over the patio an iron frame overgrown with grape vines sheltered a long thin marble-topped table surrounded by more than a dozen of the same folding iron chairs, sitting askew.

One huge tree grew to the side, its wide, generous branches arching overhead, casting a welcome dappled shade over the sun drenched terrace. Oh. What a beautiful *al fresco* dining room. A place for large family meals. Clio could almost hear the echo of voices and the laughter of children on the breeze, a memento of generations of family celebrations.

It wasn't at all a formal place. To Clio it appeared well lived-in, and well loved.

Guillermo took her hand and tugged her forward, his gaze ahead. A brittle laugh broke from him and, letting her hand slide out of his grasp, he jogged ahead. He ran down the stairs, around the grape arbor, and disappeared over the edge.

CHAPTER 11

Guillermo ran. He leapt down the second tier of steps, wove his way between the flower borders, and loped at full tilt down the grassy slope to the pool terrace, his heart pounding in his ears.

How humiliating.

How could I turn into such a blubbering emotional mess? In front of a woman I hardly know. He hugged himself, gripping his elbows, trying to settle the tremors that ran through him. A wave of grief had washed over him at the prospect of losing his home.

It was not his role to protect it; Jacopo had made the decision. And yet Guillermo felt it was his duty to save it. Perhaps it was for the best to rid themselves of the burden now, so future generations of d'Aldobrandins would not live under the weight of its yoke, like he had. Like his father had, like Nonno had, twisting their modern lives to accommodate the demands of the distant past. He, for one, was unwilling to sacrifice himself at the altar of the d'Aldobrandin legacy.

A powerful urge to strip off his clothing and dive into the cooling, soothing water of the pool for a vigorous swim ripped through him. But he had a guest. He could not do that. Instead he kept jogging past the pool, cut through a hedge and laced his way back through the kitchen garden.

The old man bent over a row of tomato vines, his broad-brimmed hat shielding him from the sun, and from Guillermo's eyes. He stood up suddenly, his hand over his heart. "Ah!" he gasped. "Signor Memmo! I did not know you were coming."

"I'm sorry, Martino. Last minute," he shouted as he ran past, and climbed another stair, cutting back around behind the place he'd left Clio.

She still stood there, serenely gazing over the edge of the dining terrace. From there, she could just glimpse some of the complex garden rooms below. He slowed, his breathing heavy, and caught his breath. Then he strolled up silently behind her.

"That is the pool to that side," he gestured to where he had just been. "It was added in the late 30's, where there was just a lawn before. My great-grandparents did not wish to disturb any of the older gardens."

She gasped and spun to face him. "My God! Where did you come from?"

"I am sorry. I had restless energy to burn." He grinned, his nostrils flaring with his still labored breathing. "This is one reason I have to escape Firenze frequently. It would seem odd for a prominent architect to be seen racing like a boy through the streets of the city."

She laughed, shaking her head at him, her brow furrowed.

He put his hands on her upper arms and spun her back toward the view. In the distance, the same undulating forests and fields they drove through rolled away to the purple horizon, and the blue silhouette of the Apennine mountains in the distance. He pointed. "And over there, the kitchen gardens, Martino's pride and Marcella's joy. Below them, the fruit trees and over there, the formal gardens. Around the corner, there," he swung her to the left, "the grotto."

"I'm amazed. Astonished. I thought... I don't know. I imagined something much more rustic."

"What would you like to see first? We will only sample today, because now that Marcella knows we are here, I believe we will be required to eat some of her delicious cooking very soon. Tomorrow I will take you around and show you every piece of the grounds."

Clio's face lit up, bright with pleasure and anticipation. Guillermo's pulse pounded as he watched her. This was perfect. *This is why we are here.* For *amore*. *I don't know what came over me.* That cannot happen again. There is no sense becoming sentimental or maudlin about the old place. *Que sera, sera.*

"So?"

"Perhaps the fruit trees?" She gave a tiny shrug, peering at him with those large, aquamarine eyes, slightly slanted and wide set, like liquid pools, serene, waiting for him to plunge in. She licked her wide pink lips waiting for his response, and a coil of warmth unfurled in his stomach. He wanted to kiss her. But no, it was too soon for this skittish kitten. *Why do I find her so fascinating?*

He gently pressed her arm and guided the way to the orchard. They skirted the boxwood edge of the kitchen gardens, and he noted how badly they needed trimming. It broke his heart. He knew this would be driving Martino crazy. He loved his gardens, but he could not keep them up without help, and the last of the undergardeners was let go over three years ago. Despite Jacopo's disdain, Guillermo kept track. And of course Marcella would make sure Martino focused on the kitchen garden, for without that they would have little to eat. Marcella took great pride in her table, even if she only had herself and her husband to feed now. *I wonder when Jacopo has last bothered to visit?*

Maybe a new owner would be able to care for it properly. Someone able to purchase a run-down old Tuscan villa surely would have deep pockets, and a deeper love and respect for the history and beauty of the place. It would be okay. It would. It would begin a new life.

He began to sing to her, leaning closer to tease her with the warmth of his breath on her ear. She jumped, and he was gratified to see how quickly the blood ran in her veins.

Bocelli's lyrics came to him unbidden, and he sang of meeting a woman, who got inside of him and stayed there. Of how he lived for her because she shook his soul. As he sang, he wondered if it was possible to feel such devotion, even as he felt it could be happening to him.

Her eyes widened, frozen in place until he finished, and she blinked. Blinked.

While he sang just under his breath, he touched her hair, and caressed the side of her neck with his fingertips, keeping his eyes locked on hers. *Si, Bella.* Surrender to me, *Bella.* Gooseflesh rose up on her delicate skin, and she shivered, one corner of her mouth twitching. Oh, how he wanted to kiss that little twitch, and run his tongue from her earlobe down her neck, where the skin danced to the beat of her pulse just below the surface, to the hollow of her collar bone. He gently pushed at the collar of her shirt to expose her neck, and bent his head, not touching her with his lips, not yet, but allowing his breath to warm her. His nostrils filled with the sun-warmed scent of her, feminine and floral, blending with the aromas of the garden, making his senses whirl. His own blood raced, sending a most urgent, demanding surge to his groin, throbbing. A shudder ran through him with the effort of pulling back. She was going to kill him.

She gave a nervous little laugh, swallowed and turned to walk away.

"You're a fan of Bocelli?"

He groaned. She needed to know what she did to him. If he gave her that power, it would awaken her own desire. At least he prayed fervently that was true. "Through there," he indicated the gap in the hedge. Guillermo gritted his teeth while he adjusted his trousers, and followed her into the *frutteto*, orchard, where she tilted her head back and took in the array of fruit trees. Fig, apple, quince and lemon.

"Oh, lemon. How wonderful." She strolled over and caressed the small green and bright yellow fruits hanging from its lowest branches. In Guillermo's mind, it was his hands that palmed and stroked her pendent breasts. He felt dizzy.

He sighed, and felt his throat grow thick with desire, his pulse throbbing there, as elsewhere.

"*Ecciti i mei sensi, Bella.*"

"Excite your senses?" Clio turned to him, her voice clipped. "You are the silliest man I have ever met."

"It is my natural cultural disposition." He smiled wryly, coyly referring to her thesis, poking a little fun at her serious ideas.

She pulled back. "I... didn't think you were listening."

He closed his eyes for a brief moment, breathing in and out. "Oh, I was listening. Shall we go inside? I'm betting you will like the interior even better than the gardens."

She nodded, subdued.

The moment was past. He squared his shoulders and led the way back to the house. Just as he was feeling a little lighter, he heard her voice behind him.

"You simply must do something to save the villa from being sold, Guillermo. It would be a crying shame to let it go after it's been in your family for over four hundred years. It's your duty to at least give it a try."

He groaned. She was going to kill him.

"Senior Memmo!" The old man intercepted them as they entered through an arched set of double doors from the terrace into a wide tiled hall. He followed them, talking so rapidly that Clio's Italian almost failed her. "Marcella is very angry with you. You did not say you are coming. You did not come to say hello. You did not say you bring a guest."

"*Si, si*, Martino. I am a very bad fellow. I know." Guillermo stopped to embrace the old man, and kiss his cheeks.

Martino stood still as a post and glared at Guillermo, his wrinkled eyes darting in her direction.

"Martino, please allow me to introduce my friend, Clio Sinclair McBeal."

Clio smiled and put out her hand.

The old man, Martino, peered at her through squinty eyes, his weathered face serious. Then he nodded and took her hand in his. It felt like rough tree bark, hard and stiff. "Well-a-com-a, Signorina Macca-a-beal-a. Macca-a-beal-a. English, eh?"

"How do you do Martino. Please call me Clio," she said in her fluent Italian, and his face broke into a wide smile.

"*Si, si*. Clio." He turned away nodding, and mumbled as he left, "Marcella is serving dinner in one hour, in the kitchen." He shot Guillermo a look over his shoulder as though daring him to contradict. "We eat early. Because you no warn us. You best not complain. Marcella make up rooms for you - Le Conte for you, Signora Gemma's for Bibi, and the *Stanza Acqua* for Signorina Clio. I put the bags in. You show, eh?"

Guillermo bit his lip, seemed to worry over something, then glanced at his watch and nodded. "Okay. *Grazie*, Martino."

He turned to her. "We'd better be on our best behavior for the first while, or Marcella will poison the soup." He grinned, raising his dark brows with mock fear. "Come, let's freshen up for dinner, then I will show you what we have time for before dinner is served." He led her up a sweeping staircase along one side of the grand, timber-ceilinged hall. A large portrait of a beautiful dark-haired woman hung at the landing.

Before she could ask about it, a voice echoed from below, "Memmo. There you are. Are you going to introduce me to your friend?"

Clio lurched to a stop. A very thin young woman with long straight brown hair stood in the centre of the hall, her hands on her narrow hips. She swung her head and flipped her hair around like a cape.

Guillermo greeted her with a broad smile. "Bibi. You're here."

"Of course I'm here. I'm motivated." She smirked and shook her head up at them, her gaze questioning as she peered at Clio.

That made no sense to Clio, but Guillermo threw his head back and gave a belly laugh that bounded off the walls. "Bibi, Clio, Clio, my baby sister Bianca. Happy? See you at dinner."

"Of course," Bianca replied as she strolled away. "I'm looking forward to getting to know you, Clio."

Clio gave a little shrug and a wave down the stairs at Bianca before Guillermo ushered her along a corridor.

Guillermo led her to a door, stopped abruptly and swept it open with a flourish. "The *Stanza Acqua*. Meet you here in twenty minutes?"

"Ok," she said, and slipped inside as he carried on down the hall. She quietly closed the door of the chamber and looked around. Unlike Pia's restored farmhouse, this villa bore its years with patient good grace, but had clearly not been modernized or even freshened up in recent decades. It was a lovely room, nonetheless, in all the quintessentially Tuscan ways. Square, with a sloped timber ceiling. The palest blue stucco on the walls was chipped, gouged and faded, though this patina lent it character. She touched its scarred surface, wondering at the stories its centuries old skin held secret. An old fashioned black iron bed with an ornate headboard dominated the simply furnished room. It was draped with a light printed coverlet that fell to the floor and bunched there, as though it were a lady in the midst of a curtsy. There was a small bedside table and an old dresser in dark polished wood.

Wondering why it was called the Water Room, Clio stepped to the tall rectangular casement window, pulled back the formal but faded blue drapery, soft on her fingers, and looked out.

Below, she overlooked what she had not yet seen in the garden, partly obscured by dark green oleander and silvery olive branches, a large rectangular stone pond adjacent to the formal Italian garden, with dark, still green water in the basin but none flowing from the central fountain figure - she could not make it out. From the basin ran a narrow channel that led to another long rectangular pond along the side wall of the single story wing that Guillermo had mentioned, the soft sound of the trickling water drifting up to her. Along the wall, on a kind of shelf, interspersed with terra cotta pots of greenery, Clio could make out a series of figures in weathered buff stone. She would have to take a closer look at the latter to see how old they were, and of what quality.

Clio rolled her shoulders, reaching back to pinch the tight muscles on the sides of her neck. She was tired. It was a long drive down, and she'd been keyed up all day. She sat on the edge of the bed, drooping a little, and let her eyes close. She was happy to have an opportunity to see the villa, but it was such a strain being with Guillermo. He was relentless with the flirtations, despite his promises. She had to constantly be vigilant to keep her cool around him.

Ridiculous man. Despite half growing up in Italy, she could never understand how they could pour out emotion all day long. And for what? Although they were as inclined to have a genuine temper tantrum over one thing or another, they were just as likely to be putting on a performance - for what reason she still had not perfectly worked out. Something to do with *bella figura*, she supposed. To look good, whatever that meant in their eyes. To be charming, friendly, warm, enthusiastic - no matter what they were feeling on the inside. It was emotionally exhausting.

Her parents, despite their academic interest in the Classics, always kept the Italians and Greeks at a comfortable impersonal arm's length. They themselves maintained a cooler, more reserved northern demeanor that suited their important lives, their important academic careers, and their important circles of academic colleagues.

I suppose that's why they were so distraught when they caught me making out with Hektor– black haired, golden skinned, dark eyed, like Dionysius, so comfortable in his skin, such a sensualist, and so effulgent with his emotions that he simply swept her off her feet– literally. Oh, how she had been carried away by him.

She imagined if she were to get involved with another Mediterranean man, they would lose it completely. And perhaps she would too, in another sense. *Can't let that happen again.*

Pity she was so attracted to them. Despite the complete lack of logic in their behavior, she couldn't stop the flustered, hot feeling that shook her whenever a man like Guillermo got too close. When he looked at her with those lively laughing blue eyes, flashed his careless bright white smile, leaned too close so that she felt the heat of him, smelled his stirring male scent, touched her hair or let his hot breath fan over her sensitive skin, she melted into a puddle of pure, mindless sensation. Her brain went completely numb at moments like that. It was such a distraction, she was unable to hold onto a coherent thought, never mind string a sensible sentence together.

She'd deliberately given him more than he'd bargained for in the car, when he'd asked about her thesis. She knew he didn't really care, and was only humoring her. That's the type of man he was. So she'd decided to humor herself at his expense.

He'd surprised her with his sharp intellect. He seemed to share her interest in the arts and history, and was so knowledgeable. He was clearly more than a pretty face. The combination was hard to resist. Neither was she prepared for the chemistry that surged between them in close proximity. The more she spoke, the hotter his looks became. And the more his bedroom eyes burned into her with desire, the harder it was for her to concentrate on her words. She felt fevered under his gaze, and desperate to escape before she did something uncharacteristic, like throw herself into his arms and suck on those beautiful sensual lips. A tremor shook her, and she opened her eyes. There was her bag on the floor by the wall.

Clio got up to change her clothes and wash her face and hands for dinner.

What a relief to arrive and meet the old man, and the spunky sister, Bianca. She wanted to laugh at the warm playful banter between Guillermo and Bianca. Clio didn't have brothers or sisters with whom she could share that close, familiar kind of relationship, and felt a pang of jealousy. And the affection between Guillermo and the old man, Martino, was touching. Almost like they were family, too.

Clio felt these two could help her, and the formidable Marcella, whom she had yet to meet, but seemed to rule the roost here at the villa, be her allies to keep the randy Guillermo at bay. Otherwise, she'd never survive the weekend intact.

After Clio washed, and changed her clothes, she ventured downstairs. He'd said to meet him on the landing, but it couldn't be that hard to find the kitchen, so she started down alone.

"You're a fool, Memmo. I can't believe you think this is going to work."

Clio froze on the stairs, nerves prickling. Bianca was just below her...

"It's worth a try." Guillermo laughed. "There's no harm in that, surely."

"You're smarter than that. Or you're even more arrogant than I thought."

"I think I know a little bit more about the art of love than you do, little sister."

"Hah! Love, what do you know of love? You have stars in your eyes, *fratello*. I don't know where you found her, but I could see right away she's not your type. In fact it's worse than that. She's vulnerable. It's unconscionable, what you're trying to do."

"Bibi. You insult me. I'm no monster."

"No. You go too far this time, Memmo. It's different with your women in Firenze. They know you by reputation before they begin. Not everyone is amenable to your stupid one-night stands, and this is no way to go about it, anyway. You have to set some limits to these games of yours. Have some integrity."

"*Pish*. You're one to talk, Bibi, with your musicians and footballers."

Clio stumbled, and caught herself before stepping down silently another step or two. Her breath was locked in her throat, and she swallowed, trying to find more air. She gripped the baluster to steady herself. Her eyes tingled, hot and filled with pressure.

Vulnerable? What am I doing here? I don't belong here.

"You can't continue with this charade, Memmo. I won't– *shht!*"

"What?"

"I hear something."

Clio forced herself to breathe deeply and calmly through a ribcage that felt as tight as a vise. It's okay. She wasn't out of control, anyway, despite the sensations that his silly flirtations stirred up in her. She wasn't naive. Now she would know better. Now she would be extra vigilant. She wouldn't be put in a vulnerable position this time. She knew what was at stake.

She stepped blithely down the last steps into the hall and turned to face them with a smile.

"Ah. *Ciao, Bella*," Guillermo said.

"Oh, hi. There you are. Am I late?"

"No. Come on. Marcella will be expecting us." Guillermo extended a hand to guide her.

Clio followed Bianca through a stone archway into a corridor that stepped down immediately to the kitchen, Guillermo bringing up the rear. A wall of warm air met them, like another medium, and Clio wondered whether there was a breathing apparatus she ought to be using.

"Memmo." An older woman, small and wiry, tossed aside a tea towel and lurched toward Guillermo, gripping him tightly in her strong arms, smothering him with kisses. Then she shoved him roughly away. "So this is how you treat Marcella. You come and go as you please, you ignore me. Hmph." She turned back to her work, retrieving her tea towel and grabbing a bowl.

"I'm sorry Marcella, *cara*," Guillermo said, and bowed his head repentantly. He grinned, and the old woman's sour countenance broke into a reluctant smile. "This is my guest, Clio Sinclair McBeal."

Marcella's face was a wonder to behold. It tensed and pinched and twitched as she thought about...well Clio didn't know what she was thinking about, but it made her wonder if there was something inherently wrong with her name. "*Buongiorno*, Signorina Seen-clair."

"*Buongiorno, Signora* Marcella," Clio replied. "I feel terrible that you were not warned of our arrival. I thought the plans had been made days ago. Is there something I can do to help you with dinner? I would like to make up for our bad manners."

"Whose?" Guillermo guffawed.

"He-heh," Bianca laughed.

Marcella peered at Clio, seeming to evaluate the sincerity of her offer, though clearly Clio's proficiency with the language had impressed her and raised her in Marcella's estimation. "*Grazie, signiorina*, but no. Lucky for this young pup that I have things from my garden. But you will have to be satisfied with a simple country meal."

"I am very happy. That is my favourite kind of meal. Simple and pure country food, lovingly prepared," Clio responded.

Marcella glared at Guillermo. "At least some people's children have been properly raised," she said, returning to her bowl.

CHAPTER 12

After a delicious, though simple meal of salad, vegetables and pasta, the tension had subsided, and it was clear to Clio that Marcella, recovered from her earlier displeasure, doted on Guillermo, even more than on Bianca. She pampered and spoiled him, patted and tweaked him, brushed lint from his sleeve and wiped sauce from his chin. He took it all in stride, clearly enjoying the attention, showering her with smiles.

Once they were finished eating, Guillermo gave Marcella a big bear hug, not very subtly dismissed Bianca and led Clio back to the hall.

"Which rooms would you like to tour tonight?"

Despite her indignation at being the clear object of Guillermo's predatory games, Clio curiosity about the villa had not diminished. However there were two more days in which to see and enjoy every part of the historic residence.

"Perhaps you could show me a couple of the public rooms down here. Then I think I'd like to get some rest, if you don't mind."

Guillermo's eyes assessed her narrowly. Clio could tell he sensed something off, something had definitely changed in the temperature of their exchanges since their time in the gardens, but he didn't know what. It's just as well. Clio didn't know how she would act if he knew she'd overheard his humiliating conversation with his sister. More effusive compliments, more empty promises. He couldn't be that calculating and selfish. No one could.

"*Tutto bene*. Come this way," he led her through a double arched doorway to one side of the hall. "In here is the principal salon. It is actually the smaller of two, but on the other side of the villa…" He shook his head sadly, "…*allora*, it has been neglected. The furniture is very old, and repairs are needed." He swung an arm out and let it flop back down to his side. "We have not used that wing for a long, long time."

For the moment, Clio forgot her irritation with his personal scheming, and felt a wash of empathy for him and his family. How sad to lose a home that meant so much to so many for so long. She stepped through the doors beside him, and her breath stopped in her throat.

In awe, she glided to the fireplace, ran a hand along the carved stone mantle, admiring the metal candelabra and small busts that decorated it. The high ceiling was vaulted and plastered between the exposed stone arches, with painted frescos decorating the vaults.

The color was mainly a creamy white, with cherubs and gold bunting along the crown. The centre of the vault had a series of hexagonal gilt egg-and-dart bordered medallions, each with a figure or two in colorful robes, some with pastoral scenery. It took her breath away.

"Oh, oh my," she sighed. "I had no idea. These are original."

"Yes. From the late sixteenth century."

"What have you done to preserve them?"

"Nothing lately." Guillermo snorted with disgust. "My Nonno was a little better at consulting experts. We are very fortunate that the climate here is very dry, and relatively free of atmospheric pollution. They have come to little harm. We have much greater challenges with the conservation projects I oversee in Firenze."

Clio turned to Guillermo, registering but pushing aside his brusque response. "Your father's father?"

Guillermo's smile was wide, but she sensed tension in the lines of his face. "*Si*. The last *Conte*. He's in a nursing home now. It would break his heart to see what is happening here. You can see the gilt is tarnished and the frescos cracked. And there has been a little water damage in areas where the roof has leaked."

"Your grandfather is alive?" She had thought he had no one but his siblings.

His eyes dropped, and he released a deep sigh. "*Si*. He's been there a very long time."

"Well then, doesn't that mean... isn't he...?" Clio sputtered. "I'm confused."

Guillermo rubbed his hands along his face, and threaded his fingers through his long hair. He released a breath, glaring at her. "Nonno had a massive stroke. He has dementia. He's been... deteriorating... gradually...for over ten years, since before my father died. Jacopo has power of attorney." His voice was thick with emotion. "And Nonno doesn't really know what's going on, most of the time." His shoulders sagged.

He smiled sadly, turned and strolled across the room, dragging a hand lightly over objects as he went. The camel hump back of an upholstered chair. The bust of a horse. A long credenza against the far wall. To Clio, it seemed as though he was memorizing each object in its place.

Her heart squeezed. "I'm so sorry. Were you very close?"

Guillermo nodded. "We still are. Sometimes he remembers me."

A great weight seemed to have settled on him, and he walked with his chin lowered and his eyes downcast, lost in thought. His bright flame seemed to flicker, his normal fiery energy dimmed, as though a cold wind had blown over him, a menacing presence. He was complex, this man. There was more to him than the smooth, charming carefree adventurer that met the eye.

She moved closer. "Guillermo?"

He circled round and stepped toward her, glancing up, trying to lighten his countenance and succeeding only in pasting on a false facade, restive and brittle.

She reached forward and rested a hand gently on his arm. "I... I'm sorry. I'm sorry about your grandfather, about your parents, about your brother. I really am. I can see how much they mean to you, and how much you have already lost."

Guillermo shrugged and flicked a hand, as if to dismiss the seriousness or heaviness of his emotional burden.

"But, you know..." she hesitated, capturing his gaze as he lifted it to meet to hers. Dark blue. Unreadable. She drew a breath. Plunging in, as into a dark pool of unknown depth, its potential dangers hidden. "You know, you *can* save the villa. You really must save the villa. I can see how the responsibility rests with you. And..." A sharp groove appeared between his dark brows, and his normally full and shapely mouth flattened into a line. A muscle jumped in his brow, a tic. She smiled weakly to soften her words. "And I can see you really don't want to accept this, but... you *have* to do something. You just have to."

He spun away, and strode toward the door, his voice booming suddenly. "You mistake the situation, Clio." He stopped in the doorway. "Come, we have time for one more room before we retire."

She quickened her pace to catch up with him. "Guillermo!"

"Tut, tut." He crooned, slipping his hand into hers. He tilted his head nearer and looked into her eyes, his own dark and slightly wicked. The corner of his mouth tilted up suggestively. "I have another surprise. Something you will like very much."

He led her up the stairs, and she caught her breath, her pulse speeding. He couldn't possibly think that, after one personal and strained conversation, he could take liberties– *oh, shit*. She sounded perfectly Victorian.

Bottom line was, she couldn't trust him. For all she knew, he made up half his troubles and put on his melancholy airs just to draw her sympathy. There was no secret what he wanted, that he'd brought her here with the intention of getting her into his bed. That's who he was, after all.

At the top landing, he turned opposite to the bedroom doors, and led her to the end of the hall. Through a pair of tall narrow green-paneled double doors at the end, he led her out into a space, neither interior nor exterior.

The sun had set, and in the dusky light, she could just make out where he'd brought her. One corner of the *piano nobile*, the upper floor, was in fact an open portico. Large stone arches, inset with iron grates were open to the night air, though a solid vaulted ceiling covered them overhead. She could see the shape of a hexagonal lantern suspended from above, though it was not lit. A ghostly figure stood against the wall on a plinth, some statue in robes, a classical figure.

"Who is that?"

His voice was distracted, murmuring. "One of the Contes. An earlier Gabriel."

"Who else is a Gabriel?"

"My father, my nephew. It is also my second name."

The night air was cool, pleasant. She walked to the grill, gripped the cool metal bars and pressed her face to the gap between. The night was still, but she heard the faint trickle of water from nearby. A crescent moon dipped low over the dark treetops. She filled her lungs and let it out, feeling the delicious sweet country air glide over her face, over her arms.

Her heart swelled. "I'm so sorry," she whispered, not sure if he was listening.

Warm air competed with the cool, tickling the skin between her shoulder blades. A shudder ran down her neck and back, the hairs standing to attention. Clio sensed Guillermo's heat directly behind her. Then his hands rested lightly against her upper arms, rubbing gently up and down, releasing her perfume, mingling with his own masculine scent. Her pulse quickened, fluttering in her chest, and she trembled again. *Oh, stop! No, please, don't stop.*

She was about to turn around when his mouth touched down on her neck, his lips brushing ever so lightly on her skin, like feathers. "*I miei sensi sono pieni di te.*" Her senses were filled with him, too. Dangerously so. The pressure of his hands increased, and her knees went weak. She buckled against him, feeling the solid strength of him holding her upright.

"*Bella. Mi hai stregata.*"

She was the one who was bewitched. In his skillful hands, she gave like warm modeling clay surrendering to the artist, as he turned her to face him, holding her firmly against the length of his body. His hardness pressed into her, and his labored breathing left no secrets between them. He moaned softly, words or just sounds, sensations, as his mouth fluttered over her cheek and neck. She no longer knew. She felt herself becoming whatever he wanted her to be. Galatea to his Pygmalion.

His mouth closed over hers. She heard a high pitched groan. Was that her? Her chin lifted of its own volition, begging for more, just at the moment his hot tongue traced the gap between her lips, coaxing them apart. She gave in too willingly, opening to him, allowing his tongue to enter the dark hungry cavity of her mouth, thrusting and stroking in imitation of the most intimate act. Liquid heat slid down her core, stirring a fire in her belly, flaring, demanding satisfaction. She moaned again, and slid her arms around his neck, pressing herself closer, trying to pull him into her, wrap herself around him. She couldn't stop herself. What was happening to her?

Guillermo pulled his mouth away, gasping, and bent his head to plant passionate kisses at her jaw, her neck, her shoulder, leaving a trail of fire on her skin. His hands gripped her hips tightly, moving with a sense of desperation and need, and he found her breasts.

"*Cara, Bella.* I knew you had the secret fire. I knew you had passion waiting to be freed. I feel it. *Dio, Io arerei,*" he growled.

His delirious words penetrated her fog of lust. Good God! Plow me? That woke her up like a bucket of cold water in her face. She pulled back and shoved him away. "What did you say?"

"What?"

"What do you think you're doing?"

"Uh..." Guillermo swallowed loudly, his expression confused.

She shoved harder, creating more space between them, making it easier to breath, to think. Cool air rushed around her heated body, helping to clear her head. "You promised."

"I...um. *Bella*, I'm-a..." His voice held a pleading tone.

"Inarticulate, clearly. I can't believe you. I'm going to bed."

"Hmm?"

"Without you!" She strode away across the portico toward the hall.

"Con il tempo e posto e io." With you I forget time and place and self.

Again with the sentimental romantic Latin gibberish.

"Oh, stuff it."

CHAPTER 13

"Excellent, Marcella. *Grazie.* Everything looks *perfetto*." Guillermo rubbed his hands together. Marcella could always be counted on to set a good table, and when he had asked her to serve a romantic breakfast for two on the portico, she did so enthusiastically, while assessing him with her squinty x-ray eyes and shaking her head.

It might be a bit obvious, to have breakfast in the place they had shared their first kiss, but it was all in the way it was handled.

"Bibi got her breakfast in bed?" he asked, suddenly concerned she would frustrate his plans.

"She will, when she shows some sign of living," Marcella replied, giving the table setting one last polish and tweak.

Thankfully, his little sister was not an early riser. Whether in the city or the country, she always found ways to entertain herself until the wee hours, and could always be counted on to skip a civilized breakfast table, in favor of *cioccolato calda e pane* in bed followed by he-knew-not-what kind of elaborate spa ritual that usually took several hours. The perfect chaperone.

He bounced on the balls of his feet, anticipating the morning alone with Clio. He checked his watch again.

He closed his eyes, letting the remembered sensations shimmer through his blood. He was still buzzing with the effect of their hot kiss. Who knew? He thought to tease, to plant the idea of an embrace, a kiss in her mind, with the romantic evening setting, always one of his favorite spots at the villa, and a little strategic intimacy. He had *not* expected her to melt like honey in the sun.

"You look very handsome today," muttered Marcella. He glanced up, but she looked away.

Guillermo blinked and ran his hands over his torso and hips. "You think so?" He smiled. He knew he looked good, but he wanted to be irresistible to the young scholar, so he'd dressed and groomed with extra care this morning, keeping her background and tastes in mind. He thought with satisfaction that he looked a little like a young professor away for the weekend.

"Eh. You are always easy on the eyes, Memmo. But today you try harder. Why? What's up with this one?"

His chest filled, his heart tripping, and he sighed. He placed an open hand over his chest "Ah, Marcella. I believe I am in love."

"Pah! You are always in love, you young fool. But this one is…" She shook her head, pulled a face and shrugged.

"What?" He frowned at her. What had she seen? How could she not like the straight-laced, ladylike Clio? Was she not forever scolding him about his loose-moralled, glitzy models and actresses?

Another face, indecipherable. Her eyebrows raised, a pursed mouth, another head shake, a *tsk*, but no words of wisdom. Hmph. He dismissed it. Marcella had good instincts, but she was always worried about him, always giving him unwanted advice. Never mind. He plucked a fresh cut pink rose from the vase Marcella had arranged on the table.

"Well," he said as he stepped out the door, "this one requires a bit more effort, eh?"

Martino's voice from below. "Ah, ah, ah, I take for you, Signorina Clio. Where you want it?"

"*Grazie*, Martino. You can put it by the front door, *per favore.*"

"You are leaving us? So soon?"

"An unexpected change of plans, yes. I'm sorry for the inconvenience. As soon as I have a quick coffee, Signor Guillermo will be taking me back to town, or at least to Stazione Montepulchiano."

"Oh, that's not right," mumbled Martino.

Guillermo's stomach tightened. He strode out onto the landing. Martino was half way down the stairs with Clio's weekend bag, while she stood on the landing, rummaging in her shoulder bag.

"Clio? What's going on?"

She started and looked up. "Oh, Guillermo. I can't stay, I'm sorry to make you drive back so soon. This was a terrible idea."

"No, no. Martino, stop, bring her bag back, *per favore.*" Guillermo turned to Clio, searching her eyes. "Please stay." He realized his grip on the rose was crushing it. He extended his hand to her.

She paused, looking down at the rose, not taking it from him.

Martino paused on the stairs, turned and started up again.

Her head gave a tiny shake, then reluctantly she took the rose, holding it loosely at her side like a pencil, flicking its stem back and forth. "I can't stay, Guillermo. And you know why. I came here only to see the villa. You gave me your word." Her movements were choppy and she slashed her hand through the air, almost knocking her bag off of her shoulder, fumbling to hang on to the rose. "Martino, please take my bag down."

The old man stopped, his eyes scanning from her to him, from him to her. His chest heaved, and he started down again.

Guillermo reached out both hands, palms up. "I'm sorry. *Scusami, ho sbagliato.* I made a mistake last night, Clio. It was an accident. The night, the air, your eyes, your lips—"

"Stop. Stop it. That's what I mean. You can't control yourself. And I know why *you* think I am here, but you are mistaken. I came only out of curiosity and concern for your villa. I wished to see it.

You mistake me if you think I am not a serious scholar, Guillermo. I am very *passionate* about my studies!"

As if she realized the double-entendre of her word choice, she looked away and her face suffused with color.

"It won't happen again. I promise."

"Your promises are worthless. I don't believe you anymore."

"*Bella.*" Guillermo reached for her hand, hesitated. Then he dropped to his knee, his hand still poised in the air, imploring.

Clio's eyes widened at his gesture. He could see her reacting, judging, deliberating by the fleeting expression in her eyes. Her face was so readable, so open.

"*Scusami, scusami.* I am most sincere this time. I have been a terrible host. At least stay until I have had a chance to show you the villa. *Per favore*, have a little breakfast, and I will give you a proper tour, an academic tour. I have a great deal knowledge about the villa and garden that I can share with you."

She hesitated, fiddling with the stem of the rose. His heart surged with hope. Why was he was so motivated to keep this woman near him? He couldn't let her go. Not yet. "Martino, bring the lady's bag back up, please."

Martino rolled his eyes, hesitated and turned up the stairs again.

"No, Martino. Please. I will be leaving today."

"After the tour." Guillermo stood up, nodding encouragement. There was still time to change her mind. The tour could take a while.

Clio turned to Martino, about to speak. Martino froze.

Guillermo's chest squeezed, and he jerked forward, patting the air with his hands. "Okay, okay. I will take you back later today if that is what you really want, but first, the tour. A proper thorough tour. We will have a nice breakfast, and then I will show you the study. We have drawings, books, antiques, records—"

He'd said the magic word. Her eyes lit up. Hooked.

The last thing Guillermo needed was to revisit and reflect on the beauty and history of his ancestral home detail by detail. It would be like salt in his wounds. She would kill him, this woman. But he had her. He set the hook a little deeper to make sure she was invested in all that he could show her. "In fact, let us quickly go to the study now, and make a plan. Then we can discuss the details over a leisurely breakfast. Marcella has set a table for us on the portico." He gestured to the door.

Clio slanted a skeptical look in his direction.

He lightly touched her back, guiding her down the stairs. Martino raised his salt and pepper brows in question. "Just set Signorina Clio's bag there in the hall, Martino. Out of the way. We will be a while yet."

Marcella came out onto the landing, scowling, hands akimbo. "Where are you going? Breakfast is ready."

"We'll be right back, Marcella. In *un momento*."

"A quick breakfast only. I want to get started so we can head out early," Clio said, back straight as a pike, chin high. "Perhaps I can identify something to help you save the villa. I have some ideas—"

"*Si, si*." Guillermo humored her. He'd bought a little time, that was all that mattered. "It's possible."

Martino shook his head, sighed and preceded them down the stairs with Clio's bag, muttering, "There are no quick meals in this house."

~

Clio agreed to a tour only to placate Guillermo and his caretakers. He was winding up to lay his extravagant charm on as thickly and cheaply as Cool Whip on tiramisu, and when he dropped to his knee on the landing, her first reaction–lurching heart, flushing cheeks– had been purely emotional–*how romantic!* But then her inner critic, far more sensible, had taken over. It was more of his typical Latin melodrama, and she'd had about all she was prepared to take. The sooner she got away from here, and from him, the better. Although she was very curious about the villa, she needed to be back in Firenze working on her thesis outline. And soon.

And it was a good thing, too. When she awoke, she was all resolve and determination. But when she saw him stride out onto the landing this morning, she'd almost swooned with remembered desire. Damn his eyes.

He was wearing red leather sneakers with skinny black jeans that hugged his narrow hips so casually, a cashmere v-neck sweater stretched across his contoured chest in a sky blue the color of his eyes, and casually tossed around his neck was an ivory silk knit scarf. He looked like a model in some Italian designer fashion magazine.

She could have laughed. Even her stuffed-shirt academic father knew how to don khaki and flannel for a country outing. But then Father was a Scot, and Guillermo Italian. Except Guillermo was so achingly beautiful her eyes smarted with unshed tears. His dark hair tousled with waves across his forehead, tucked behind his ears, and she was struck with a wave of remembered passion from his touch the previous evening. Her pulse began to race. The feeling of liquid heat burned through her, unfamiliar and disorienting, making her legs watery and weak.

She really had to get out of here, and soon.

Instead, she grabbed her camera bag and followed Guillermo across the hall and through a doorway further back and opposite the salon he'd shown her the night before, in the wing that supposedly was unused and run-down.

He led her into a modest sized, rectangular study, with a large arched window on the far wall, and a timbered ceiling. Bright morning light streamed in, casting the room in deep shadow. This part was not neglected. The sunlight reflected off of the broad surface of a wooden desk in front of the window. Its surface was bare and highly polished. The room was clean and neat, but it did not look lived in, or much used.

"I have plans for both the villa and the garden in here somewhere," Guillermo said, striding in, leaving her standing just inside the doorway. He opened a credenza on a side wall and crouched to search its interior. "*Stronzo*." He stood and came back, flicked on a light and returned to rummage through papers and files. "Hmph." Standing, he crossed to a bookshelf on the opposite wall and scanned its contents, frowning. "I'm sure this is where I left them last time I was here. Jacopo must have returned them to the library."

It would be good to see the plans, and get her bearings. Then she could decide how long it would take to have a quick tour before she left. And also on which areas to focus most of her attention. She wouldn't want to overlook any artworks–

He turned to her. "Hey, come on. Come this way." He waited for Clio to move toward him and then turned to another door beside a modest marble fireplace in the centre of the sidewall. "I expect you'll like this."

Clio followed him, curious. The room was tasteful and traditional, but seemed to have been redone in relatively modern times. Or at least parts of it had. A spontaneous trill of giddy laughter escaped her lips.

"Oh my God! Is this for real?"

The study was a mere anti-chamber to the room she now faced. It was five or six times larger, as wide as the study was long.

Guillermo stopped and turned to her, a wide grin slicing across his features. He stared at her for a moment, his eyes sparkling. "I told you."

"I... I would not have expected... such a room, here. I mean, it's a lovely, lovely villa, but..." It was hard to find breath, and she found herself gasping.

"*Si*. The villa is special, worthy of preservation, though not museum quality. But the library has always been a favorite project with my ancestors. It is..." He circled a hand in the air, indicating both the room itself and the substantial collection of antique books and artifacts and even gleaming brass mechanical devices that packed the shelves.

It defied words. It wasn't as large as the public libraries she'd seen, nor as ornate, especially as those she'd seen at monasteries and universities. But for a modest, and she used that word lightly, family library it was exquisite. It had a certain charming intimacy that those grand libraries often lacked. The proportions of the room, the painted vaulting of the ceiling, the lovely wood bookshelves flanking both long walls, interspersed with more of the long, arched windows– every detail was perfection. Where the study had but one, this room hosted three windows on the long side, and another on the end wall. This would take longer than she had anticipated.

Clio floated further into the library, her body weightless, gliding around busts and small figures that perched on pedestals in the centre of the room. There were two long marble-topped trestle tables flanked by six chairs each, with a cozy reading area wrapped around another fireplace, opposite the windows.

"This is where I...where we did our homework. Whenever we were here, that is. We actually attended school in Firenze and abroad." Guillermo's voice was soft, wistful as he gazed up. "But here is where I fell in love with history, with art and architecture. When my maths were too difficult, or Machiavelli's concepts too obscure, I would stare at the walls and ceilings and daydream of a time long ago." Guillermo's voice slurred, as though he were talking to himself.

"Is the collection catalogued?"

He did not respond.

"Guillermo?"

"Mm? Partly. Some of it is older than others." He shrugged. "Some more valuable."

"Guillermo! What are you going to do?"

He blinked at her. "What do you mean?"

She threw her hands up and slapped them against her thighs. "How can you sell this villa? What will happen to all of this?"

"It is not I who am selling the villa, if you recall." His lips flattened. "I suppose the new owner will keep it, or if he doesn't want it, it could be sold at auction. There are collectors of such things, I believe." His voice was deliberately flat and emotionless, facile.

Clio released a theatrical groan. "Don't be obtuse. You. Your family. It is all the same." She shook a finger in his face. "You can't simply dispose of it for money. That's criminal."

"Hmph." Guillermo moved off, scanning the shelves for whatever it was he could not find in the study. "Criminal is what my brother apparently did with his investments, and with the contracts awarded by his ministerial portfolio. Selling the villa is just a 'crying shame', as you say. An embarrassment. But...what can be done?"

Clio felt a sense of outrage that eclipsed her immediate need to escape Guillermo's company. At the moment he was more ornery than horny. How could he be so blasé? How could he abdicate all personal responsibility for the villa. If it were her own, she would do anything; she would fight to the death to save it. Through clenched teeth she said, "I'll tell you what can be done. First of all, you can sit down and apply for historic preservation funds. I know there is a lot of competition, but certainly with your expertise, and your connections, and furthermore your family's importance, you could write a few persuasive letters?"

He reached for a roll of drawings on a shelf. "Here they are."

"Secondly, you can work to find new streams of revenue." Her voice was becoming shrill, and her face hot. Clio wanted to scream. *Calm down. It's not your villa. It's not your problem to solve.* She had to let it go, but blood raced through her, making her head hot and her muscles clench. She pinched the bridge of her nose, slowing her breathing, calming her rapid pulse.

Guillermo carried the drawings to one of the long study tables and unraveled them, leaning over them with one hand on each edge, holding them flat. "Come and see. These are the villa plans–"

A series of loud bangs echoed from the front hall, reverberating through the open doorways and against the walls of the library.

Clio yelped.

Guillermo frowned and stood up, letting the heavy drawings recoil with a swoosh and a thud as the roll closed in on itself.

The sounds seemed to bounce off the vaults. It was quickly followed by a cacophony of muffled voices, punctuated by shouts and barks, and the scratching of nails on the marble floors.

"What the hell?" Guillermo tucked the drawings under his arm and stomped toward the door.

"Signor Memmo. Signor Memmo, come quickly." Marcella's agitated voice preceded her through the doorway from the study. Bursting in, she sighed dramatically when she saw them, and held a hand to her heaving chest. "Come. *Che bufalo* is here to buy the villa!"

CHAPTER 14

"He is here now. Signor d'Aldobrandin is here now," Marcella announced as she led them into the hall, her hands flapping like they did when she shook dishwater from them.

Stronzo! The hall was filled with flashing color, people and dogs. Dogs barking and scrambling and scratching around everyone's legs, adding to the mayhem.

"Jiggy Thang! Lil Peppa, come here!"

"Oochie Bone, settle down, don't chew on that."

"Shuddup you dogs!"

"D-Wayne, don't touch that thang!"

It was too hot, Guillermo's head buzzed, his heart thumped in his chest. Putting his fingers into his mouth, he whistled loudly, the shrill sound reverberating off the walls of the tall, tiled room.

When the noise died away, even the dogs cowering and whimpering, everyone stared in his direction.

"*Buongiorno.* What can I do for you?"

An enormous muscular black man stepped forward out of the throng, a slender, sexy woman gripping his arm. "Yo. Bon journey. Ah am Mad Masta Richie R a.k.a. Sling DoomZ, and dis be my boo, Foxy Diamond." He gestured with a massive Rolex wreathed hand to the glamorous woman at his side, who waved and cocked a hip. Guillermo squinted. They both wore white. White from head to toe. The man wore a long baggy t-shirt, crushed velvet tuxedo jacket, faux leather pants that scrunched and rumpled all the way down to his gleaming white high-top sneakers with their fat tongues lolling not unlike the menagerie of dogs squatting around his ankles. One of every breed, apparently. *I wonder which one is Jiggy Thang?* The slender woman wore a mini dress that appeared to be painted on her, and oversized sunglasses.

A skinny black man, a good six or eight inches shorter than the giant, skirted around him, leapt forward and thrust out his hand. "Hey man, I be Slim QTip, agent and manager for Masta DoomZ, here." The skinny guy wore an oversized graphic muscle shirt printed with a massive, collarbone to crotch-spanning Virgin Mary that made Guillermo inwardly cringe. *Mama would roll over in her grave. Twice.* Slim QTip's sinewy bare brown arms were riddled with swirling blue graffiti, inscribing large spiky letters that Guillermo could make no sense of. His neck was swathed in enough golden bling to break his skinny neck. More scrunched leather pants, in black. On his head, backwards, was a ball cap that appeared to be made of black crocodile skin.

Guillermo paused, blinked. *Who are these people and why are they in my house?* He strode forward, fists on his hips, about to grill them when QTip spoke.

"My boss has come to look ova the villa, like we discussed on the phone, Mista Fitucci. If dis goin' happen, then what we gotta do is have a good look around. See the potentialities. Experience the place, yo?"

"Hmm." Guillermo, nodded sagely, rubbing his fingers across his brow, at a complete loss for words. *What's the best tactic here—stall?*

He attempted a welcoming smile and offered his hand. Slim QTip pounced on the offered hand, shaking it, rotating into a thumb grip, sliding back to hook fingers, and then thumped his fist on top of Guillermo's, which Guillermo clumsily returned, mentally shaking his head. He deemed it best to speak in English.

"As-a my housekeeper mentioned a moment ago, I am not Signor Fitucci, I am-a Guillermo d'Aldobrandin. This-a is my family home. We were just about to sit down to breakfast in the portico, gentlemen, lady. Would you..." He noticed two boys lurking in the doorway behind the adults. "...and your family care to join us? Then we can-a talk at our leisure while we await-a Signor Fitucci's arrival." Presumably he was on his way. He'd better be.

They all looked at each other, checking in. Some voiceless consensus was arrived at, then Mr. QTip said, "It's like, whateva, yo? We gonna, like, take yo up on that oppatunity. We gonna eat breakfast witchu, Mista D."

Guillermo turned, pulled a face at Marcella, Martino and Clio, who stood behind him, frozen with mouths agape. He appealed silently to Clio. What could she be thinking? The subject of her leaving seemed to be moot for the moment. "Let us-a go up." They nodded like marionettes, and he could completely relate to the blank, stunned expressions on their faces.

He offered his arm to Clio, she took it, and he practically dragged her leaden body back up the stairs and out the green door to the portico, while Marcella scrambled back to the kitchen to fetch more place settings and work some miracle of loaves and fishes to multiply the amount of food provided. She was in her element.

∼

And on that side, you see the formal Renaissance gardens. My great grandfather built the pool." Guillermo explained, pointing out through the arched opening of the portico at the grounds below.

Clio watched the muscles flexing in his back and shoulder as he raised and lowered his arm. There was tension bunched there. A muscle in his eyebrow twitched as he forced a smile that looked nothing like the charming one she'd seen and dismissed so often as fake. Clearly he was barely holding himself together. *He really does care.* Her heart ached for him.

The sleeve of his sky blue sweater was pushed back, and her eyes lingered on the smooth golden skin and dark hairs of his exposed forearm. He too wore a gold chain around his wrist, albeit a much smaller and more subtle one than Mad Masta Richie's. He shook his wrist repeatedly, an agitated gesture, and she wondered what he was thinking. Scheming. She could sense the gears turning in his clever head. His veneer of civility covered the powerful emotions he held in check. He was capable of diplomacy, able to observe and analyze, playing it cool, waiting before reacting. He was a mature business man after all, not the loose screw he'd seemed at Pia's place.

A shiver darted up her spine, tingling at the back of her neck, remembering his breath, his touch and their kiss from last night. *I have to put it from my mind!* All she wanted was to get away from him, from the temptation of his piercing looks and his heat. She found it difficult to follow the conversation. Her head felt too light, as though it would lift off and float away like a hot air balloon. She pressed her fingers against each temple, trying to focus her attention. The day was warming up quickly, and she plucked at her shirt, sticking to the sheen of sweat that had formed on her chest and back. Now they were forced to deal with this unexpected intrusion. She glanced at the cool, glamorous Foxy with her overt sexuality. The heat didn't seem to bother her. Clio's wish to go home had just got bumped down the list of priorities. Way down.

"I respect your person, Mista D," said the big guy, Mad Richie, apparently a successful rap artist and record producer from the States, among other business interests such as shoes, clothing and liquor, which his wife Foxy apparently ran. Clio wouldn't know a famous rap artist if she fell over one. Too bad he wasn't an opera singer.

But he and his entourage smelled of money, loads of money. "I gotta family, too," he was saying. "An' my family, we got needs, see? My opinion is dat this a cool crib but it need a few things to, to *modernize*. No disrespect to yo gran'fatha, but it gonna need a *new* pool, wit a pool shack and a bar down there." He pointed, his thick gold chains chinking together. Richie grinned at his wife and kids. "We gotta have some place to be chillin, yeah?"

"That sounds great, Richie, honey. The boys is gonna like that. Ain'tcha boys?"

"Yeah, Ma." The older one's eyes were locked on his smartphone.

"Can we have ATVs?" asked the younger one.

Clio cringed. So far Mad Richie hadn't said much about his intentions, but it did not seem like a good fit. Wasn't he just having a look? Why was he talking like it was a signed deal? Hopefully Guillermo's brother hadn't agreed to anything yet, or signed any papers without talking to this guy. Surely he wouldn't sell the villa to a buyer like this, who was just looking for a luxurious vacation home for his family, and maybe an old-world status symbol. She tugged gently on Guillermo's sleeve, clearing her throat and murmuring, "Guillermo, maybe you should call Jacopo. Do you think he–?"

"Here's-a the *caffe*," Martino came out with a pot in each hand, Marcella having recruited him to help serve the suddenly enlarged crowd. His face was pinched, and his dark eyes darted around the table, as though he expected someone to pull a knife at any moment. Clio imagined he'd encountered few blacks in his rural existence, except those stereotyped in American movies.

Marcella entered directly on his heels, carrying platters. "Please sit down-a and enjoy-a." She set the platters on the table, and went out for more, while Martino circled the table pouring coffee and steamed milk as everyone took their seats.

Guillermo sat at the head of a long table that had been set, their breakfast for two having been swept away by an efficient Marcella, both his hands resting on the table in front of him. He leaned back, his fingers drumming restlessly on the tablecloth with an incessant tattoo: *drrrt, drrrt, drrrt*. Clio peered sideways at him, noticed his jaw working. He kept his eyes trained on Richie, like a cobra ready to strike. Guillermo was flanked by Mad Richie and his wife Foxy. Clio sat opposite QTip, and the two children, boys about the ages of ten and twelve, sat at the far end, each of them now engrossed by games on their smartphones. Thankfully, the three dogs had been banished to the front terrace.

"Yeah. Now dat's sick coffee. Dat's why I gotta connection wit Italy, yo? Italy is, like, da shit. I had a dream to have dis crib, a crib like dis, to get away. I'm from Chicago, yeah? I love Chicago, it's where I'm from, it's part of who I am, but dis bourgeous thang, we caught dat vibe. Me and my family, we gotta get away from America sometime. Evabody in America intense, yeah? We gotta chillax."

"Boys, put those away and have some manners, here. You's wit Italian royalty, here. Have some respect."

"Erm..." Guillermo grimaced, his neck flooding with color, though apparently no one but Clio noticed.

"Yeah, Ma." They made no change.

Guillermo swallowed, and Clio nodded. She rotated her shoulders, rubbing her arms, trying to ease the hot tingling sensation on her skin. This wouldn't happen. This couldn't happen. Her heart squeezed painfully. *What must Guillermo be feeling right now? Couldn't he just ask these people to leave?*

Marcella and Martino brought more platters of food, fruit and eggs and bread.

"*Grazie*, Marcella, Martino. Did Andreas, uh, Signor Fitucci provide you with plans? Do you know about the layout of rooms and such?"

QTip replied, "I seen some of dat, yeah, but Mista DoomZ here he wanned to see it fresh. If dis is gonna happen, den it gotta have the right vibe, yo?"

"It's very old, Richie," said Foxy. "I'm worried about the bathrooms. There's a funny smell. The kids have to have their own bathrooms, baby. And so do the guest rooms."

"Don't worry 'bout dat, sugar. We gonna figure it out. We gonna eat and Mista D. gonna bust out de tour, and den we'll see."

"Your... er, wife is correct," Guillermo said. "It's over four hundred years old, and really it hasn't been modernized much. You might find it doesn't meet your high standards of comfort."

"You bo janglin', Mista D," said Richie, chuckling. " I don't have no ego. I'm cool wit de old-ness of it. It's all in how you interpret it. I'm a artist, yeah. I can look atta old place like dis, and I can see it's got hella possibilities. We gonna change it up a little, dat's all."

Clio spoke before she'd considered her words. "I just want to point out that, of course, whomever buys the villa will be responsible for all the historic artwork. There are paintings and sculpture..." Clio had no idea what else. She hadn't even seen the place yet. But if the library was any indication, she supposed the villa was full of valuable artifacts.

"It's like, you know what? I really appreciate dat, missus. I'm a artist, yo?"

"Um. Mm. There might be some laws protecting some of it. But, perhaps the collection might go to one of the universities?" Clio said. "Or even...or even, the University of Florence Art History department might be interested. They might want to send someone out. It could take awhile to–"

"Never mind the art. What kind of internet connectivity do you get out here?" Foxy asked, turning to Q-Tip. "Do you think you could set up a hot spot that would run the online shop without interruption?"

"What did you have in mind, Richie?" Guillermo asked, his tone flat, infinitely patient, though his fingers continued to drum, and he hadn't touched his food or drink.

"Guillermo, I don't think this is what Jacopo wanted," Clio mumbled. "Maybe it would be better to wait for Mr. Fitucci before getting into specifics."

He smiled at her, but there was hardness behind the smile, as though he'd resigned himself to something brutal, and was steeled to it. His face was becoming familiar to her. "It's alright, Clio. I know *exactly* what Jacopo wants. Let's hear what Mr. DoomZ is looking for. Maybe he won't find this villa suitable."

The sober emphasis Guillermo placed on Mad Richie's ridiculous nickname told her exactly what he thought. If the villa fell into this man's hands, it would be ruined beyond recognition, beyond salvation. And he held out little hope.

"Let's make sure that he doesn't," Clio murmured in Italian, drawing an approving snort from Marcella.

"No, man, no. I mean, I think we gonna hop on dis. We check out some otha villas, but yeah, what they be *callin'* villas is just fugly old farm houses. Dis place got all dat. I can feel a connection already." He took a big bite of Marcella's bread and drowned it with coffee. "So, the reality is, dis place is kickin. I gotta make a few changes, yeah, to fit our lifestyle. Nothin' major. We gotta find a place for a media room and wire dat up. Gotta have a media room. An' a recording studio. Jes' a small one, in case I get the inspiration while I'm here, yo?"

QTip piped up at that thought. "You was gonna invite Brotha Hood Stubbs and Sinista Kool Dawg fo to jam and maybe cut a record togetha, right, Richie?"

"Yeah, yeah. Dat's right, Slim. But I don' wanna work alla time here. Dis crib be fo chillin, nizzle."

Clio addressed Guillermo in quick Italian. "Yes, but... Guillermo, there are only so many large rooms. Where would they fit a media room and a studio? That's—"

His eyes, shadowed by his furrowed brow, caught hers, and with a small head shake, silenced her. She gripped her knife tighter and cut her melon, and the piece flew off her plate while the knife skidded noisily across the china with a screech. She set down her cutlery and gripped her hands together under the table. Her breathing was quick and shallow. This wasn't her home or her business. She sat back, taking a deep breath. *Calm down and think strategically.* Guillermo was clearly biding his time until the real estate agent showed up, and didn't want to slam any doors shut.

She could see he had a point. It wasn't every day someone showed up at your door with deep enough pockets to buy a historic villa and property and have enough left over to contemplate renovations. And at the same time rescue your brother from humiliation and ruin. Clio had to see it from Guillermo's point of view. She sipped her coffee glumly. Maybe he was right. But...

"Weren't you telling me just the other day," she caught Guillermo's eye, asking his forgiveness for her license. "That the roof was leaking and damaging the frescos in the smaller salon?"

"Hm? Oh, *si, si*. It leaks in winter. And you'll need expert restorers for the frescos."

One of the dogs yipped, launching all three of them into a ruckus that momentarily distracted everyone.

"Shaddup down there yo stupid mutts! Yeah? Dat's cool. I got the chips. We fix dat up, too."

"Most likely you can *fix* that for under a million. With the proper experts involved, of course, at additional cost. But I wonder about the plumbing. You see, we are very accustomed to it, having grown up with it, but your wife might–"

"No, no–"

"Yeah, ye-ah. It's the truth, Richie. I gotta have good bathrooms and guest rooms. You know my designers and marketing people are *not* gonna put up with skanky toilets. Not to mention the Italian buyers I want to wine and dine."

Clio observed Foxy carefully. Whatever business interests she was talking about, clearly she was more than beautiful arm candy. It wasn't what Clio expected from such an overtly sexual and fashionable woman. She radiated power. Clio squirmed, suddenly self-conscious of her childish and prudish shirt and trousers. It put the lie to her mother's warnings.

According to her parents, being perceived as a sexual object was the gravest danger for a woman academic. Even an established one like her mother could suffer a career setback if she was perceived by her colleagues to be frivolous or loose. Clio thought wryly that her career ambitions were very likely the reason she was still only dreaming about finding true love instead of living that dream. Foxy seemed to have it all.

"Don'tcha be worryin, baby. You gonna have yo toilets, too. Dis crib got lotta rooms. You–"

"And wi-fi, Richie. We've got to have good wi-fi."

"Signor! Signor Richie Sling-a DoomZ-a!"

A tall, pink-faced man burst onto the portico, heading straight for Mad Richie. "I've been looking everywhere for-a you!"

"Yeah, well we been right here, yo?" said QTip.

"I'm so sorry. I wait-a for you at the gate." He stopped and scanned the scene, the table, everyone present. "And then there were the dogs-a." He waved a vague arm toward the front of the house and smoothed the front of his suit jacket. His brow furrowed, and his dark eyes glinted. He zeroed in on Guillermo, speaking Italian. "You are very familiar, signor. You are…?"

Guillermo shoved his chair back and stood up, offering his hand. "Guillermo Gabriel d' Aldobrandin. Jacopo's brother. And you, I presume, must be Andreas Fitucci, at last." He placed a pointed emphasis on the last, and Signor Fitucci had the grace to blush. "We have been having breakfast with your client and his family, and discussing his needs."

"*Si, si. Grazie* for your patience. My deepest apologies, Signor d' Aldobrandin. I arranged to show the villa with your brother Thursday, and with your housekeeper, but they said nothing about any of the family being here this weekend. *Scusami.* We did not mean to intrude on your privacy, *Signor.*" His eyes darted to the remains of the spread on the table, licking his lips, clearly regretting his tardy arrival.

Guillermo's face stilled, and he rotated his head toward the door, where Marcella hovered. "Is that so?" He narrowed his eyes at her, and she escaped, her face culpable. "Not to worry Signor Fitucci. I was not expected. Well, we've been awaiting you this past hour, but I believe everyone has finished breakfast now, so perhaps we can begin the tour of the property."

"*Si, bene, bene, signor.* Right away. We give you your privacy." Again his eyes darted longingly to the coffee pot, and he sighed.

At that moment Bianca appeared in the doorway, elegantly put together in shredded jeans and a t-shirt, showing more tanned golden skin than fabric. She tossed her long mane of hair off of her face and squinted at them. "I couldn't find anybody. What's going on out here?"

CHAPTER 15

"We'll join you on the tour, Andreas. I was just about to show my guest around." Guillermo turned to Clio. "This is Signorina Clio Sinclair McBeal, a Doctoral student at the Accademia di Belle Arti in Firenze. She's here to study the artifacts at the villa, and advise the family on the best course of action regarding their handling, under the present circumstances."

He watched her double-take, but she squared her shoulders and shook Andreas' hand, and he felt a smile tug at his mouth.

"Er. You ain't the missus?" QTip asked.

"No. Senior d'Aldobrandin is not..." Fitucci trailed off.

Her smile was tight as she shook her head. She was like a mother bear, fiercely defending her cubs. Her delicate redbrown brow was lowered menacingly, and she peered at the real-estate agent as though she would as easily eat him for breakfast as shake his hand. Without knowing why, he needed to comfort her and reassure her, though he had nothing to offer. He placed a gentle hand to the small of her back, rubbing with his fingertips.

For a moment he reveled in a sensation of perfect harmony, and imagined what it might be like to have someone like Clio always at his side, sharing his battles, his joys and sorrows, belonging to him, and him to her. But that was folly; exactly that kind of romantic notion he made a point of avoiding. A jolt of anxious energy coursed through his veins, pulsing, demanding movement.

Guillermo would like nothing better than to grab this beautiful, surprising woman and run away. Either jump in his Alpha and drive away as fast as he could, or even better, take her hand and run, run, run. Run through the gardens, and run away into the fields and vineyards, losing himself in her arms, in the silent rows of vines, under the blue dome of the Tuscan sky.

But that wouldn't do. His desire for freedom and escape warred with his need to stay, to fight, to protect his home and do his duty by the family. Acidic bile, the symptom of this conflict, stung the back of his throat bitterly.

The entourage moved from room to room through the villa, examining each one with a critical eye. The minor modifications Richie mentioned seemed to expand in scope and magnitude as they went along and absorbed the general state of stately decay. Every one of the historic salons and bedchambers seemed to take on a new identity as Mad Richie and Foxy visualized how each would be repurposed and transformed.

Guillermo felt quite sick, his guts churning uncomfortably, despite having eaten no breakfast. He said little, simply listening, thinking, letting Andreas lead the tour, pointing out where they were on the floor plans he'd brought along. Guillermo'd given up trying to persuade Richie that the villa was too dilapidated and out of date to suit his needs, or would cost too much to bring up to his exacting standards. The man was on a mission, and no amount of restoration, or renovation expense daunted him. He was evidently as rich as Croesus.

The tour of the villa moved at a snail's pace, and he thought it would never end. This was not the pleasant experience he'd planned on sharing with Clio. Bianca tagged along for about twenty minutes before uttering a painful muffled mewling noise and excusing herself. He ground his teeth. This had all come up so unexpectedly, there had been no time for any of them to get used to the idea, himself included.

Poor Bibi. For her this would be hardest of all. She was still a teenager when their parents died. Still spending a good deal of time here at the villa. For her it was still and would always be home. And she'd never really settled anywhere else since she'd finished school, running a little wild with no prospects of any kind laid out for her future. None of them were equipped to finish the job of raising her, though she was now twenty-two.

What she needed was a purpose. Something or someone to love, to anchor her life and give her a sense of belonging without need to hang on to the past.

Clio hung back, listening and watching, her eyes scanning each corner of the villa like laser beams. She had pulled out her camera at the start, and now held it up like a shield, snapping hundreds of pictures, judging by the sound of the shutter's digital snicking.

When Fitucci led them into the seventeenth century ballroom addition, accompanied by exclamations of *Ay yo trip!* and *Boo-yah!* whatever they meant, Guillermo pretty much had all he could take.

That's when Richie began to talk about his cars. He had apparently amassed quite a collection of Italian sports cars, *whips*, he called them: a Maserati, a Ferrari, and a Lamborghini Veneno on order from the factory.

"Dis here area be jus right for the garage and games room, eh, Slim?" He sidled up to one of the large arched double doorways and began to pace off its width. "Dis be wide enough for a garage door! Dis seal the deal fo me."

Andreas' face was pink with excitement. He at least was thrilled with the possibility of selling the villa to the first buyer to cross the threshold.

"You're getting a bit ahead, Richie," Guillermo spoke up now.

"My brother Jacopo is technically the owner, and he hasn't even arrived yet. There may be a number of issues...actually..." He turned to Andreas. "Was there a price on the listing? Has this even been discussed with Jacopo?" He heard his own panicked voice rise in pitch. He rubbed his chest, easing the sharp pain that shot from his shoulder to his gut like an electric shock. *What had Jacopo asked for?* The thought of applying a specific Euro price on his ancestral home felt like an atrocity.

"Rise up, foo. Tell me what you lookin' for bruvva, and we'll get the deal rollin.'"

Andreas shook his head, no, in response to Guillermo's question. The prospect of this deal had made his eyes glassy with anticipation. He could probably retire on the commission, or take a really, really long holiday at any rate. Guillermo sent him a silent warning to back the hell off.

"Well clearly we have to slow this whole process down. My brother and I need to have a meeting before any offers are considered. We need to know where we stand."

"Mista D, this hasta happen. I'm sold now, we jes gotta find a happy place."

Guillermo shook his head. There would be no happy place for the d' Aldobrandin family. "We'll talk, Richie. Leave it with me."

"Don't leave me hangin'. I mean we gonna figure it out, yo?"

"Are you ready to tour-a the gardens and outbuildings?" Andreas asked.

"That's dope. Maybe later. We gotta roll out."

Andreas hesitated, his mouth poised to speak, but nothing came out. Likely he had no idea what Richie had just said.

Guillermo crossed his arms over his chest, fighting for breath in his tight chest. He nodded. "Signor Fitucci has your contact information, *si*?"

"Yeah, yeah," QTip answered, busily scrolling and clicking on his smartphone, distracted. "We gotta jet, Richie. Blade's gettin' impatient."

"Yeah, yeah. We're gone." He turned to leave, gathering up his family, who had straggled over to look out a window. "Hey, bruvva. Is dat yo whip outside? The Alpha? She's tight!"

∽

"Mar-*cel*-la," Guillermo peered meaningfully at the old housekeeper, once Richie and his entourage had departed, and they'd all sat down for *caffe* and a debriefing in the kitchen. He seemed relieved to be speaking his native Italian after the trying morning. His tone was clearly annoyed, and it made her annoyed in turn.

She gritted her teeth. What difference did it make, anyway? It seemed to her he was just going to give in to Mad Richie's outrageous demands in the end. How could he rake Marcella over the coals for a minor breech of communication? If he had no intention of getting involved, he ought to leave the poor woman alone.

"Why did you not mention to me last night that Signor Fitucci was bringing a buyer to the house today?"

Marcella lifted her chin, stubborn defiance in her dark eyes. She set a plate of biscotti on the table and stood, scowling, twisting her tea towel between gnarled hands.

"Oh, sit down, Marcella," Guillermo snapped. "Quit glaring at me like that."

She sat, while Martino continued to hover at her side protectively.

"I am very sorry this whole thing caught you by surprise, Signor d' Aldobrandin. I had no idea–" Fitucci began.

Guillermo waved away his concerns. "No, no, Andreas. You could not have known I was coming. I am only wondering why my devoted housekeeper failed to mention it to me when I arrived, since she knew on Thursday that it was scheduled."

"You know why," Marcella muttered.

"Do I?"

"*Si.* You would have left. You would have run off."

Clio choked, almost spewing coffee. That was likely true, given Clio's limited experience of Guillermo. He dashed off at the slightest provocation or discomfort. She twisted her mouth ruefully, and was rewarded with a scathing glare. His heavy dark brows were truly formidable when he lowered them like that, threateningly, and he clearly knew it. She wouldn't want to be the child of such a man, and be scolded for some wrongdoing. The thought made her insides twist. *What kind of a father would Guillermo make?*

"And what if I did? I had no desire to experience that... that circus!"

Andreas cleared his throat, fiddling with his coffee cup.

"I told you." Martino said, clearing away the small plates from which they'd eaten their bread, olives, salami and cheese. "Did I not tell you he would be angry?"

Clio shrank back. It was not her affair.

Marcella squeezed her wrinkled hands together in front of her on the table, the white bones of her knuckles showing through her thin brown skin. She sniffed. "I thought you would want to be here. It's your home, after all."

"It's not mine."

"Then whose is it?" She rebuked, then softened her tone of voice. "When Jacopo called to say he would be late—"

"Jacopo's coming?"

She nodded. "When he called to say he was delayed, I knew it was a sign. A blessing. The Lord had sent you, and prevented him from coming. You were *chosen* to be here. This was meant to show us."

Guillermo's dark brows shot up. "Show us what, Marcella?" His tone was patient, but the expression on his face brooked no nonsense. It seemed he was accustomed to her thought processes.

"That this is not destined to happen, Memmo, *caro.*" Marcella threw her hands up. "Jacopo is not capable, forgive me..." She crossed herself. "You are the only one who can fix this. You always were the one with sense, the fixer. Only Memmo can prevent this from happening, I said to Martino. God arranged for you to be here when Signor Fitucci brought those people. So you could see the *travestire* with your own eyes!"

Clio held her breath. *What would Guillermo say to that?*

Guillermo stroked his eyebrow, his eyes half closed. Then he braced his forehead with his hand and shook his head, sighing. "I can do nothing, Marcella. It is not for me to interfere in Jacopo's business."

That's not true. Clio bit her lip. She had to show him that he *could*. He could do many things. And if she helped him, maybe together they could pull it off.

But no. They were not a *they*. Why was she thinking of them as a couple, as friends, even? They hardly knew each other. She didn't care. She couldn't afford to care.

"Jacopo's business. *Pah!* It is not Jacopo's business. It is d' Aldobrandin business. The whole family. All the ancestors and the children. Jacopo has no right." Marcella's voice quavered, her eyes filling with tears, and Clio's throat burned in sympathy. This was home to Marcella and Martino, too. But more than that, the old couple really seemed like part of the family, which, if they'd been around since before Guillermo was born, they truly were. "Have you been to see your *Nonno*?"

Guillermo's face fell. "No," he whispered.

"Well I doubt Jacopo has either."

Marcella implied Jacopo wouldn't be visiting or consulting with Guillermo's grandfather anytime soon.

"What is the point of upsetting him, Marcella? He is better off not knowing." His voice, thick and aqueous, was so permeated with a trenchant sadness, that Clio's head flushed with sympathetic heat, her eyes filling.

Who was she kidding? *I do care!* How could she not?

Marcella sniffed. "You should go."

Guillermo grunted.

"Am I too late? I thought I heard my name." An overloud Italian tenor from the doorway.

They all flinched at the interruption. Marcella's indrawn breath echoed in the silent room, and she crossed herself again.

"Signor d' Aldobrandin," said Andreas, a hint of relief in his voice.

A tall, thin man in a suit strode into the kitchen and stopped in the doorway, his face smiling. *How much had he heard?* On seeing the somber faces of everyone around the table, his smile slid off. "Who died?"

Guillermo drew a deep breath and straightened. "Speak of the devil." At his tone of barely suppressed rage, Clio's eyes flew to his face.

"Oh, so you *were* talking about me."

"We were talking about Nonno, actually." Guillermo stood up from the table, his hands hanging at his sides. His manner was intense and brooding, like a boxer.

Jacopo did not reply, his lips thinning.

He was very like Guillermo, and yet completely different. One would easily place them as brothers. But there were some significant differences. Guillermo's brooding dark brow overshadowed his vivid fiery blue eyes. His broad shoulders were squared, as if for a fight, and his hands, at the end of well-formed, muscular arms, clenched into fists.

Jacopo's eyes seemed dark brown, and he was frailer, less athletic, with slightly hunched shoulders, as though he'd spent his life bent over a desk, instead of running in a field. He seemed more the aristocrat, with a narrower face, a slightly more hooked bridge on his nose. His mouth too, was thinner, a little weaker, less defined.

Guillermo crossed his arms over his chest. "Marcella thinks I should visit him. Perhaps ask his opinion about the villa."

Jacopo's face darkened. "Are you trying to provoke me, little brother? Do you think I do this to hurt the family?"

Guillermo sucked his cheeks and looked away.

"What? You can't look at me now?"

Guillermo appeared to be fighting with himself, deliberating, his tongue working his teeth, his eyes darting back and forth. He caught her eye in passing and his face crumpled with pain. Clio held her breath. She wanted to lay a calming hand on his arm, or wrap her arms around him, as though she had the power to sooth him. *What is he going to do?*

"You told me Fitucci was vetting potential buyers. What kind of criteria did you provide him? How much money are you expecting from this little deal? How damned much did you pull out of the estate already?"

Andreas Fitucci pushed back his chair and stood up, tentatively. "Em. I could explain—"

Guillermo continued, "You should have been here, Jacopo. You should have seen the guy Fitucci brought. It was very enlightening." He laughed without humor. "I thought you had some principles."

She no longer doubted that Guillermo cared. That made it all the worse.

Jacopo's eyes flared. "Come to the study, little brother. It's time we had a talk."

CHAPTER 16

Guillermo burst into the study, banging the door open as he went. Jacopo was hard on his heels, but turned and calmly shut the door behind him. Turning to face Guillermo, he sighed heavily.

Guillermo paced back and forth from the desk to Jacopo and back again, pausing with his back to Jacopo, trying to calm his racing pulse, and relax his taut muscles. He rubbed his neck, thinking.

"Are you going to tell me who Fitucci brought that got you so riled up?"

Guillermo swung around, planting his legs wide, and swept his arms out. "Are you telling me you don't know?"

"Of course I don't know. I wasn't here. You were."

"And it's a damned good thing I was, or we wouldn't have a clue what these people are like."

Jacopo's brows slid up in question, waiting.

Guillermo's muscles were so tense he was quivering. He clenched his fists, imagined knocking Jacopo across the room. He visualized him crashing backwards into the wall with a satisfying crunch. His blood surged. The muscle in his brow twitched involuntarily and he rubbed it roughly, dismissing his violent fantasy with a huff.

"A distinguished British businessman, of course. A millionaire with a passion for Renaissance art and architecture who can't wait to restore the villa to it's original glory. You should sign the documents without delay."

Jacopo's brows came together. "Really?"

"No! Not really."

"Memmo."

Guillermo pressed his lips together, gathering his thoughts. Jacopo really had no idea. "Some filthy rich American rapper and record producer. Tons of money. Looking for a little vacation place for his family."

Jacopo shrugged. "That works too, doesn't it?"

"Except for the fact that Renaissance to them means old and smelly and inconvenient. He was more than willing to pay for the restoration projects, I think, but he has a list of planned renovations, the cost of which would make the price of the villa seem like chump change."

"Then they won't offer for it. Someone else will come along."

Guillermo drew a deep breath. "I'm sure men that rich are just lined up at the gates waiting to see it." He gave his head a shake. "In any case, he was quite enthusiastic when he left this afternoon." Guillermo swept a hand out. "He was thrilled to discover that the doorways in the ballroom were wide enough to accommodate his new Lamborghini Veneno when it's delivered from the factory."

"Oh, *cazzo!*"

"*Si.*"

Jacopo seemed to mull that over. "Well, at least he won't ruin the original sixteenth century part of the house. And perhaps it will be alright, if he just parks them there." He flopped down into an armchair next to the cold fireplace, his entire body sagging with defeat.

His head was pounding. "You kid yourself, Jacopo. They have

no respect for our tradition. They will mess with every part of the villa and the gardens, modernizing and adding luxuries that don't belong here. They would rip out great-grandfather's swimming pool."

Jacopo's face was strained. "I don't know, Memmo. I don't know. I don't see what choice we have. Where will we get the money to pay the mortgage? Never mind the ongoing costs of repairs. You know what it's been like."

Guillermo paced again, grasping at ideas. "Why did it all have to be so fast? Could your creditors not have waited? You could have paid them back in installments. *This* is irreversible, Jacopo. Once it's sold, the villa will be lost to us forever!"

Jacopo buried his face in his hands, scrubbing.

"Is that the legacy our generation will leave? Everything gone? Everything in ruins?"

Jacopo's head shot up. "I understand you are angry, Memmo. Of course you are angry."

"It's not just me. Pia is broken up about it. And Bibi..." He threw up his hands. "What about Bibi? She's too young. She has no home, no roots, no place. What will happen to her when you take away her last connection with Mama and Papa?"

"Stop it!" Jacopo's chin quivered. Tears leaked from his eyes and traced down his face.

Guillermo stopped. His hands and feet felt cold. But a roiling heat churned in his belly, and his head continued to throb. His pulse slammed against his temples. Never had he hated Jacopo as much as he hated him in this moment. His weakness, his righteousness, his literalness and lack of imagination, his pedantic rule-following. Always lording it above Guillermo, always being right to Guillermo's wrong. Bending to their father's will and their father's coaching. Making himself into a version of their father, only more-so.

What was the point of continuing to do what had always been

done before? How had that saved them? And where did it get him? Where did it get any of them? Generations of failures.

He frowned, flooded with sadness. Even Nonno, lovely sweet-tempered, romantic Nonno, who he loved dearly. Even Nonno who loved the villa and the family history more than anyone, could not save the family from financial ruin.

"Sometimes I hate this family," Guillermo said. "Certainly I hate the men of this family."

"You don't hate Nonno."

Guillermo shrugged. What did it matter?

Jacopo wiped the tears from his face with the heels of his hands. "Don't hate me, Memmo. We are brothers."

Guillermo glared at him.

"I know I was not the best brother to you." He sighed heavily. "I always felt the pressure, the responsibility. Father made it clear I had to take over. And then he died before I knew... before I was ready."

Guillermo tried to hate him. He tried to hang onto his anger, but it ebbed away.

"And then Valentina..." His voice was ominous.

"Valentina what?"

Jacopo's lip quivered again. "Valentina is leaving me. She's taking the kids to Rome."

"What?"

"She was the one who pushed me to take risks in the first place. Now she says she is humiliated by my mistakes, can't live with the scandal. She won't subject the kids to all the negative press."

Guillermo's chest squeezed. "Oh, Lapo."

His use of the old pet name Mama had used caused Jacopo's face to crumple, and more tears to flow.

"She won't leave you. I'm sure it's just been the stress."

"She will. She will if I don't make everything right again, Memmo. There's more..."

"What more?"

Jacopo swallowed before answering. His head dipped to the side, his eyes downcast. "There was a woman…"

"*Stronzo*." He hadn't known. No one knew. That was something his proud sister-in-law would not tolerate. "How did she find out?"

Jacopo shook his head, flicking his open hand. "That was before the financial scandal. I thought we were working it out, but now… I don't know what's worse, living without the children, or living without Valentina."

"Is it settled then?"

"No. I hope… Maybe not. Maybe I can persuade her to give me another chance. But not if I'm unemployed and ridiculed. Not if I'm destitute. That's why…"

Guillermo drew a deep breath, trying to dislodge the knot of tension in his gut. "I see. I get it." He raked his hands through his hair.

"I love her, Memmo. I can't live without her. I am nothing without her."

Guillermo nodded.

"I'm so sorry. I'm so ashamed. I don't know how to solve this any other way. Mortgaging the villa was all I had left. We have to let it go, Memmo. Just let it go."

There was an excited knock on the door.

Guillermo raised a hand and stood up. He strode to the door and opened it a few inches, blocking the gap with his body, so that no one would see his brother in this state. It was Andreas Fitucci.

"Signor d' Aldobrandin, *scusami*. I am sorry to disturb you, but… I have just received a call from Mister Richie."

Guillermo's heart thumped.

"He has made an offer. A most generous offer."

Guillermo realized he and Jacopo had still not discussed the price. "How much?"

Fitucci's answer shocked him.

He stiffened, a sudden fist of ice forming in his centre, almost knocking him over like a sucker punch. He heard Jacopo gasp behind him, and the air in the room went still. "*Grazie*, Andreas. Leave it with us."

It was so much money it would pay the mortgage and then some. It could not be refused. The villa would be sold to Mad Masta Richie despite Guillermo's opposition and Jacopo's regret.

~

They had watched Andreas Fitucci scurry from the kitchen, his cell phone gripped in his hand, "*Si*, Signor Richie–"

Martino wiped his hands on a tea towel, disgusted. "I'm going to the garden." He left through the kitchen door, leaving it ajar, grinding his hat onto his head and bending into his stride.

Marcella tsked, standing to clear the remaining cups and dishes.

Clio realized she was still holding her breath. "What will happen, Marcella?"

Marcella shrugged and wiped the table in broad, practiced circles. She walked to the sink, rinsed and wrung the cloth, hung it up. "What I have seen many times, is that they will talk, then they will disagree, then Guillermo will get worked up, and then..." She shrugged.

"He'll leave. He'll run away again." Of course. *I wonder if he'll leave me stranded here?*

Marcella nodded, a wry expression on her old face.

Several minutes passed during which Clio realized they were listening. For what? The slamming of a door? The sound of feet crunching on gravel? The roar of an engine from the drive?

What is he running away from?

Instead the peaceful sounds of the Tuscan countryside drifted in. Songbirds chittering and grasshoppers clicking. The fountain trickling in the grotto below the terraces. The faint distant rumble of a farm vehicle.

They waited.

Marcella finally shrugged.

"What did you mean? When you said to Guillermo, 'You always were the one with sense, the... the fixer.'?"

Marcella rubbed her chin and perched back onto the chair opposite Clio. "This family." She thought a moment. "I knew their parents, *si*. And their grandparents, too. You know about *Le Conte*?"

"Guillermo's *nonno*?"

"*Si. Le Conte* was still running the estate when I came here, still the patriarch, until his stroke." She closed her eyes and shook her head back and forth sadly. "A big stroke. No warning. And that was the end of him. He was never the same after that. Very quickly he moved to the home. That... oh, well, that seemed to steal the hope from them all."

"Why?"

"They have been struggling with money for so long. Several generations back. Long, long ago, there were some successful businessmen in the family. But not lately. Some, like Guillermo's *nonno*, were the romantics. They held out hope. Others, like his father, and Jacopo, were the other sort. Determined, but slow witted, *rigoroso*, unimaginative, conservative and pessimistic. All of them failed to make significant changes. All of them passed up on opportunities that might have made a difference, and passed the troubles on to the next generation."

"I'm no business person, but, but there must have been something–things– they could do. What did they spend time on?"

"Politics," she spat. "I believe it all went wrong when they got involved in politics. *Bene*, they were good enough at that. They are intelligent men, democratic and fair, and they were popular. But if you cannot keep your personal affairs running smoothly, what business do you have running the country, eh?"

"And how does Guillermo fit in? Or doesn't he?"

A wry smile twisted Marcella's lips. "He's different, *si*?"

"So I'm learning."

"When the others were preoccupied with their education, or their careers, Memmo was living. He spent more time here than

Jacopo, growing up. He was always outside, *doing* something." Marcella gestured out the open door. "Exploring, working on a project, helping Martino. He knows this place better than anyone. No one was surprised when he became an architect. He had a way of... of understanding how things were made, how they were put together, and how to fix them. Common sense, *si*?"

Clio nodded.

"His common sense stretched into other areas of life. If there was a crisis, Memmo would step in and somehow, almost effortlessly, solve it. Money, health, broken machines, the villa repairs, a car that wouldn't start, his sisters' wardrobe crisis, a boyfriend problem, broken hearts. Memmo was there. And he always knew what to do."

"I'm confused. It seems to me he's rather averse to responsibilities. Isn't that why he's always... running?"

Marcella nodded. "Maybe. But he has a way of always stepping up. Well, until the old man's stroke, he did. Memmo worshipped him. He took it hard. Then is seemed like overnight, Gemma was gone, cancer, and then Gabriel soon after- he never recovered from her death. He doted on her. Everyone did."

"But Guillermo seems so selfish, so superficial, so reckless. So determined to look out only for himself."

"Determined, yes. He won't let himself care too much. He's afraid, Clio. He sees his family falling down around him. He sees a connection between this villa, the title, the burden of responsibility- and how it has sucked the life from them all, even Jacopo, young as he is. Memmo is so full of life. I think he is a little bit like a wild animal, or a bird. You cannot tie him down or a little bit of him dies. He needs to be free."

Clio did see. And yet she also saw that Guillermo did care. More than he was willing to admit, even to himself. What would happen to him and his family now? How could Clio walk away without trying to help?

"You love him very much, don't you?"

Marcella's eyes met hers, sad but also shining with love. "*Si*. Memmo is my boy, my favorite boy, just as he was Gemma's favorite. He is so full of life and love and passion. Martino and I... we could not have our own children, and so... Memmo is the child of my heart."

~

"Come," Guillermo took her hand and led her to the kitchen door, a bottle of wine under his arm and two glasses in his other hand.

She looked over her shoulder at Marcella, whose expression said she was just as gobsmacked that he had strolled calmly into the kitchen a few moments earlier. What happened to the hasty getaway?

"Where is Jacopo?" Marcella asked.

"He decided to head back to town right away. He and Andreas have some papers to go over, and he has dinner plans with Valentina tonight."

The two women exchanged another look. What had happened?

"Where are we going?" Clio asked.

"I never got a chance to show you the gardens."

"Oh. Ok-ay. Um. Should I bring my camera?"

"No. You can go back in the morning if you want to photograph." He paused in the doorway. "What have you got planned for dinner, Marcella?"

In the morning? "What about returning to Firenze?"

"Shh, Bella." He squeezed her hand tightly, and she frowned.

"Mm. I have a *filetto di maiale*, pork tenderloin. Some early peas, spinach and carrots..."

He thought a moment, his eyes unfocussed while he searched his imagination. "*Filletto in latte e risotto primavera?*"

"*Si*." Marcella nodded thoughtfully.

"Don't start until we return. I am cooking tonight. Find Bibi and tell her, too. Oh, and chill a couple bottles of *Bianco delle Regine* for dinner, *per favore*?" He led Clio out the door and along the path.

She kept her tone light, concealing her frustration. "Are you celebrating something?"

"Maybe."

Clio couldn't ask what had happened. It was none of her business, if he didn't want to tell her. Whatever it was, he seemed... elated. Not upset. Certainly he hadn't run away as he had from Pia's, and she had that to be thankful for. He *seemed* happy, but there was a kind of brittle determination about the *way* he was happy that made her worry. This wasn't over yet.

He led her down the stairs to the *al fresco* dining area they had passed when they first arrived, but this time he took a left under the huge chestnut tree and released her hand to go down a narrower staircase to the level below. The sound of trickling water grew louder as they descended through the robust shimmering oleanders and stubby, twisted olive trees that flanked the slope.

When the foliage opened out, she at last saw the secret grotto she had caught a glimpse of from her bedroom window. It was almost Moorish in design. A huge, rather shallow rectangular pond with a wide stone border. In the center rose a trio of figures, three lithe female figures clustered together, their arms entwined.

"Who–?"

"Who do you think, Clio?"

"Um... nymphs?"

He laughed out loud. "Come on. You can do better."

Clio grimaced. "They aren't muses."

"You have a problem with that?"

She groaned. "Which ones?"

"Calliope, the eldest." He pointed, and at once she recognized her writing tablet. "Terpsichore." Holding a lyre, of course. "And..."

"Clio." The third figure held a book. "Why didn't you tell me?"

He shrugged. "I am showing you."

"Why these three?"

"Who knows? There are so many choices, but these are the three that my ancestor chose. Personally I like these three. Epic poetry, song and dance, and history." He shrugged.

"One beautiful, one vivacious, and one seriously dull."

He looked confused.

She looked at him. "History is the dull sister to the arts."

His face darkened, and for a moment he seemed almost angry. "There is nothing dull about history. Why would there be a muse of history if it were boring?"

She rolled her eyes, crossed her arms tightly over her chest and moved around the perimeter of the square fountain. How could she explain? She'd always felt that way. The arts held so much potential, so much emotion and sensation, and the muses seemed to encapsulate all that creativity and beauty and pleasure. What was Clio, the muse of history, doing there at all? "Well, she is dull. I don't think she belongs."

He paused, eyeing her, a quizzical expression on his face when she glanced back to see why he was so quiet. "Seriously?"

She shrugged.

"Why do you study history, then?"

"My parents believe it is more worthy. Thus my name." She made a small bow, and he would have laughed, but she seemed so sad and pitiful. "But I choose to study the history of the *arts*. My more glamorous sisters."

"You mean...you are trying to compensate for... what? You are trying to absorb the other muses into yourself because you feel... somehow inferior?"

Clio felt a flood of heat wash over her. She pushed both hands down to her sides in protest. "Why do you have to say it out loud? It's horrible."

Guillermo's laughter jarred her. She shot him a look. *How can you judge me?* She felt so small. So insignificant. He sighed. "Clio, Clio. Why don't you do what you *want* to do? Would you rather be an artist than a scholar?"

She shrugged. "I love the arts. I love painting, sculpture, architecture, music, dance, poetry..."

"Everything but what you are."

"What am I?"

He shot her a sardonic look. "Like all the muses, formidable when crossed." He smiled, a broad knowing smile that bore no resemblance to the rakish, flirtatious, cocky smiles she was becoming used to. He lifted a hand to push back strands of her hair that had escaped their ties, the pad of his thumb grazing her temple, lifting a shiver that raced down to her shoulder blades and arms. "Where would we be without history, *cara*? She already includes all the others. They are her servants. Without history, we would have had no Renaissance at all."

She met his gaze, for a moment so lost in the sublime sensation of his touch, she'd thought he'd said something altogether different. "You are strange." A man who could talk intelligently of history, psychology, art and still make her feel desirable all in the space of a few minutes, was a man to whom she could lose her heart.

"Do you believe in destiny, Clio?"

What a question. She strolled past the big fountain to the long narrow trough of water along the wall. There was a series of shallow niches, each with a statue. Nymphs, gods and cherubs, as though they'd been added over time at the whim of various owners.

"I don't know. Why?"

"I think... I believe that you, Clio, were brought to me for a reason."

If her heart were a dove, trapped in the cage of her ribs, it had just flapped its wings violently. "Oh? Why? So I could watch the destruction of your family's history?"

He walked away from her, dragged his palm over a stone figure, suddenly sobered. "That was harsh."

Clio grimaced, squeezing her eyes shut and covering her face with her hands for a moment. Oh, wretched harridan. She didn't mean to hurt him. *It's not his fault.* Why blame him for his predicament, or punish him for her own fears? Her voice came out in a whisper, slightly tremulous. "I'm sorry, Guillermo. I didn't mean..."

~

Guillermo turned and strode toward her. He could feel her tension, and that was not what he wanted. He had wanted to entertain and to woo her. He wanted her to help him take his mind off of the atrocities of the day. She was too tense. This was going in the wrong way. He gave himself a shake, letting the worry go. "It's fine, *Bella.*"

"It's only that I'm so frustrated. What happened in there? What's going on? I know I have no right to ask, but you..." She fluttered a hand at him. "You are so enigmatic. One moment I think you care deeply, the next..."

He raised a hand and gently pushed back a tendril of fiery red hair from her forehead, letting his fingers slide down to caress her smooth pale cheek. He wanted to kiss her there, on that translucent skin. Her blue-green eyes flashed in recognition of the spark of heat, the attraction that flowed between then. He also saw something else, fear. *Go slow, Memmo. Go slow.*

She was so exquisite. He could not remember being so enamored, so hypnotized by a woman. And there had been many, many women, but none before that seemed to keep him so tightly wound, so fascinated and feeling so helpless. *What does it mean?* "Of course, I care, Clio." He let his voice drop a register, to a quiet, intimate timbre that he knew from experience resonated with a woman's organs. *Come to me, Bella.* His hand dropped lower, tracing the lovely white line of her neck, the delicate bones of her shoulder. Her lips, wide and rosy, quivered in recognition of his touch. Her breath faltered. The moment for another kiss had come, at last. He dipped his head–

She drew in a sharp breath.

"You can't surrender, Guillermo."

He straightened, clenching his teeth. This woman would be the death of him.

"You don't know how valuable this is," she said. "It's not only the historic value, the importance of preservation, the art, books in the library, historical documents, everything intact, unchanged, the educational value." She paced away. "It's also the personal value. Your family heritage, your personal memories. Do you not realize how unique, how special and how priceless that is? Not everyone has that blessing. You can't let that go." She pounded at her chest with a tight fist, and he resisted the urge to smile at her earnest and fiery zeal lest she take offense.

He sucked on his teeth, pondering. "You have seen it is beyond my control, Clio. No matter what I might want, I cannot have it. Do you believe we can have whatever we want in life?"

"No, of course not. But you can't lie down and… and…"

"Surrender without a fight?" He sighed. Perhaps if he surrendered to her, she would exhaust herself to the hopeless cause of his family estate, and then she would fall into his arms. "Tell me, *cara*. What would you have me do?"

She hesitated. "Really? You want to know?"

He took her hand and led her out of the grotto, past the clipped boxwood hedges of the formal gardens. It felt so normal, so right, to have her hand in his, and to walk by her side, he wondered how he had ever managed without her. "Yes. I want to know. I can tell you've been giving it some thought."

"I have. Since I met you, I've been racking my brain. I would need to investigate, but… but I'd be willing to do that. I could offer a bit of my time to help. I know a lot of people, in the universities, in the various non-profit agencies, and in government."

Now that she was thinking about him and not herself, she was quite altered—bold, beautiful, intelligent. What was it about her own life that made her seem so caged? He wanted to shake those feelings out of her.

He was swamped with a powerful urge to kiss and hold her, to make her his own, to repair whatever damage she had experienced that made her feel small and unworthy.

Since when did he care so much about the well-being of a woman that wasn't one of his sisters? One he'd only just met?

Guillermo said nothing, merely caressing the palm of her hand with his thumb in slow circles, accidentally-on-purpose brushing her shoulder with his as they strolled along the pea gravel paths past the potted herbs and shrubs. He could not pull her into his arms and crush her to him with the passionate kiss that he burned for. But he allowed himself to breath in her scent, to revel in the feel of her nearness, and to let his blood sing with unquenched desire. There was something to be said for anticipation. He knew how to slow down and enjoy the anticipation.

Though he was not accustomed to waiting for the surrender of a woman. Usually they fell into his arms most willingly. But Clio left him feeling as though the wait, the effort, would be well worth it. The pleasure they would bring each other would surpass all those other cheap encounters.

He led her diagonally through the flowerbeds, past the weathered obelisk at its centre, and beyond toward the framing pine and cypress trees that formed the backdrop to the formal gardens, dividing the estate proper from the farms.

She talked. She outlined all the possibilities: government grants, corporate sponsorship, space rental to educational institutions, even vacation rentals.

"You know, the more I think about it, the more sense it makes. I know they have whole satellite campuses for Renaissance studies in Sienna, in Abruzzo, in Perugia. And not only are the major American and British universities eager for these kind of arrangements, but once they are established, there is a need for residencies, and all of the domestic requirements that go along with that. That's additional revenue. And think of the conferences and summer programs! Retreats! Weddings! And once you were set up for that sort of thing, then you could begin to advertise for vacation rentals. There is very good money in that, and I know there are many old families that are making that work, and even maintaining part of the property for their own residence."

"And who would live here, and manage all of this that you envision?"

That seemed to give her pause. "You? Yes, I thought you."

He smiled and gave a small quiet laugh. "I have a career, you know."

Her brows came down in consternation. "Well. Well, you could think about it. Maybe part time or something." She brushed it away, flicking her hand.

By this time they had meandered between trim rows of grape vines, their entwined hands bridging over as they walked down parallel paths. She didn't even seem to notice where they were, or that they were holding hands.

The distraction of his predicament, her absorption in the problem and her myriad angles to the solution caused her color to rise. He felt his own blood race as he gazed at her rosy, flushed cheeks, her bright, sparkling aquamarine eyes, so wide set and large and almond-shaped, they mesmerized him. Sunlight flashed on her bright auburn hair, and as usual, when she was absorbed, she'd brushed it with her hands, knocking strands loose that now flew away, glinting like bright flames.

Her enthusiasm was rubbing off. He felt his own excitement building, and even a sense of hope. It was enough to make him almost believe her schemes could work.

From the vineyard they emerged into a meadow with tall grasses and wildflowers. Golden seed heads and a sprinkling of blue flax, red poppies, pink phlox and tiny white daisies danced in the gentle summer breeze, rolling away from them down the slope into the valley below. This was a good spot.

He set down the wine bottle and glasses and looked at her. Still talking. Though his mother had been dark, like Pia, she had possessed a vivaciousness and vitality that Clio channelled now, and he adored. He sat on the ground, tugging gently on her hand, and she complied, sinking onto her haunches. He tugged more, and she landed with a thud.

"What? Where are we?"

He laughed. "Relax a moment. I need to rest. You have worn me out with your ideas, *Bella*."

She blinked at him.

He pulled a corkscrew out of his pocket and opened the wine, pouring a generous amount into each glass, handing her one. She took it, gave him a tentative, charmingly confused smile, and followed his example when he raised his glass, clinking rims.

"To us. To this beautiful afternoon. Just the two of us alone. A beautiful woman in a beautiful summer meadow." He reached to pull a thin strand of her hair from her mouth, and again was lost in the inviting soft pink cushions of her lips.

That seemed to bring her back to the moment. She pulled a funny face at him. "You're at it again."

"Indulge me, *Bella*. Just for this afternoon, let us relax and enjoy each other's company. Let me look at you and admire you." He took a sip of the Orvieto. It was no longer very cold, but still pleasantly refreshing. She drank as well.

Guillermo released a breath. There now. At last he'd achieved his aim. The garden, the meadow, the soothing view of the Tuscan countryside. A beautiful woman at his side, a glass of good wine.

She was watching him closely, curiously, as though wondering what he would do. A drop of wetness lingered on her full lower lip, luring him. His groin tightened in anticipation of their touch.

He leaned toward her, dipped his head, lightly licked the drop of wine. She shuddered, but didn't pull away. "Mmm. *Bella*. You drive me mad with your beauty and sensuality. You are a women who is made for love." He pressed his lips to hers, so gently, allowing the jolt of pure pleasure to resonate through his veins, like the echo of church bells across the valley. So soft, her scent making him drunk with desire. *But slow Memmo. Remember, go slow.*

He pulled back, gazing into her eyes. They were wide, a little stunned. Like clear shoals in the Ligurian sea, turquoise glass through which he could see white sands, sparkling fishes, lost truths, pieces of himself. His heart thudded in his chest, and he ignored a quiet voice in his head that asked, *What is it about this woman that keeps you fascinated? Be careful Memmo. Be careful.*

"*Nei tuoi occhi c'è il cielo, cara.*" Heaven is in your eyes.

"But Memmo." She swallowed. "Won't you at least try?"

Guillermo was caught in the web of her passion, and he didn't know why he said the next words that came out of his mouth. "For you, *Bella*, anything."

CHAPTER 17

The remainder of the evening went by in a blur of sensory pleasure.

Guillermo shooed Marcella out of the kitchen, donning her apron and forcing her to sit with Martino, Bianca and Clio at the adjacent table with glasses of wine, and bottles to replenish them. Then he proceeded to entertain and amaze them with his considerable culinary and operatic talents, as he repeatedly broke into song while chopping vegetables, seasoning meat, and stirring risotto, serenading them. Marcella kept jumping up to help him find things, or tell him what to do. But he would simply set down his knife, or whatever he had in his hand at that moment, and swoop her up in his arms to swing her around in a few dance steps, laughing and depositing her back in her chair with a kiss. Love and devotion shone in her eyes as she indulged him, like the favored son he was.

And he returned the affection unselfconsciously.

Clio couldn't pull her eyes from him. He was like Dionysius, or Bacchus as the Romans called him, the god of wine, merry making, theatre and ecstasy. Clio found herself wondering what it would be like to be loved and treasured by him, as his family clearly was. He created warmth and brought exuberance and delight wherever he went.

"*Buon appetito!*" Guillermo lifted his wine glass in a boisterous toast.

They ate at the kitchen table, like a family, relaxed, laughing, sharing stories of the days when the family were all together, the children growing up and spending summers and holidays at the villa. The pork tenderloin and risotto primavera that Guillermo had expertly prepared were delicious, and carried her senses to a new level of contentment. Clio closed her eyes, reveling in the wonderful flavors and textures of well-prepared food. He and Marcella alternately tasted and complemented the food and engaged in playfully competitive banter about their cooking skills, while he winked at Clio, laughing. The wine flowed freely, and it seemed to her that her glass was never empty.

Clio couldn't remember being so immersed in a moment, or so relaxed and enjoying the company of another, since, well, since she'd been very young.

Summers on Mykonos and Crete came to mind, when she was fourteen or fifteen. She was old enough to wander unsupervised while her parents worked, and she made many friends, both local Greeks and other foreign kids on extended vacations, like herself. It had been a dizzy, giddy, sensual time of pure pleasure. They all came of age together in the warm air and sultry light of the Mediterranean summers. All the rules and rigor of their families and the school year faded away in the ecstatic youthful glory of their shared company. And there had been Hektor to share it with. Hektor to tempt her and stir her fledgling senses.

A surge of burning humiliation flooded her head and chest as she recalled the episode with Hektor on the beach on Mykonos. She had been just fifteen and naive as could be, eager to celebrate her newly discovered femininity.

But she could never imagine a more beautiful and amazing first sexual experience. Her lip began to tremble. But the embarrassment and shame she felt when Father caught them *in flagrante delicto* on the beach, and Hektor fled to save his own skin, that memory clouded the other out. The lecture she'd been subjected to, the isolation that followed while they all waited to see if she'd foolishly gotten pregnant, had combined to ensure she would trust neither men, nor her own sexuality again. It didn't bear thinking about.

"Are you alright, Clio?" asked Bianca.

"Perhaps I've drunk a little too much wine," she replied, a hand to her cheek.

Her face ached from smiling and laughing so much. Sadly, she realized how little smiling she did these days. Except when she was gazing fondly at sculptures and paintings that she loved, her life had become very dull, very abstract. No wonder she'd said those things by the fountain. It felt like the truth.

At some point during the evening, she realized Guillermo never had answered her question about what they were supposed to be celebrating. In the back of her foggy mind, it occurred to Clio that this bacchanalian feast, and Guillermo's frenzied mood, were an elaborate ruse to distract them all, and to delude them into forgetting the upsetting events of the day, perhaps Guillermo most of all.

Dessert was a simple scoop of *gelato* pulled from the freezer, with a splash of homemade *grappa* drizzled over it, as though they were not already drunk enough.

"You have *gelato* on your cheek, *Bella*," Guillermo said, leaning toward her to wipe it off with the pad of his thumb, then licking it clean. She smiled at him, the room spinning a little, her eyes unfocused.

"So do you," she laughed, reaching with her spoon to deposit a splat of melted ice cream on his nose.

"Hey!"

She darted forward to lick it clean, and in that split second, he shifted, kissing her on the lips. A dart of dangerous lust shot through her. She pulled back, shocked, laughing, and he followed, darting and parrying until he managed to plant his mouth firmly on hers, dipping his hot and cold tongue between her sticky lips. She swooned, liquid heat funneling down through her core, finding herself leaning toward him, hungry for more pressure, more attention from his hot, sweet mouth.

A quiet moan emanated from somewhere deep in his chest as he pulled away.

She covered her mouth with a hand. *Oh dear, I must be really drunk. I'm behaving like an idiot.*

Marcella laughed and got up from the table to clean up, while Martino cleared his throat and looked away.

Guillermo grinned, and in her foggy mind, she felt her face heat with shame. He was playing her like a fiddle, and she was too drunk, or too stupid to resist him.

But truly, she had never seen such a beautiful man. Her female appreciation of his pure virile maleness, his gorgeous sky blue eyes, flashing white teeth and tousled dark waves was boundless. Better than any Bernini sculpture or Carravaggio painting, because hot red passionate blood ran in his veins, and he was eating her up with his eyes, making her feel more alive than she had a right to.

His eyes met hers, darkening with desire, glittering with wicked pleasure, daring her to set aside her restraint and swim with him in the sea of sensation in which he was so adroit.

And she wanted to. Oh, how she wanted to.

Reckless lust swam in her veins, making the room spin, and stealing all caution.

Guillermo laughed darkly. "I think I'd better help you to bed, *principessa*. You've had quite a lot of wine, no?"

"Mem-mo," came Marcella's sharp voice. "You be a good boy."

"*Si*, Marcella. I am a *very* good boy." He hooked an arm under Clio's shoulders and hefted her out of her chair, and she sagged against him like a ragdoll. He tossed her rubbery arms over his shoulders, and she managed to hold onto him as he hauled her upright.

She hiccuped. "*Scusami.*" A bubble of ridiculous, silly giggles rose up out of her.

Bibi roused herself, lifting her head from the table. She was just as bleary-eyed as Clio felt, but she managed to add a steely thread to both the look she shot Guillermo, and to her voice when she said, "Remember our conversation, Memmo. I'm watching you."

She was limp as overcooked linguine. *Stronzo*! Life was cruel. He helped her up the stairs to her room, and they stumbled inside together. Finally she was relaxed and willing, but too drunk for him to even consider taking advantage of her. Even though he'd had his share of the wine, he knew better. Not that he was a saint. He'd been known to take an inebriated woman to his bed on more than one occasion. A certain kind of woman, who clearly knew what she was getting into. But even if he *were* thinking about it, he was sure Marcella and Bianca would be listening at the door, ready to pounce on him should he dare to take a wrong turn.

Not that he didn't *want* to. The Lord in Heaven knew he was extremely motivated to get this woman into his bed and make deliriously passionate love to her. He did not ordinarily have to wait to satisfy his desire, and had never wanted or needed to control himself and suppress his needs as he had this past couple of weeks. Ever since he saw her at Pia's after the accident, clean, and vivid and so incredibly sexy in her borrowed, feminine clothes, her spectacular Titian hair barely contained after her shower. In that moment, his heart had clenched into a fist of exhilaration, and had not given him a moment's peace since then, rebelliously thumping with joy whenever she was near.

He didn't need them to tell him that Clio was different. She was no young innocent. But drunk or sober, she held herself back from indulging in the normal physical activities of modern adults. He suspected it had something to do with her high-achieving, over-bearing parents. But until that cage was unlocked, he would not be forcing himself on her.

That didn't mean he was unwilling to enjoy her beauty, her delicious womanly scent, the touch of her soft skin, her silky hair or her incredible fabulously mouthwatering lips. He was already hard, thinking about it, and suspected he would be staying that way.

She slipped away from him like a silky scarf sliding to the ground, but instead she floated up, swirling around, a soft feminine laugh escaping those lips.

"Sing to me, Memmo," she said, swaying to some music in her head. "I feel like dancing."

Huh?

"I enjoyed your singing tonight. You have such a lovely, sexy voice."

Guillermo puffed out his cheeks and exhaled. *Stronzo*. She would kill him.

"What do you want me to sing, *Bella*?"

"Mmm. That one you sang in the garden... what's it?"

He remembered. Truer words had never been written. "*...La prima volta l'ho incontrata...*" he sang softly, hoping there were in fact no nosy women hanging about in the corridor. "*...Mi è entrata dentro e c'è restata...*" She'd got inside him alright, right past his defensive walls, and shaken him somewhere deep and vulnerable and raw. Somewhere he'd never allowed another woman to go. He felt a twisting, tumbling sensation in his chest at the realization. Somewhere in the vicinity of his heart, *maledizione*.

While he sang, she danced, swirling her hips, lifting her arms over her head, pulling at her plait until it came unraveled, as though she knew how utterly wild that would drive him. Her eyes glittered at him with such sensual abandon he could only stand and listen to the mad rhythm of his own heart pounding in his ears.

He felt like a helpless fool standing there.

Then she spun and spun toward him as though he were

drawing her on a cord, until she brushed up against him, draping herself backwards over him, lacing her arms around his neck. *Che cazzo!* She writhed and wiggled her incredible ass into his already tumescent groin, and the blood rushed from his brain, making him dizzy with desire. He grabbed her hips to still her torture and push her away. But she dropped her hands over his and held them there, and he knew it was a lost cause. "Mm-mmm. Memmo?" Her voice emerged low and throaty and sensual, like thick treacle.

He cleared his throat, whispering hoarsely in reply. "*Si, Bella.*"

In answer, she took one of his hands and slid it across her stomach, soft, flat and still undulating from side to side as she brushed her shoulders against his chest. *Oh, Madonna! No!* But yes, sure enough she continued to steer his hand, up her ribcage to the full heavy curve at the underside of her breast, where she made sure his stopped and pressed against her, something he'd been fantasizing about since the portico last night. Was it only last night that he'd kissed her? It seemed like a lifetime ago.

He gritted his teeth. He had to stop this or he wouldn't be responsible for what happened.

"*Cara.* I think maybe you've lost your inhibitions in a bottle of *Bianco delle Regine*, eh?"

In response, instead of coherent words, she moaned softly, massaging his hand into her breast in delectable circles. *Oh, Bella.* He couldn't help himself. He kneaded and squeezed her fullness, then drew her taut nipple between his fingers, pinching while her moaning increased to a frenzy pitch.

Soon she'd directed his other hand over her hipbone and was sliding it downward toward the inviting vee between her legs. *Oh, Dio, no! This wasn't happening!* Her heat seared his hand, and he needed no help knowing what to do once his fingers felt her hot mound, slipping into the hot groove at her centre, especially with her twisting and squirming in circles against his hand, using him for her wanton pleasure. His *erezione* pressed against her soft ass. *Si! Ah, si.* How he wished he could peel off her clothes and let himself go, then he'd show her what he could do, not only with his hands, but with his mouth.

"Memmo, oh, Memmo, yes!"

Her moaning increased, joined by gasps of pleasure and little high-pitched squeals as her head fell back against his shoulder and her breathing became fast and labored. He dropped his mouth to her shoulder, breathing through her shirt, burrowing his face into her hair and neck and jaw, kissing, licking and nibbling wherever he came into contact with skin. "*Sono ubriaca di te*," he murmured. Never mind the wine. I am drunk with you. Lifting his head, he regarded her profile. Her eyes were closed, and her lips parted seductively, plump and red, her tongue lashing and stroking her teeth.

"Please, Memmo."

"*Ti voglio baciare.*" His hand left her breast to turn her face to the side so he could bend to devour her mouth, thrusting with his tongue to enter and possess her, mimicking the act he could not realize, their tongues dueling feverishly. They moved together, slithering and sliding and thrusting together in rhythm while she panted and her moans of delight got louder and more urgent, reverberating in his own throat. His legs trembled uncontrollably, and he struggled to brace them both, he was so hard, reeling with desire for her. "*Ti desidero, Bella, Bella, Clio.*"

Gesu! He was going to pay for this.

And then she broke, shattering and dissolving in his hands like sunlight through a prism, her legs giving way as she collapsed completely against him with a long moaning cry of ecstasy. "*Ah, Bella*, Clio. *Cara.*" He caught her hard to him, holding her upright, then slowly letting her sink down as he rotated her to face him. He picked her up in his arms, keeping their mouths fused in a soul deep kiss.

Abruptly, her mouth went limp and her head fell back. He realized she had passed out. Fainted? Fallen asleep? She was dead weight in his arms. He strode to the bed in three long strides and laid her gently down, stepping back to gaze at her in the golden light of the small bedside lamp. She didn't wake, but lay there, her head back, flushed lips slightly parted, her wild coppery hair tumbling around her like a halo of fire, frozen in the image of ecstatic release.

He released a long breath and swallowed. *What the hell had just happened?*

He scrunched his eyes closed, knowing that he would take the image of her to bed with him, along with her feel, smell, and sounds, and that she would likely keep him up all night tossing and turning in misery.

CHAPTER 18

Bands of steel were crushing Clio's head, and sharp knives pierced her eyeballs. She could see the fires of hell burning through her tightly closed lids. She lay a moment, gathering information, sorting through the thick fog in her head. Her mouth was woolen and dry and tasted of old socks. What had happened to her? Was she sick?

Another few minutes went by before bright flashes of memory began to insinuate themselves on her foggy mind's eye. Sensuous food, rivers of wine, a whirling dervish, opera music. Images of beautiful Bacchus, half naked, with Guillermo's laughing face, surrounded by his entourage of raving *maenads*, their heads wreathed in snakes, dancing in a state of ecstatic frenzy, bearded satyr's with erect penises tripping after him in a parade of wild abandon. She squeezed her eyes shut to block out the erotic images.

Why would she dream of…

The strands of myth and memory slowly separated, and Clio began to feel an oppressive weight press in on her, and a sickening twist of nausea in her stomach that was more than the after-effects of too much wine. Bacchus indeed!

Oh, holy hell, what had she done?

Did they have sex? She sat up abruptly, looking frantically around her in the bed, hands to her breasts. Rumpled sheets, but thankfully she was alone, and fully dressed in her wrinkled clothes from last night. Sharp pain lanced her eyes and pounded at her head, and she fell back with her eyes closed, keening. Whew. At least she hadn't slept with him...

There was a soft knock on the door.

Clio froze. Who could that be? She couldn't face anyone. She had to get out of here and get home somehow. Quickly and invisibly would be preferred.

The door to her room opened a crack. "Clio?"

It was Bibi.

"Mmrnph."

"Are you awake? Can I come in?" Bianca asked, but came anyway without waiting for a reply. "I brought you a strong coffee. Thought maybe you'd..."

"Yes. *Grazie*," she murmured, pushing herself slowly and carefully into a sitting position. "Time'sit?" Her voice scratched.

"Almost noon." Bianca carried a tray toward her and set it on the side table, then perched on the side of the bed. "I guess you're not used to drinking much?"

Clio rolled her eyes, and they felt like the sockets were lined in acid. "You think?"

Bianca chuckled softly. "Here. Drink." She held the *caffe* steady as Clio rose to one elbow and drew it to her lips, sipping strong sweet black coffee that turned into liquid energy in her veins, chasing away some of the fog.

Clio waited a few moments, then sat up higher and took the cup from Bianca, drinking more.

"There you go." She was being so nice. They had hardly had time to get to know each other this weekend, until last night's fun and games.

Clio stared at her, wondering if anyone but Guillermo had

any idea what had happened last night after they retired to her room. Even she didn't remember how it ended. What did they think of her? Oh, how could she ever face him? The shame. It was horrible! Worse in some ways than anything that had happened to her as a young girl on the beach in Mykonos. She ought to have more self-control. She was no longer an innocent girl, to be throwing herself like a sleazy tramp on a man like that. Clio knew better.

She was terrified of this part of herself, the part that lost all sense of reality and time in the liquid heat of a sensual moment. She knew from experience that that kind of sensual abandon led only to shame and regret. After getting caught in Hektor's arms, her parents had dragged her home, half clothed, humiliated in front of her friends and neighbors, not even waiting for the privacy of a closed door before shouting at her.

How could you embarrass us like this Clio? After all the advantages you've been given. Is this what we've raised you for? Is this how you thank us for raising you and educating you? Are you nothing but a cheap slut that throws yourself away on every oversexed teenaged boy that dares to look at you? Have you no self-respect? Have you no shame? How will we live this down? What will people think of us?

And that was only the beginning of her shame. Afterwards, there were more lectures, insults, more dark glares, as though her actions were a betrayal of everything her family stood for, as though she was no longer worthy of belonging in their elite circle of society, as if it were about them. She was sure they would have disposed of her if they could. A complete loss of freedom in every aspect of her life, as though she were worthless and too stupid to live, and could never be trusted with free will again. And her body was the biggest traitor of all.

Now she had done it again. Or nearly. How could she so completely lose control? *I'm a fool.* She was utterly humiliated. If only she could disappear.

Bianca stood up and said, "A long hot shower's the thing. You'll feel like yourself again. Trust me. I know." She nodded sagely and slipped out, closing the door behind her.

Clio finished her coffee and took Bianca's advice, slowly showering, dressing and packing up her things, as though by stalling she could avoid the inevitable. But the sooner she got this over with, the sooner she could return to her life in Florence and never have to face charming, sexy, dangerous Guillermo Gabriel d' Aldobrandin ever, ever again.

Clio didn't know whether she was more afraid of him or herself. Well, it didn't matter. This time she knew better. She would never again allow herself to be used and discarded by a man like that.

An hour later, after Clio had slipped downstairs and outside to photograph the fountain with its three muses, and the statuary of the grotto and the formal gardens, she returned tentatively to the house by the kitchen door. Voices from the front hall told her where they were. Guillermo, exchanging quiet words with Martino, looked up when she entered.

"Ah, there you are, *Bella*."

The room seemed to tilt and spin as she dragged her feet forward, holding her camera bag in front of her like a shield. As though that could protect her from the judgement and scorn in his eyes. She felt utterly exposed. Her face flashed hot with fever.

She held her breath as her eyes met his, but she dropped her gaze to the marble tile pattern on the floor, swallowing hard. A cold sweat swamped her shrinking, crawling skin.

Expressionless, he looked away, turning to Marcella. He pulled her into his arms for a warm hug and kissed her cheeks. "I'll be in touch. Don't worry. We'll take care of you no matter what happens, *cara*."

He straightened and spoke to Clio without really looking at her. "The bags are already in the car. Are you ready to go?"

Her ribs squeezed, crushing her chest painfully, slowing her heartbeat to a sluggish thud, thud, thud.

She closed her eyes and drew a breath, swimming in a sea of mortification. Just put one foot in front of the other. You can get through this. Behave in a dignified fashion and you'll get through it. Maybe she'd dreamt half of what she remembered after all.

She cleared her throat, forcing a light tone. "Um-hmm. Yes. Sorry to sleep so late." She smiled shyly at Marcella and Martino, murmuring her thanks for their hospitality, even though, technically, they were staff and Guillermo was her host. Now that she'd faced him, she was impatient to leave.

Stepping out onto the gravel drive, she watched his strong, lean body move around his Alpha Romeo, his muscles bunching in his t-shirt and jeans as he opened the passenger door and waited for her. She slunk in and sank down, gripping her bag on her lap and her knees tightly together. As he strode confidently around the hood of the car and got into his side, pulling the door closed with a soft thunk, she couldn't help a shudder of appreciation for his gorgeous, sexy masculinity and a sizzle of remembered heat.

She should have known better. How could someone like her withstand the persistent company and attentions of a man like him? He was way out of her league. And exactly the kind of man she made a habit of avoiding. The kind of man that only wanted one thing, and would never appreciate her for her intellect, and her accomplishments. What would Father and Mother say if they knew what had happened? Another wave of mortification rippled through her. Thankfully she wasn't a fifteen year old girl anymore.

He waved and pulled out slowly, tires crunching over the gravel. "Are you alright with the top down?"

She nodded, dashing a quick glance at him and then locking her eyes on the road ahead. The wind noise would inhibit conversation. Good.

They drove for some time without talking. At length, the afternoon sun became oppressive and he pulled into a rest stop to close the roof, while she used the restroom and bought a couple of bottles of water. She, at least, was seriously dehydrated and still battling a tremendous headache. Once inside the quieter, cooler confines of the car, he broke the ice.

"I take it you're not feeling too well today," he ventured.

"I have a bit of a headache, yes," she admitted.

Another several minutes of silent road noise passed.

"Clio, I–"

She shot up a hand, palm out. "Don't. Please, don't. I would just rather not." She clutched her elbows, avoiding his gaze, trying to find comfort in the confines of the car, unable to escape his knowing eyes.

"*Tutto bene.*" He kept his eyes straight ahead, his hands on the steering wheel. She clutched her bag on her lap, her chest tight, her breath shallow.

More time passed in silence.

"Clio, listen to me. I want you to know, I think you are so beautiful. Please don't hide yourself away from me. I'm so sorry I left you. I think you are the most sensual woman I have ever known. Last night, I–"

"Guillermo, pleeeease!"

"Clio, you are so incredibly hot, I thought I'd die for wanting you, but I couldn't take advantage."

She moaned and buried her burning face in her hands. She felt hot alright, as though she were on fire, burning with humiliation, sweat blooming between her breasts and shoulder blades.

"I'm trying to understand. I don't know why you hide yourself, why you run away from–"

"Running?" She jerked back, her blood pounding in her ears. "How can you, of all people, accuse *me* of running away?"

"What?"

"You are the expert on escaping, aren't you? You are always running away. What *was* last night anyway? You seduce everyone to join you in your dangerous, chaotic, mindless escape from reason and order and responsibility. You lead everyone on a crazy dance, Guillermo, yourself most of all."

He hesitated, just a beat. "You blame me for getting you drunk?"

"Yes. No. That's not the point. How could you even orchestrate such an evening with everything that had happened yesterday?"

Guillermo scowled. "You are afraid to *live*. That is your problem."

"No, *you* are afraid to live. You hide from everything that is real."

He gaped at her. He sputtered, unable to form words.

"Life is not all fun and games, Guillermo. It is embracing your destiny and... and rising up to deal with it. Being the best that you can be."

"Is that your belief? Really? *Phhtt*. Life is choosing, Clio. *You* decide what you want, how you want to live, who you are."

Clio turned her head to gaze unseeing out the passenger window, waiting for her pulse to slow, for her heated body to cool, for her tense muscles to release their ruthless grip on her. Her thoughts were jumbled, too tossed by emotion and passion to make sense of. The countryside rolled by, anger and frustration radiating off of Guillermo like the hot Tuscan sun off the pavement that unfurled before them in an endless strip.

At last, calmer, she said, "I know I offered to help you with research. To look into some programs for you, and whatnot."

He scowled, shot a glance at her that said, *What the hell are you talking about?*

"About the villa. I'm afraid I'll have to retract the offer. I don't know what I was thinking. I have to focus on writing my thesis now. I'm really out of time, and Dr. Jovi's patience is running thin." Her voice was cold. Formal. Distant.

There, that took care of that. Now they'd have no further need to see each other. That had been worrying her for quite a few kilometers. She couldn't have him calling or dropping in to ask for help, confused about their relationship.

He drew a slow, deep breath, and his voice matched hers, curt and hard-edged. "It doesn't matter now. Yesterday, Mad Richie called Andreas with an offer, and after Jacopo and I discussed it, we decided it was too generous to pass up. That's why Jacopo went back to town. The papers are being drawn up now. The sale will go ahead in thirty days." He paused, but she said nothing, just stared at his hard profile, aghast. "So you see, although I appreciated your offer of assistance, Clio, it won't be necessary after all." His smile was hard.

"How could you?" Her voice was tremulous. She blinked, shaking her head. "You're running away again. You're not the man I thought you were."

His dark eyebrows rose up, and his beautiful sensual lips twitched as he worked to suppress a smile. "You're not the woman I thought you were."

"Oohh!" She released a guttural roar. "You insufferable, obnoxious, detestable man." A hot flash shot through her body, making her suddenly sweat as her pulse kicked up again, pounding in her ears. She flung her water bottle at his head, and he flinched and ducked as it bounced off his deflecting elbow.

"*Gesu*! Calm down, woman." He laughed. He actually laughed.

"I hate you."

He pinched his mouth together and had the sense to say nothing while she fumed, her brain a disordered mass of thoughts and emotions. She withdrew inward, unable to focus on one thing, except to know that she didn't want to look at him, or hear him or touch him ever again.

For the remainder of the ride, other than shooting her a glance from time to time, he did not attempt further conversation. Once they entered the Firenze city confines, he had to concentrate on the mad crush of Sunday traffic. Then at last, thankfully, he pulled up in front of her apartment and cut the engine. He stepped out, going to the trunk.

She flung her door open and lunged onto the side of the road, desperate to get away from him. She marched toward her building, stalled, and spun to find him standing right behind her. She yanked her suitcase from his hand. "Thank you for showing me the villa."

Without warning, he gripped her head between his hands, covering her mouth with his. She tried to protest, pushing him away with her free hand while struggling to hang onto her bag with the other. Her head buzzed as blood shot through her veins, her heart pounding wildly. She twisted out of his grip with a gasp of protest.

He broke the kiss and pulled away, peering at her with a roguish grin on his face.

"Good bye!"

"*Grazie, Clio. Mi hai incantata, Bella*," he murmured. *You have enchanted me.*

She spun on her heel and left him standing on the sidewalk.

Guillermo sat at the table with his head in his hands, his face down. He found it almost impossible to meet the eyes of his siblings, who sat around the table with him at Andreas Fitucci's office. *Why was he taking so long?* He wanted to get this damned thing over with and go home. He wanted to crack open a cold beer and sit on his sofa watching Formula 1 racing or some other mindless numbing thing. He wanted to be alone.

"I'm glad you made it to town, Pia," Jacopo said. His tension was visible in every line of his face, in his hunched shoulders, in the way his Adam's apple bobbed each time he swallowed, as though his mouth was too dry.

Pia's face was pinched, her complexion grey-tinged. "It's all right, Jacopo. It will be all right. We will be all right." She laid a hand on his arm, briefly, then removed it, as though he were a too hot pot on the stove.

Jacopo nodded but did not seem convinced, repeatedly stroking his lips with the fingers of his left hand. The gesture was familiar.

Guillermo remembered how Jacopo used to have a favorite blanket, and how he always stroked his lips with it when he was stressed or overtired. How Mama pleaded with him and argued with him to give it up when it became soiled, tattered, and when Jacopo was patently too old to need it anymore and it became an embarrassment. Now, Guillermo couldn't recall when or how he had finally let go of it, and adopted this mannerism in its place.

"I'm sorry, you know I am sorry. I would undo it if I could, but there is no way. It is too late. The debt just too large. I was never cut out for this, the estate management. You know that."

"Yes, I know it."

"And you also know this train wreck has been waiting to happen for years. For generations." His voice was strained, and cracked a little at the end.

"Yes, Jacopo. We all know that. It's not your fault."

Guillermo sniffed and rubbed his nose.

Jacopo shot him a look, as if to ask, *What?*

What? Guillermo shot back his own frown of incomprehension. Jacopo was going to be impossible to live with now, carrying this new burden of guilt around on his shoulders, instead of the old one of responsibility, history and debt.

He sighed heavily, stretching his shoulders back, trying to release some of the tension that was building up in his chest. He glanced at his watch.

Bianca slouched sullenly, texting on her phone. She didn't look up. Guillermo was pretty sure she would have refused to come if he had not talked to her, made her understand that her signature was not necessary on the sale documents, but that he felt it was important that they do it together. That Jacopo needed their tacit approval, and that they all needed to move forward together.

"It's not like we're the first family to give up an old place," Guillermo said. "It happens all the time these days. People move on." The words came out flat, without feeling. Just the way he felt them. He felt his pulse thud dully in his chest, as though it struggled to beat. He rubbed his chest, trying stimulate blood flow with the encouragement, but even his arm felt too heavy.

"*Si*, Memmo. You're right. Modern life doesn't make it easy. We are holding on to ghosts. And no one has time or money to take care of old properties," Pia said. He gave her a tiny smile of thanks. She tried so hard to be nurturing. He appreciated it, even though it was a lost cause.

The door opened.

"*Scusami, scusami*. I talked to him. He will be here any moment. He is very sorry for the delay."

It was as if the fates had designed this miserable meeting to take the maximum emotional toll on them all. There would be no easy, quick in and out. No way to avoid the full impact of the villa's sale on each of them. This way, they had to take away their own suffering, and also share in their siblings' pain. *Cazzo*. He'd had enough.

And then Mad Richie and QTip were entering in a whirlwind of black leather and bling, and introductions were being made all around.

"Yo. Bon journey," boomed Mad Richie. When Andreas introduced Jacopo, Richie attempted to give him a hip hop handshake, but he didn't get very far. After the first bit, Jacopo just stared at his hand, blinking, and Richie turned away, in search of a better foil.

"There's my man, Mista D," he said, his white teeth flashing when he recognized Guillermo. This time Guillermo made it all the way through the handshake, Richie's chains clinking. Then had to repeat the entire process with Slim.

He clenched his jaw, forcing a smile. How had *he* become the hero here?

Guillermo observed Jacopo take it all in, his eyes scanning Richie and Slim's flashy, rapper wardrobe, sliding over Slim's elaborate blue graffiti'd skin like he'd never seen a tattoo up close before. He would have laughed at Jacopo's stiffness, if he weren't feeling like his face, his limbs, his heart were made of lead. Pia handled it better. A little. At least she didn't have to contend with the handshake.

Bibi lifted her eyes from her phone, narrowed them at the two Americans, and returned to her texting. Guillermo gently kicked her under the table. She was old enough to put on a good face, no matter how she was feeling. Their eyes met, he squinted at her in warning, and she shrugged with her sandy brows. He sighed. How could he scold her when he felt the same way. But there was nothing to be done about it.

Andreas deposited a stack of papers onto the table and began to sort through them.

"This will not take very long at all." He explained what the papers were, and where everyone had to sign and initial. The papers were slid from person to person, pens tossed and passed as needed. The four d' Aldobrandins signed their ancestral home away.

Then Mad Richie cleared his throat.

QTip straightened. "Mad Masta Richie don't wanna mess up dis deal, yeah? He respect yo all. But he gotta axe fo one more thang, before we sign these papers. We got one more condition we gotta add to dis here sale before we sign."

Andreas paused mid-sentence, his hand pinching a stack of papers, and the room went so quiet and still that Guillermo could hear the voices of people talking through the walls. He glanced at Jacopo, and when their eyes met, Guillermo saw the fear there: *Don't let the deal fall through. We need this.*

He spoke up. "What's the matter, Richie? What's on your mind?"

"It's like dis, Mista D. We been talkin' to our lawyers and accountants and such. And the consensus is dat we need some details before the deal close."

Jacopo drew in a long slow breath through his hands that were folded in front of his mouth, and apparently held it.

Guillermo seemed to be the designated negotiator, if only because Mad Richie was addressing him directly and ignoring everyone else. His chair squeaked as he sat upright, his muscles tense. Andreas sat silently waiting, and Guillermo could almost hear his silent prayers drifting heavenward. "What sort of details, Richie. I'm sure between us we can answer any questions you have."

"We already talked about what we need, yo? Dat old villa's kickin' already, but we gotta change it up a little," Richie said.

"I got a list of thangs we need right here." QTip pulled out a stack of his own papers, handing it over to Andreas, whose eyes went wide as he took it in, and Guillermo could see that it was more than a casually written list. They'd clearly been consulting with some experts and prepared for today's meeting.

QTip explained, "If dis is gonna happen, den the crib gotta have these changes, but Masta Richie, he gotta know about the costs, and the technical re-quirements."

Guillermo nodded, frowning.

"I got to be able to visualize it, see? An' who got the expertise to figure all dat out? Who the man with the reputation around here that gonna give us the bes' service?"

"So, we axe around town. An' even though we got a few names, Masta Richie, he–"

Seeing where this was going, Guillermo jumped in. "There are many qualified architects in Tuscany who could advise you. I don't think–"

Richie cut him off. "Don't be worryin', Mista D. We gonna figure it out. It's only that I gotta see the possibilities before it's settled, yeah? So, I says to Slim, Slim? The bes' way we gonna get all these ideas crammed into that old villa is if we get Mista D doin' it hisself."

Guillermo sat back in his chair. A hard knot was forming in his stomach. They couldn't be saying what he thought they were saying. God couldn't be that cruel. He could feel his brother's and sisters' eyes on him, questioning.

Richie continued. "You met my family, yo? I feel dat you know me, man. You the top dog in Florence. Dis kinda thang be yo specialty. And even more than that, you got the inside track, yeah? So you're the man I want to realize all the possibilities of dis villa. No body gonna know dis villa like you do, Mista D. No one! Ain't dat right?"

Guillermo swallowed, trying to take in more air, but his lungs felt suddenly too small, and his breath too shallow to dislodge the tension twisting his gut. He swung his head back and forth slowly, trying desperately to come up with arguments.

"Dis be a good thang for all of us, yeah? You and your family gonna be a lot happier knowing you be the man dat advising me how to take good care of your place. You the man dat knows about the leaking roof and the experts we be needing fo the frescos." Richie looked around the table, as though convincing Guillermo's family was the key to getting him on board.

"I respect your person, Mista D. You be the man fo the job, I jus' know it. This hasta happen. I mean we gonna figure it out together. Yo, Slim?"

QTip nodded, his lips thinned in determination, backing up the boss. "We jus' can't sign the papers until you agree, Mista D. Mad Masta Richie always get what he want, see?"

Guillermo felt a tingling sensation in his fingers, and a restless twitching energy in his legs. He cleared his throat, trying to focus his mind on a response. The room was so stuffy and hot, he found it harder and harder to find air. Beads of sweat broke out on his upper lip, and he wiped it away. *No, no!*

"Don't leave me hangin', Mista D. Say you'll do it."

Guillermo pushed back from the table and slowly stood up. "*Scusami. No, scusami.*" He strode to the door. "I can't do that." And he was running.

CHAPTER 19

Guillermo didn't run past the exit door to Andreas' building, but he didn't stop there either. Frustrated that he didn't have his Ducati, he came out onto the street and hesitated. He didn't want to go back to his office. He found himself pacing briskly toward the historic centre of Firenze, winding his way on a familiar route, to the Duomo, past the Uffizi, over the Ponte Vecchio, his stride long and agitated.

Is this it then? Is this my duty? Does my family really expect me to do this horrible thing to save us?

He stopped for a quick espresso, tossing it back, and crossed back over the bridge, working his way across the piazza and through the empty market streets to the Ospidali degli Innocenti and the Palazzo Vecchio.

Does God really ask this of me– when it feels so wrong? Is this my personal punishment for all my selfishness and hedonism?

He didn't have to stop and study any of the beautiful historic monuments around his city. They were as familiar to him as the feel of his Ducati's leather seat between his legs. And it was as comforting as sensing the surrounding countryside as he whizzed past on his bike. It was always magical to see the faces of the tourists that thronged in the piazzas and lanes. He never resented the crowds during the summer. Instead he felt pride in his cultural heritage.

Stopping on via del Pucci, he stared at the ground. He was torn. In one direction lay Michelangelo's Laurentian Medici Library on Piazza San Lorenzo, where he'd been headed. One of his favorite places and one he often went back to when he needed to think. In the other direction, not far away, l'Accademia di Belle Arti on via Ricasoli.

And Clio.

She pulled him like a powerful talisman. Why he should feel the need to find her and talk to her now, he didn't know. Only that somehow she would bring him comfort, and help to settle his mind.

Scowling, even knowing that he wouldn't like the reception he would receive, he turned in the direction of l'Accademia and walked quickly, listening to the rhythm of his shoes on the pavement, a man possessed. When he arrived, he burst in and strode past reception, ignoring the protests of the woman sitting there.

Clio's head came up, her shock at seeing him standing in her office doorway obvious.

"*Bella.*"

"What are you doing here?" She scanned his face, frowning and turned her gaze away.

"Clio. *Per favore.*"

She turned back, and their eyes met. A silent moment passed. "What is it?"

"Come with me?" He reached out a hand, palm up. "I know you don't want to see me. But... I need you. *Per favor.* I'll explain if you let me."

She frowned. "Uh... I'm working." She stood and came toward him, glancing sidelong down the corridor past his shoulder, and his heart betrayed him, leaping in his chest with joy at her proximity.

He felt dizzy with the familiar old-fashioned floral scent of her skin and hair. All that spectacular Titian hair ruthlessly pulled back and plaited tightly. It made him smile, and then remember images of her hair loose, flowing over his arms as she went wild, and then spilling over her pillow as he left her there, spent and unconscious. Heat rippled through his limbs, bringing his libido suddenly to life. His Clio. Beautiful, passionate. His. "Come!"

"Where?"

"Don't ask. Trust me." He continued to hold open his hand, and she stared at it, deliberating. *Please, cara. Don't think, just do it. Fly with me.*

She frowned a little, and pursed her lips, ignoring his outstretched hand. She blinked and picked up her handbag, lifting her brows at him in question.

Si! "*Grazie, Bella. Grazie.*" Whatever embarrassment she was feeling on Sunday, she was willing to move past it. To trust him. And at the very least to spend a little time with him, to indulge him.

He led the way out, walking quickly. Once on the street, he kept up the fast pace, refusing to answer her stammered questions. "Wait, just wait." After a few blocks, she gave up trying, sensing that he had a plan and a purpose, and they walked in silence.

At last they arrived at the Library and he led her in.

"The Laurentian? What's up?"

At the desk, he flashed his pass and a smile at the guard. This time he took Clio's hand and she didn't resist while he practically dragged her into the famous stair vestibule. Pulling her over to the far wall, he slumped back and gazed up at the classical staircase in all its mysterious glory, the paneled walls, the clerestory windows high above, bright beams of light cutting through the softer interior twilight.

"Ahhh." He released a breath, but kept a tight hold on her hand. This was good. Very good.

"Guillermo?" There was a hint of worry in her voice.

His eyelids burned, and he felt wetness gather on his lashes. Without letting her go, he pressed the heels of his hands to his eye sockets, rocking forward and back, compulsive laughter welling out of him. He suppressed it, resulting in shaking shoulders and a muffled giggling in his throat.

"*Bella, Bella.*"

"What is wrong with you? What are we doing here?"

It was several more minutes before he was able to calm down and control himself.

He filled his lungs with air and released a huge breath, and with it some of his pent up emotional tension. "Let's go up." He took her hand again and led her up Michelangelo's magnificent Mannerist staircase, entering the stately library hall, and pausing again. It took his breath away, as it always did, and he stood a long while drinking in the exquisite proportions of the room, the regular rhythm of the fifteen bays and coffered ceiling, the repeating patterns on the inlaid red and white marble floor. This was a kind of bliss for him, and it brought him a measure of peace that could override anything life threw at him. This was something universal and lasting and profound and mysterious.

And it was somehow made immeasurably better knowing Clio was at his side.

What was going on with him? His entire life was turning upside down and inside out. He didn't recognize his life, and he could hardly recognize himself.

They slid into one of the reading benches and sat down side by side. It felt very like a pew in church, and in a way, though he still attended church, this was a place of more profound worship for him.

"Do you believe in God, Clio?"

She hesitated, drawing back. "I don't know. I was raised by godless heathens. I don't know what to think."

"You don't contemplate... oh, I don't know. The hows? The whys?"

She nodded. "Sure. Doesn't everyone?"

"I am Catholic, of course."

She nodded, a question in her eyes, and he scrambled to explain himself. What was he trying to say? And why was he compelled to speak to her this way? He'd never spoken to anyone, least of all a woman he desired, about these ideas and feelings.

"I believe in God, and I even attend mass, now and then."

She waited, focused intently on his face. Guillermo struggled to find words to explain the connection - between God and his world. Between faith and form.

"But for me, God is experienced in... in my work, and in the works of Michelangelo, of da Vinci, of Bernini. In beauty, in form, in mathematical proportions that somehow stir the soul. My attempt at practicing faith is to work in this medium, always searching for ways to express that intangible, unknown, immeasurable connection with... God, I guess."

She listened intently, and he sensed that his ideas resonated with her on some level. That she was taking his words and translating them somehow into terms that made sense for her. He'd seen her exquisite drawings and photographs. He'd heard her speak of her thesis, and so he knew, he knew she felt something similar, even though she would likely never express it in these terms.

"I understand. I feel something... something like that when I experience the art that I love. The Bernini sculptures, the Brunelli's, the Caravaggio's. A..." she took a deep breath, "...force. A force that moves me... here." She pulled a fist to her center.

He made a sound in his throat. His stomach tightened in sympathy. That ball of fire, yes!

"I also feel God when I drive."

She frowned.

He forced air through his nose, a small laugh. Okay so that she didn't get. "When I drive all night on my Ducati, or race through the country in my Alpha." Guillermo lifted both hands up, open but clenched into passionate claws, straining to help her see. "It's like a meditation. The speed...erases human thought, and raises me up, or breaks me down to the level of the atom. God's building blocks, *si?*"

She kept her gaze pinned to him, her eyes glistening, her head tilted slightly, her brow furrowed. His blood stirred, and his fingers tingled with the desire to grab hold of her and pull her to him.

"In those moments, I am one."

"Mmm." Her eyes narrowed slightly, processing his words.

"There is no separation, of 'I' from everything. You know?"

She pondered a moment. "There is also the connection that happens with another human being. Isn't that the same?"

He searched her aquatic eyes for understanding. A kind of electrical current flowed between them. He felt physical desire, yes. But more than that, a burning desire to merge with her, spiritually as well as physically. He needed to bury himself within her, for comfort and protection, but also to cover her, hold her, wrap her up in himself. He wanted to be both inside her and all around her, and his blood pulsed with his need. *I know why she moves me so. She understands me.*

She dipped her head, then looked at him again. "That's why I feel that we cannot escape the circumstances of our idiosyncratic existence. Who are we to say that these random events we face day to day are not... significant? Perhaps it is simply being in the moment and engaging fully with whatever comes our way that is the measure of... or the manifestation of..." She lifted a hand, palm up.

"I understand." He nodded, and as their eyes met, he knew... "Well, if that is the case, then I must do this." He shrugged. "I suppose the universe is telling me that I will both serve the greater good and find my own personal resolution by facilitating this renovation."

"What renovation?"

He harrumphed and smiled ruefully. "Mad Richie wants *me* and *only* me, to design and oversee the changes to the villa before he will sign the sales agreement."

She gasped, splaying a hand over her mouth.

He nodded, feeling a cold resolve settle into him.

Clio sat at her desk at the university, wondering why Guillermo had sought her out and practically dragged her to the Laurentian Library. After the disastrous weekend at the villa, she'd sworn she would never see him again. Even if he'd wanted to see her again, which she'd strongly doubted, despite the baffling good-bye kiss. Why had she agreed to go with him? She didn't understand the force that kept pulling them together.

Her gaze fell on the photographs and drawings pinned to her wall, her eyes tracing the delicate features of St. Theresa's face, her closed eyes and open mouth. She was so lovely in that moment. Transported. Clio took a deep breath and sighed loudly.

"Clio. Oh, Cli-o," Jonathan's voice called softly from across the room. "Where are you?" She ignored him.

And yet she did understand. Guillermo felt it too. As their subsequent conversation demonstrated. When he struggled so heroically to explain his feelings, her skin tingled all over in acknowledgement. Clio had never felt so connected before, as though the words they spoke were heavier, more significant, for being listened to so intently. And despite her advice to him about engaging in the moment and living fully, instead of running away, it felt as if she were talking to herself. There was a sad and frightened girl trapped inside of her that needed to hear those words as much or more than Guillermo did.

And when he'd confessed his predicament, and their eyes met, her heart bled in sympathy. She couldn't imagine how Guillermo could face such an ordeal. He didn't deserve this. She wanted to help him. She needed to save him from that pain. Because she knew that playing a role in systematically destroying his beloved family estate to meet the idiosyncratic desires and specifications of Mad Masta Richie would destroy him, too.

Clio gnawed at her cheek, frowning.

Guillermo might not believe there was any hope of saving the villa, but Clio could still cling to it. And as long as she did, she would do whatever she could to prove it to him.

Dr Jovi's face popped into the frame of her open doorway. "*Ciao*, Clio. How is your work going today?"

She sat up and blinked. This interruption she couldn't ignore. "Um. Very well, *grazie*, Dottore."

Their eyes met, an implicit challenge telegraphed from him to her, and back, as she forced her slack features into an agreeable smile.

"She's been working like a dog. I can vouch for her," Jonathan piped up, his clipped British accent vaguely annoying today.

Dr. Jovi's laser vision scanned her face, her desktop, her workspace, measuring, assessing, as though he could discern her progress from some invisible clues. "*Bene. Bene.*" He nodded and moved along down the corridor.

Shit. Shit shit shit.

She *was* making progress, but so slowly. Her attention was, without a doubt, divided. *Back to work.* She stared at her monitor, the words swimming meaninglessly before her eyes.

She drummed her fingers on her keyboard, *clickety-clickety-click*, not even remembering her place, or what she was supposed to be writing about. Pushing her chair back, she stood up and strode to the end of her office, spun and paced back, ignoring Jonathan's panning gaze. She pulled at her hair, strands unraveling from her braid as she tugged. *How can I sit here and ignore what's going on?*

Her stomach twisted. *What could I do anyway? I can't solve his problems for him. If he wants to design a modernization of his family's four hundred and fifty year old Renaissance villa, and turn it over to an American bigwig musician, it's none of my business.*

Clio slid her chair hard up against the desk and attacked the computer.

She checked government websites and read about heritage restoration programs, historic resource preservation grants, laws and regulations, other funding opportunities. She surveyed all the Italian universities, and several foreign ones, compiling a list of research institutes and partnerships, satellite campuses and conference facilities, making copious notes. She emailed several colleagues who worked at similar small research institutes and grilled them.

"What *are* you doing?" Jonathan asked, his voice falsely innocent.

Clio jerked, her fingers pausing on the keyboard. "Nothing."

"Oh. I thought your thesis was going rather well. Your energy picked up all of a sudden." A smirk snaked across Jonathan's face.

Clio frowned. "Shut up."

Laughter.

Dr. Jovi's hunched form shuffled past the door. Was he moving around more than usual? He was spying on her.

She leapt to the door and peered down the hall.

Stay calm. He'll tell Father I'm not going to make my deadline. I have to get back to work. That's all there is to it. I must put it out of my head and focus on my work. She pushed back her sleeves.

"Aargggh." She plopped into her desk chair with a groan, her head in her hands, torn between the demands of Dr. Jovi and Father, and the needs of Guillermo and his family. *What am I doing?* She should be finishing her thesis and getting on with her own life. But she felt more passionate about the real problem of saving Villa Cielo and its frescos and sculpture from possible destruction than she did about her own abstract work. *What does that mean?*

Jonathan said, his tone conversational, "I read in the online newsletter that Cornell is negotiating with the university of

Bologna about a joint venture research centre. I suppose it's early days yet…"

"Why didn't you say so earlier?"

Jonathan rolled his eyes. "You said you were working on your thesis."

"You know perfectly well that's not what I'm doing."

Someone walked past the open door, and Clio flinched. It was only the departmental secretary, Signora Carlo. Clio released the breath she was holding and turned back to Jonathan.

"Is that Dr. Bensen do you think?"

Jonathan nodded. "Probably. The article didn't say."

Clio pulled her braid to one side, tugging it, and scratched the back of her neck. She'd met him once, at a conference with Father.

Before she knew it, she'd dug up an email address and banged out a brief query. Her finger hovered over the send button. *What am I doing? Raising hopes when it's not my business. Not in my power to change anything.* She amended the wording of her email slightly, increasing the tentative quotient. Then she pushed send, and looked up.

Jonathan's gaze slid over to her, eyebrow raised, the corner of his mouth curled.

∽

Three hours later, when Clio had managed to tear her thoughts away from Guillermo and his villa, and dig into her research chapter with determination if not enthusiasm, her incoming message dinged. *I should leave it for the end of the day. It's probably nothing.*

"Aren't you going to check?"

"No." Her heart wouldn't allow her to maintain a facade of disinterest. It thumped in her chest, insistent. *Check*, now *Check*, now. *Check*. "Oh, alright." Her voice emerged sharp and impatient, at odds with Jonathan's nonchalant, ironic inquiry.

He chuckled softly.

Opening her email, she saw a few routine messages. One from Mother. *Later.* Then–*there*. Dr. Bensen's reply. She double clicked and scanned. Oh! It was true, they were negotiating with Bologna –multi-disciplinary research institute– slightly different agendas– Bologna had no suitable space– were indeed open to considering– "Ooooh. This might work." A bubble of hope filled Clio's chest, her breathing accelerating.

Before replying Clio carefully re-read the message. The one snag was that the funds were limited. Oh, drat. That was the one thing they needed a lot of, and they hadn't yet been able to identify a director for the new institute, someone to spearhead it's setup and manage day-to-day concerns. Someone based in Italy.

Hmm.

I wonder what Guillermo's degree is, and whether he'd qualify for the director's job? Curious, she Googled his name–*oh, my. I should have done this before.* The d' Aldobrandin name wasn't common, and except for historical references, the first four pages of real estate were owned by Jacopo. Naturally. Scrolling down, Clio finally found references to the architect Guillermo Gabriel d' Aldobrandin. She learned the name of his firm. There were awards and certificates. Many of them. He was a *very* prominent, successful architect in Tuscany, and in the city of Florence in particular. There were photos. *Just ignore them.* Despite herself, she clicked through anyway, landing on a page of Guillermo's handsome face repeated over and over–making presentations, accepting awards, his charming white smile flashing. My God, he was good looking. She sighed. A shiver of pleasure rippled through her, lifting the hairs on her arms and neck, fluttering in her chest. *Oh, put it away. Stupid girl.*

Forcing herself to close the window –but wait, she bookmarked it first– she clicked through for information on his firm, and eventually found reference to his education. A Bachelor's degree in history from the University of Rome. A Master's degree in Architecture from the Harvard Graduate School of Design? He studied in the States? He never said a thing. And some additional coursework at the University of Florence in historic architectural restoration and preservation. It was all pretty relevant. But would it do?

Clio had no idea if Guillermo would like to be a director of a Renaissance art and architecture institute. But he certainly had the knowledge and experience. And she had no doubt he had passion for the subject...

But it would be a very different life for him. Perhaps if he were older, nearing retirement. Right now, he was on top of his game—successful financially and highly regarded as a specialist in heritage restoration and re-use. It was an idyllic career for a young architect. Very sexy. He was probably quite content.

And yet she knew in her heart he wasn't.

What he really needed to do was take responsibility for himself and his family's estate in order to achieve self-respect, and respect from his family. That would make him happy. Remembering her conversation with Marcella, Clio knew he was a natural leader, and problem-solver, that his family turned to him for guidance and strength, even though none of them realized it.

But she couldn't say this to him. Not yet. He wasn't ready to accept the idea, and would refuse to have anything to do with the whole scheme if he found out what she was thinking. She rubbed her damp hands on her thighs and chewed her lip. But if it meant saving the villa...

CHAPTER 20

Guillermo fervently wished he were working at home. *There at least I could numb the pain with a strong drink. Or ten. Stronzo.* How was he going to get through this any other way?

He lifted his head out of his hands and stared at the sketches and plans on his desk. The smartest thing to do would be to delegate the whole damned project to someone else in the firm. Mad Richie would never know. And yet, it was too personal. Guillermo could never let anyone *else* cut and slash his family estate to pieces. It wouldn't be fair to his staff. Only he could do this dirty deed. And though it would in some ways be easier to work on it at home, it was a paying job –he'd made damned sure Richie was paying top fees– and he needed to use and bill his time accordingly.

"Someone to see you, Guillermo," his PA, Ignacio said from his open doorway, pushing his round glasses up his long nose.

"I'm not expecting anyone. Did I forget an appointment?"

"Eh. I don't think so." A lifted eyebrow and a twinkle in his dark eyes. "It's a girl," he said in a sing-song voice.

A girl? What does he mean–girl? What kind of girl would seek him out here? A fluttering sensation raced through his stomach, like a lone leaf lifted on a breeze, rattling against his ribcage. He ignored it.

"*Tutto bene*, I'll come out."

A moment later, the mystery was solved as he stepped into the front reception area to find Clio bouncing on the balls of her feet, her hands clasping a folder in front of her. The flutter in his chest returned with vigour. When she saw him, her teeth sank into her luscious full lower lip, and her wide-as-an-ocean eyes lifted to meet his, a little guilty smile flitting across her face. And a question: is this okay?

Beautiful. Heat infused his chest, tingling through him. He felt his face stretch into a smile of welcome. *Dio*, he was glad to see her face. "Clio, *Bella*!" He stepped forward and placed his hands on her shoulders, kissing her cheeks in welcome, feeling strangely pleased by the way her eyelashes grazed her cheeks shyly, and her blush of color at his greeting. "What a pleasant surprise. Come in, *per favore*, come in."

As he guided Clio forward with his fingertips on her lower back, toward his office, he caught curious glances between Ignacio and the receptionist, Anunziata. Over his shoulder, he narrowed his eyes at them in warning. He didn't need them teasing him today. His nerves were too frayed.

Closing the door, he offered Clio a chair and sat behind his desk. "I'm surprised to see you, Clio. How are you?"

"Me? I'm fine. Just fine." She leaned in and dropped her voice. "How are you?"

Her warm sweet breath fanned his face. Hmm. He tipped his head to one side, then the other. "I'll manage."

Her eyes pierced his, and he felt his own gaze wavering under her scrutiny. There was something different about her. "Did you change your hair?"

Her hand shot up, smoothing her wild red locks, which seemed more voluminous and present than usual. "Oh! Not really, I just... didn't have time to... it's just a ponytail."

"A pony-a-tail-a," he said in English, grinning. *I'd like to grab that ponytail and give it a pull.* Something about her girlishness made him feel like a mischievous schoolboy. "It is very pretty. More, eh..." –he gestured with his hands– "feminine."

Pink flooded her cheeks, her gaze dropping again, and he covered another grin with his hand.

"I should have called first, or texted, but... well I had an opportunity to slip away from the Accademia, so I just grabbed it. I hope it's not inconvenient."

Their offices were not that close together. He felt his chest swell with joy that she would seek him out. He swept a hand over his sketches. "No. You know what I am doing." He shook his head. "This *dimenticato* commission. I struggle away." He shrugged, but found it difficult to meet her penetrating gaze.

"I have it all worked out. I think." She appeared strangely happy and excited about his misery.

He didn't know what she was talking about. "*Si?*"

"*Si.* It's all in here." She dropped a thick file folder on his desk. "I recorded all my phone calls and research, in case we have to backtrack for any reason, and so you will have the information at hand, and the contacts." She pushed the file folder toward him over the desktop.

He opened the file, scanning the top sheet. Cornell University... blah, blah... Bologna University... blah, blah... *instituto di ricerca di Arti i Architettura Rennaisance...*

He tensed. "What is this?"

She began to explain. How she'd looked into funding for the preservation of historic sites, and that these applications had been filled out and required only his signature. How designation by the Ministry for Heritage and Cultural Activities, Director General for Landscape, Fine Arts, Contemporary Art and Architecture, or perhaps the DG of Enhancement of Cultural Heritage, as an historic architectural asset would facilitate approval of available funding. Guillermo pressed down a bubble of hope when she said how this alone would not generate sufficient funds to save the villa from sale, only prevent desecration. "But it's a good start, right?" How she'd thought of renting the space to a university or two, and she listed several examples of this kind of arrangement, as a satellite campus, summer institute, or research center.

"And this is a list of potential appointees to the board or directors. Just people that I know. You will want to add to it from your circle of influence."

Guillermo leaned forward, hardly daring to breath. *What had she done? How had she done this?* As she spoke, his chest filled with a light, bubbling sensation, as though he were hollow and would lift off his chair and float away. It was as if he was detached from his body, and watched himself from across the room, listening intently to Clio's inventory and explanation. Her elaborate scheme was improbable. He was afraid to believe her, and yet he wanted to. Oh, he wanted to. Was it possible?

She got up and rounded the desk, leaning beside him to shuffle papers and show him. "There's more. Of course there's more. It's awfully complicated," she continued, her eyes gauging his reaction, wide and full of hope. The rose and gardenia scent of her filled his nose, making him light-headed, and concentration difficult. "Between the mortgage payments, ongoing maintenance costs, repairs and renovations to accommodate the changes in use, we'd have to be even more resourceful. But I think, if you would be willing to consider some hospitality business as well, the two would tie together nicely. In addition to room and board within the villa, and conference facilities, to support the academic functions, visiting students and faculty, for example, improvements could be made to various farm buildings and cottages on the estate so they could be rented as vacation properties."

Guillermo frowned, thinking of his family. Would any of them be interested in such a scheme? Would they be offended by it? Would Jacopo be able to manage it all? Business, of any kind, was not his strength.

Her curling cinnamon hair bloomed around her glowing face like a halo of fire, her cheeks flushed, and her aquamarine eyes flashed brightly with optimism and excitement. He reached up and tucked a coiling tendril of hair that had escaped its ties behind her ear, his fingers tingling. She shivered under his touch. It fueled his own excitement, and an undercurrent of desire blossomed in his veins. She was so beautiful, and so completely oblivious to her beauty, his chest ached. A remembered image flashed in his mind, of a wanton woman, completely uninhibited, consumed by passion, swirling and twirling, gyrating in his hands, shuddering in her release, and his body tightened in response. Her ecstatic face, utterly spent, in repose as she slept, surrounded by the red cloud of her untethered hair. He wanted to take her into his arms, cover her plump red lips with his mouth.

"Ah, *Bella*. You are amazing." He couldn't resist, he pulled her down into his lap and wrapped her in an embrace. She responded, as he hoped she would, by coiling her arms around his neck and squeezing tightly, her firm full breasts pressing against his chest. The blood rushed away from his head, and he felt dizzy. She was so excited, her quick breath tickled his ear. He ran his hands up and down her lithe back, feeling her long muscles and the bumps of her vertebrae under his sensitive palms.

She pulled away, and their eyes locked, bright and hot. Then without Guillermo doing a conscious thing, their lips met. Oh, *Dio*. Their tongues tangled and he felt himself swell to hardness with need, her soft round bottom pressing down into his lap.

They shifted their position, and their mouths broke apart just long enough for her to gasp, and him to growl, and they locked mouths again, teeth clashing as they devoured each other, their passion building.

He caught a glimpse of movement through the sidelight in his office door, and his heart rate shot up like a rocket. *Gesu*! He was at work. He'd completely lost it. Pulling away, swamped with regret, he said, "Clio. Um. We cannot do this here, *cara*."

She sucked in a breath, blinking. Clearly she'd lost sight of that fact, too. She shot up, her hands smoothing nervously over her hair and shirt and thighs, as his eyes followed hungrily. "I'm so sorry. I... I was overcome with enthusiasm."

He grinned, his eyes meeting hers, heat flaring. "Not as sorry as I am," he chuckled.

She blushed a furious red, right to the tips of her ears.

Location notwithstanding now was not the time for him to be thinking of seduction. As much as he felt she would surrender to him in her current state of agitation, it wouldn't be fair. Clio. Clio. A woman of big ideas. A woman of overwhelming sensations. Of beauty and dreams. His heart squeezed with an unfamiliar tenderness. He wanted her. Oh, how he wanted her for his very own. But he couldn't take advantage of her in this moment, when she had given so much of herself to help him. He couldn't afford to frighten her away with another lust-filled moment of abandoned reserve that she would later regret. He mentally shook himself, dragging his focus back to her ideas. "I got carried away with your presentation."

"Hmm." Her gaze darted across the surface of his desk, and she began to gather her papers together, clearly embarrassed at her own loss of control.

It was so much. It was all too much. He was filled with admiration for her. Why could his family not have been so optimistic, clever, and daring, to come up with these creative ideas, when there was still time. Then his bubble of hope popped, and he deflated and sank back to earth.

"It will work, right?" she asked. "I know it's complicated, and it's a huge task, but... it *will* work, yes?"

Guillermo shook his head, smiling wryly. He raised a hand. "No. Not so fast, *Bella*."

Her face fell, a shadow of concern darkening her eyes. "What do you mean, no? Why not?"

Guillermo gathered himself together. *No, don't give up on me,*

Bella. "I mean... I mean what you've done is astonishing, Clio. I'm very impressed, and you've given me hope where I had none."

"So, so you agree? We can set the ball rolling? We should do this?" Her excitement was palpable. He couldn't bring himself to quash her hopes or his own. And he didn't want to. He needed to keep this alive, and he needed Clio. He couldn't afford to alienate her, or hurt her. He would do nothing to drive her away again.

He opened his mouth to speak, then closed it, cautious. He drew a breath. "Let me take this file home and read it very carefully. I want to understand all that you've done, and what is involved. Okay? I... can't say anything for sure yet."

The tip of her pink tongue darted out, wetting her swollen, just-kissed lips, and he twitched with desire. "But... you do think it's possible? You think it's a good idea? Would your family go for it?"

That was a damned good question. Compared to what alternative? He ground his teeth. "I think we should keep this to ourselves for now. I need to understand better what you're proposing. The implications."

"Guillermo, we've got to try. Don't you think? We've got to at least try."

"You know, the sale is already done, the funds are in escrow. It is only a matter of completing the conditions and waiting the agreed term before it closes."

Her delicate eyebrows drew together in question. "The conditions? Your designs?" She gestured to the drawings on his desk.

"Yes, partly."

"So stop. Can't you just stop?"

He shook his head. "Not without jeopardizing the sale."

"But you won't have to sell, Memmo. That's the point."

"What if this scheme of yours doesn't work, Clio? What if some... thing goes wrong? What do I tell my family then, when we have nothing but debt?"

She straightened. "You are a coward, Guillermo d' Aldobrandin."

He placed a hand on his chest. "You wound me, *cara*. That is not fair."

She pulled herself up straighter, sniffing. "Alright then. Alright, keep going. Work with Mad Richie on the side. Hedge your bets. We'll do both. Keep your insurance, if you must."

"*Si*. We could do that, I suppose. But you do not have time for this. What about your thesis?"

"I will make time, Guillermo. It's important to me. Is it important enough to you?"

Guillermo knew it was hopeless, much as he would have loved to be swayed by her idealistic dream. It was too late for the villa. Too late for his family. But it wasn't too late for he and Clio to build something new. Something to fill the empty hole in his chest. So, even though he knew it was dishonest, he would do whatever he had to do to keep Clio near him. Perhaps in time– ah, well... "You know it is, *Bella*. I want this to happen, too. But, it's complicated. My family– *Cara, tutto quello che voglio è accontentarti.*"

"Don't do it to please me. It's your history."

"Don't be cross with me, Clio. I will work with you."

"How long do we have?"

"Thirty days."

She puffed her cheeks with air and blew out. "Well, get reading. We have a lot to do."

Once she'd gone, he couldn't get back to work. He was buzzing with ideas, excitement and frustrated desire. He grabbed his helmet and riding leathers and strode out of his office.

"Where do you think you're going, loverboy?" asked Ignacio, his chin dipped and his brows elevated, dark eyes peering over the rims of his glasses.

"For a ride," he growled.

∼

Clio knew she was playing with fire. Every hour she spent working on Villa Cielo Incantato was an hour stolen from her thesis. And though she was making headway, it was slow and tedious. As much as she'd loved doing the research –she did spend an additional two years collecting data, after all– she wasn't enjoying the documentation stage. It all felt like warmed over stew. Still tasty but not nearly as thrilling as the original hunt and discovery. I guess that's why everyone doesn't have a Ph.D.

Adrenaline swirled in her veins like eddies in rapids, causing her to wonder if she was really vibrating on the outside the way she was on the inside. She was making headway on both projects, but she felt like she was figuratively and literally looking over her shoulder, expecting Dr. Jovi to pounce every moment. Would he believe she was doing all she could? Would Father?

And yet she couldn't stop. Both projects meant so much to her. It would have been impossible to explain to Dr. Jovi, or worse, her father, how much she cared about saving Guillermo's villa. She felt five hundred per cent alive, invested in a way she had never felt about anything before, even though there was no personal gain.

She looked up at her photos and sketches on the wall, tilting her head at the familiar images, her eyes resting on the ecstasy of little Saint Clare of the Cross from the Franciscan Monastery. Was it really God who moved you so, Clare? Are you really Clare? Or some not-so-innocent country lass who modeled for her lover, burning with physical desire? What moved the artist who depicted you so passionately? What quickened the blood in his veins? Was it spiritual or earthly love? Yes, she decided, she still cared about her thesis.

She could do both. She would do both, even if it meant she had to give up sleeping, and eat every meal on the run for the next sixty days or more. Guillermo needed her help, and she couldn't let him down.

Her thoughts lingered on Guillermo and her heart swelled with urgent longing, his image rising in her mind's eye. She was so confused. They were spending so much time together in the evenings, working toward a common goal. She felt his absence keenly during the day, as though a vital part of her had been cut out, and left on the counter at home, throbbing, awaiting their reunion.

Not for the first time today, Clio opened the Google link to the page with photos of Guillermo. It had become a daily, if not an hourly ritual. I'm not wasting time. I'm reminding myself why I'm doing this. She stared at his face, lost in the impossible deep blue of his laughing eyes, imagining him here with her. Her pulse quickened, and she felt herself cringe inwardly. Was she being a fool? Why are you doing this Clio? Is it the villa? Or is it Guillermo?

"Clio?" Dr. Jovi's old man's voice in her doorway made her jump, quickly clicking closed the guilty distraction. "How are you doing, my dear? Is the writing going well today?"

"Oh. Yes, Dr. Jovi. Pretty well, actually."

"Which chapter are you working on?"

She hesitated. Where was she, again? "Um. I'm, uh..." She blinked rapidly, retracing her thoughts and efforts of the day. "Oh, I've been jumping around, doing some editing, but, uh, mainly the justifications section today." That sounded plausible. It was partly true, anyway, she recalled.

Dr. Jovi's eyes narrowed as his bald head nodded, reflecting the overhead lights like a lacquered egg. "You look rather tired, my dear. Are you getting enough rest?"

She nodded automatically. "Sure. Well. You know. I'm okay."

"I know you are working hard. I have put a great deal of pressure on you. But you know I only want you to succeed. After a point, there won't be anything I can do for you. When your time is expired, I'm afraid..." he tapered off, and she knew exactly what he was too diplomatic to say.

"You are very kind, Dr. Jovi. I could never have done any of this without your guidance, and your patience."

"Well, well." His head bobbed thoughtfully, and he absently rummaged in the pockets of his suit jacket. "It is important that you push yourself, but you seem distracted today. I don't want you to fall ill. Why don't you rest today? Take yourself home and get caught up on your sleep. Get some fresh air on the way there, heh?"

Clio scratched her head, swamped with guilt. She nodded, finding it difficult to meet his eyes. She could use the time to make a few calls, coordinate with Guillermo, and bring him up to date. And she'd still have time for a good night's sleep. "Yes. Thank you." She'd make up for it tomorrow by writing twice as much. She wouldn't let Dr. Jovi down, either. "Yes, I think that's a good idea."

"That's a good girl. Your father will be calling soon to announce his quarterly visit." He nodded, peering at her through squinting eyes as he smiled. "We want to make a good impression, don't we?"

Clio pressed a smile on her face. Oh, yes.

The walk home passed in a blur, Clio remembering to stop for a few basic food items on the way, but hardly registering the sights. She really was over-tired. When she got to her apartment, she flopped face down on the bed. *I'll just have a little nap first...*

She awoke to a sharp rapping on her door, her heart leaping.

Groggy, she pushed up from the bed and staggered to the door. "Who is it?" she mumbled.

"Guillermo."

Guillermo? Her heart thudded. Should she be expecting him? What time was it? "Uh. Just a sec." She ran to the bathroom and smoothed her mussed hair, tucked in her wrinkled shirt. There were creases embossed on the side of her flushed face. *Shit.*

He strode in when she unlocked the door, turned and took her in. She rubbed her cheek, trying to revive the circulation, and hide her creases. Smiling, he said, "Did I wake you?"

"No. No I was just…"

They both laughed as their eyes met, and she felt her face heat.

"Yes, okay. I dozed off. Dr. Jovi sent me home early."

"Well, good." He stepped forward and planted a quick affectionate kiss on the corner of her lips. "You're rested up for our work tonight." He strode to her sitting room and dropped his files on her coffee table, collapsed onto the sofa. He'd been here so often lately, he looked almost at home sitting there. He looked as tired as she felt, his eyes smudged with shadow. "I got a couple of replies today. I could hardly wait to go over them with you." He looked up at her. "Clio?"

She was standing, dozily gazing at him, feeling a buzz all over. After she'd stared at his image on her computer screen all morning like a dummy, he was finally here in the room with her, warm flesh and blood. She had to get a grip. There was so much to do.

Her stomach rumbled with hunger. "Have you eaten? Would you like a drink?"

"I'm fine. Uh, well, maybe some water, per favor?"

She went to the kitchen, filled two glasses of water. Pausing, she downed one and refilled it, dabbing cool, wet fingertips over her forehead and neck to wake herself up. Ugh. She felt like a blob of melted gelato. Or a pan of soggy tiramisu. Or a… She shook her head, grabbed a hunk of stale bread to gnaw on and took the water glasses back into the sitting room.

Guillermo was reading over some papers from his file, his laptop open on the side, and he patted the sofa beside him as she set down the water glasses. She sat, taking the letters from him to read them over. Mm, hmm. It was a letter from the Ministry, with a request for further details, and yet more forms to fill out. "This looks promising."

"They want more details." Guillermo leaned back, watching her as she read. Her eyes darted to the side, and a smile crept across her face. "What?"

He shrugged and reached forward to tuck a strand of hair behind her ear. "Bella," he whispered.

She shot him a quizzical glance. "Yes?"

He shook his head. "Just that. You are beautiful."

"Hmm." She dropped her gaze, opened her laptop and clicked on a folder, then opened a file. "Do you have this information?"

He chuckled. "Yes, I brought it." He rummaged through his file and handed her a few pages. As she scanned them and entered the relevant facts into her computer, Guillermo sat quietly perusing plans of the villa on his own screen, stroking her forearm with a lazy finger. Her arm tingled where their skin met, and the tingling spread and warmed her all over, right to her core. It was impossible to concentrate. After the day she'd had, she wanted to toss the computer on the floor and throw herself on him. She hungered for his touch, despite the fact she'd extracted a reluctant promise from him to keep his roaming hands off of her while they worked on this project. It didn't stop her from dreaming. Or him from crossing the line.

Swallowing, she squeezed her eyes tightly shut and regrouped. "Guillermo, you promised."

He was absently rubbing the small of her back with warm fingertips. "Hmm?"

"Guillermo, stop. Please." She straightened her spine, pulling away from him. "You're distracting me."

"Well, Clio. It's mutual, Bella. Being in the same room as you makes me very hot and bothered."

She turned to him, scowling, though she felt a smile tugging at her lips. "Memmo."

He caressed her cheek with his knuckles, his blue eyes shadowed with desire. "Perhaps just one kiss. And then I will be able to leave you alone."

She shook her head. "As if I'm going to believe that."

His sensuous mouth twisted. "Kiss me anyway. And afterwards you have my permission to slap me if I misbehave."

She laughed, and he took her head in both hands, driving his fingers into her thick hair, and captured her mouth with his. Oh, this is what she wanted. All day she'd been dreaming of his kisses. As his hot tongue probed her mouth, the warm tingling that he'd kindled over the surface of her body penetrated to her center, turning her insides to liquid fire.

The one kiss she'd allowed him threatened to engulf them both, as his hands pulled her towards him, and hers slid up his firm chest to encircle his neck. They'd begun to slump lower on the sofa, getting dangerously close to reclining, when a loud warbling sound erupted in front of them. They jerked, tearing apart. Wha…?"

The sound repeated, and as her head cleared of passion, she realized what it was.

"It's a Skype call." That could only mean one thing. She leaned toward her laptop and clicked on Skype, bringing it to the front. Her heart pounded. "It's Father."

Guillermo squirmed and blinked at her. "Huh?"

"My father is calling," she hissed. "You have to hide." She gave his shoulder a shove.

Guillermo stood up and staggered. He took a lurching step away from her, and then seemed to realize what was required. He stepped around the coffee table, behind her laptop screen, and squatted so their eyes were level. "How's this?" He quirked a brow at her, grinning.

She rolled her eyes at him and sighed. The call trilled again. She smoothed her hair and straightened her clothing. It would have to do. "Shhh. Don't make a sound." She clicked on Father's icon. "Hello, Father."

"Clio, sweetheart. There you are."

Guillermo's eyes widened at the sound of her father's gruff voice, no doubt surprised to hear he had a Scottish burr. He mouthed something at her, a question. She tried to ignore him, focusing on her father's blurry, lagging face. "Yes, sorry. I was just in the toilet."

"Ah. Yes. Well. I spoke to Jovi today. He seems to think you're making good headway. I wanted to check in before I booked my flight."

"Your flight?"

"Yes, Clio. My flight. I've got a small break coming up between sessions, and just enough time to pop over to see how you're making out."

"I'm well, Father. Just fine. There's no need to—"

"Nonsense. Nonsense. I want to see my little girl. Jovi tells me you're writing at last. I want to go over the outline and premise with you before you get too far into it."

Guillermo's face twisted in disbelief, his eyes questioning.

Clio stared at him, deadpanned, clenching her teeth. This was so mortifying. She couldn't explain how controlling, how domineering, Father was. She couldn't say anything to him. "I know how you like to check up on me, Father, but I'm doing fine. And I know how busy you are. Maybe I could just email the outline to you, if you want to look at it. I think it's good." As though Dr. Jovi hadn't already done so. Father just had to tinker. He had to come and put his own spin on her work, give it his stamp of approval.

Guillermo's brows came down, fiercely shadowing his eyes, rendering them blue-black. His jaw jutted forward.

"You don't look well, sweetheart. Have you been having headaches again?"

"No, Father. I'm just a bit tired. I've been working hard. You'd be proud of me."

Guillermo grinned and gave an exaggerated, mime-like nod.

"Well. All the more reason to visit. But I'd like to feel assured that you're going in the right direction. You don't want to waste time now. Jovi seemed to indicate that you were distracted. To tell the truth, I'm a bit concerned. You'd better not be stargazing again. You can't afford to mess up so close to the end, Clio. Soon you'll be one of us."

At this, Guillermo's jaw dropped open. He blinked, frowned, then stuck out his tongue at the back of her computer screen.

Clio nearly lost it. She drew a deep breath, fighting for calm, glaring at Guillermo. She stroked her forehead with her fingertips. There was no point arguing with Father. Once he'd made up his mind, there was no negotiating. "When were you thinking of coming, then?"

"In a few days. A week at most."

Guillermo shook his head and bugged out his eyes in mock terror.

She pressed her lips together to stop from laughing.

"Is there someone there with you?"

"What? No, of course not. Where are you now?"

"Athens. I'll book my flight tonight and let you know."

"Okay, then. If you insist. What about Mother?"

"Mm. She's in Prague this month."

"Ah."

Father was silent for a minute or two, gazing down at his desk, shuffling papers. Then, without looking up, not that their eye contact was real anyway, he said, "Look Clio, I sense you're being evasive. We can't afford any more delays. Jovi's time is valuable. Space at the Accademia is limited. And after that automobile incident, I can't keep throwing good money after bad. It's time you wrapped this up and got on with your life. I had a call from Dr. Broughton about a junior position."

Clio's chest squeezed, her breath thin and shallow. She could't look up to meet Guillermo's eyes.

"What are you saying?"

"I can't give you any more extensions. I have to pull the plug if you don't wrap this up."

"But, Father, I'm doing fine now. I–" She looked up and nearly choked. Guillermo had stood up, and was silently gyrating with his shirt pulled up to reveal his gorgeous, lean abs, simultaneously stroking his belly and his butt, giving her the most ludicrous, lascivious bedroom eyes.

She slapped a hand over her mouth to stifle a laugh. She coughed. "Ahem. No, Father, there's no–"

Guillermo was stifling his own laughter, and she kept her eyes trained on Father's grim, blurry face.

"You've got a month, Clio. You've got a month to submit. That's why I want to help with your outline. We can make certain you get to the finish line."

"Father. It's my thesis. And my career. I don't want to go to Ohio anyway. I'd rather–"

"Believe me, Clio. You can't shake a stick at Ohio. It's a good start for you. Success or failure will rest on your shoulders. Your Mother and I can't baby you anymore. It's high time you proved what you're made of."

"Then let me."

"Don't be peevish now. I'll see you soon."

She looked up. Guillermo was gone. No, he was lying on the floor, playing dead, apparently. She held her breath. Strangely, though Father's calls typically made her quake, this time she felt a strange sort of distance, and although she was rankled, she wasn't nearly as annoyed as she would usually be.

The moment Father ended the call, she shouted, "Guillermo. I almost peed my pants."

In an instant he was revived, and dived back onto the sofa, enveloping her in his arms, and smothering her face and neck with noisy kisses until they both collapsed from laughter and tears.

"Excuse me but... your papa is a *cazzone*."

She sobered. "Guillermo. This isn't the least bit funny."

CHAPTER 21

Guillermo could hardly contain his agitation. It was partly desire, partly rage at her exasperating, pompous bully of a father. His fists clenched with the urge to rip something apart.

He was pulsing, hard, overcome with an uncontrollable urge to ride or fight or fuck. His cock throbbed, pushing at his fly. This was dangerous. He couldn't let his crazy passion loose on Clio. It would terrify her.

To let off steam, he broke from kissing her to tickling her ribs and underarms. She squeaked and bucked under him, only fanning the fire. His hands, trembling to take her full breasts and squeeze them, slid down her ribs to her hips. He dug his thumbs into the corners of her pelvic bone, in that spot he knew was wildly ticklish. She threw her head back, exposing her creamy long neck, screamed and kicked, laughing hysterically, and they rolled from the sofa onto the floor, knocking into the coffee table.

They were breathing heavily, giggling and barking with laughter. He gritted his teeth, his eyes feasting on her gorgeous flaming hair, wild and messy now, radiating out from her face, which was flushed, her eyes sparkling, her lips parted, red, wet.

He groaned and covered her mouth with his. She gasped in his mouth, and he thrust his tongue into her, hard, dragging the tip across the roof of her mouth, capturing her tongue and sucking, thrusting again, in his mind, fucking her the way he dreamed of doing. She stilled under him.

He ground his groin into her soft stomach, slipped a leg between hers, and buried his face in the crook of her neck, moaning. They lay still, his pulse throbbing, his rigid cock pressing against her, pulsing, *thud, thud* and *thud*. Blood *whooshed* in his ears, in his head, in his cock, and he shook with the effort of being still. He must not behave like an animal. This was Clio. Clio. His angel.

She squirmed under him. He felt her hips press up into him. "Don't do that, Clio," he ground out between clenched teeth. "I am already dying here. Don't make it worse."

Her hands, resting lightly on his shoulder blades, slid down lightly, fluttering across his shirt with just enough friction to cause his skin to thrill at her touch. He shuddered. "Memmo," her voice was a feather light whisper. He heard her swallow.

"Do you want me, *Bella?*"

She exhaled. "I'm not insensate."

He waited. Could she be relenting? Would she love him the way he wanted her to?

"I'm afraid. You will take your pleasure, and then you will laugh at me. Or you will disappear and cower the way men do, afraid of the consequences of slaking your lust on a woman. And then what? Where will we be?"

"I need you, *Bella*. You don't know how I need you."

"We need each other, Memmo. For the villa. What would happen if–" She stopped.

"Don't you trust me?"

There was a long, long pause, and he felt her breathing still, and her heart pounding behind her ribs.

"Clio?"

"I want to Memmo. I don't know. I can't help thinking…"

He pushed back, and their eyes met. Hers were shadowed with

some dark thoughts, flickering with painful memories. "What? What happened to you, *cara*? Why are you so afraid of love?"

She glanced away.

He sat up, pulling her up, and they leaned back against the bottom of the sofa, shoulder to shoulder. He slipped his hand around hers, interlacing their fingers. "Tell me."

She sighed, long and pensively, and he waited.

And he listened to a story of her youth. Guillermo could picture her, fifteen years old, tanned golden, freckled, her wild red hair flowing, her womanly curves blossoming under the Mediterranean sun, on the beautiful white beaches of Greece. Free to wander, explore, and befriend the local teens, and the other ones, on vacation like herself.

But, she told him, it was a local boy that she became especially close to. Hektor, only a year older. Tall, slender, dark, strong, with sparkling dark eyes and a flashing white smile. So charming. She fell in love with his fiery nature, his sensuality, and his free and reckless ways. Clio told him that he, Guillermo, reminded her of this boy, and that made it harder. It made her want him, but even more afraid.

He stroked his thumb in circles across the back of her hand while she talked, aware of her physically, so close, and yet with this barrier between them, keeping them apart.

Clio recounted that she and Hektor walked the hills around the village, played, frolicked on the beach. And he awoke in her a passionate nature that had lain dormant. Day by day that summer, they had grown more intimate, more bold, exploring each other's bodies, awakening the hungry, carnal beast of lust.

The remainder of the day, the sun arcing across the room, the noises of Firenza outside the window, went by unnoticed. Guillermo's awareness of her body and his own was heightened. His desire for her only grew more intense as she spoke, yet he knew he could not act on it. She was trusting him with her secrets, sharing her fear. He couldn't do anything to threaten her, to break that fragile trust. His heart hammered steadily against his ribs, loud in his ears like the crash of the surf on the shores of Mykonos, as if he were there with her, so that he held his breath and strained to hear her soft voice over the thunder of the waves.

Clio knew they were young for it, both she and Hektor still virginal, but their connection was strong and their blood hot. It seemed inevitable that eventually they would take the last step. And they did. And it was beautiful, if clumsy. It would have made a beautiful memory. But her father had ruined it, like the ancient ruins he studied to death, smashing it into rubble and dust.

Clio began to shake, and Guillermo slipped his hand from her grip and put it around her shoulders, pulling her close to his side, stroking her hair gently, murmuring soothing sounds as she talked.

Her father had been searching for her. It was late, later than usual she supposed, and he had got a little worried, even though it was normal for her to be out with her friends in the long summer nights. How he knew to look there, at that particular private cove, she never found out. But he did. And though they heard him approach, saw his huge bulging shadow bearing down on them, they could not disentangle themselves and get their clothes on quickly enough. He'd seen everything in the blaze of his flashlight.

He was livid, hauling Hektor off of her by his hair, slapping him so hard he flew back onto the damp sand with a crunch, and dragging the crying Clio home, half dressed, fully, utterly humiliated.

Guillermo rubbed her shoulder and stroked her arm, trying to warm her and settle her tremors. His throat ached, and he swallowed against the tightness. Now he understood. He was relieved on the one hand, furious with her father on the other, but those feelings could wait. Now he wondered only what he could do to comfort her.

Tears crept steadily down her cheeks, and she dipped her chin, hiding her face behind the curtain of her tumbled curls. He lifted her, pulling her into his lap. He pushed her hair back from her face and wiped her damp cheeks, kissing the top of her head and her brow. "*Bella, mi cara. Grazie.*"

She continued. In the aftermath, Clio was virtually confined to their house for two weeks. Whenever she ventured out, under close supervision, her face flaming with shame, she searched the town for Hektor, but found only the smirks and laughing eyes of her so-called friends and other townspeople. Once, she thought she caught a glimpse of him, but if it were him, he'd quickly disappeared around the corner of a building. She never saw him again, even though it was a very small village. Then she was shipped back to boarding school. Forever chastened.

"Ah, *mi* Clio." Guillermo wrapped his arms around her tightly, and held her until she seemed calmer. His chest filled with gratitude that she trusted him, that she confided in him at last. It meant something. "*La ringrazio per avermi avvertito, e la ringrazio per la fiducia.*"

She filled her lungs and exhaled loud and long, with a shudder, as though in purging her secret, she had also purged her shame.

"It was wrong of him," he said. "Horribly wrong. You were young and exploring your sensuality. This is normal and good. There is no shame in that. I'm so sorry, *cara*." He kissed her hair again, and she sighed.

He paused, thinking. "Do you trust me, Clio?"

She whimpered and nodded faintly.

"Let me show you something. Let me help you." He slid her off of his lap, rotating her so she sat on the floor between his legs, leaning back against his chest. He kept his arms wrapped loosely around her. "Do you remember that second night at Villa Cielo Incantato? When we all got drunk?"

She drew in a sharp breath and stilled.

He brushed his hands lightly up and down her arms. "You felt ashamed, *si*? Because you let down your guard, forgot yourself, and you allowed yourself to feel."

She nodded, and he closed his eyes and inhaled the scent of her hair, feeling its softness brushing his face. He lifted it away from her shoulder, baring it, and dropped his face to the crook of her neck, breathing against her.

"Mmm. We never spoke about it afterwards. You were so frantic the next morning. Let me tell you how *I* felt that night. What you did to me."

"I...oh–"

"Shhh. Don't speak. Just listen. You were so beautiful, Clio. I wanted you so badly. I was on fire for you. I thought I would shatter into a million fragments, with you swaying and gyrating in my arms." As he spoke, he continued exhaling hot moist breath through her blouse, against her neck and shoulder. His groin tightened at the memory of her that night, feeling the weight of her soft curving ass against him. Now, his hands slid down to rest against her hips on either side, resisting the urge to thrust up, but not able to stop the throb of blood that surged into his cock at the thought of it. "Do you remember what you did? What you did with my hands?"

A small sound emerged from her throat, reluctant and fearful.

"Do it again, *Bella*. Trust me, *cara*. I won't hurt you. I won't laugh at you. I promise." He slid one hand over her stomach and stopped there, waiting for her. "Close your eyes and remember. I will close my eyes. It is safe."

She didn't move for so long, he thought she'd forgotten, or was too afraid. At last, her hand slid over his, then she guided his other hand up, across her stomach, her ribs to her breasts.

"Mmm. *Mi Bella*. I am so hot for you. I love your breasts. I love your body. You are beautiful and sensual. I knew it the first night I saw you. I have burned for you ever since."

She didn't speak, but left his hands there, cupping her breasts, her chest rising and falling against them. He gently kneaded them, rubbing them with his palms, feeling her nipples harden, and his cock respond.

Her breathing became more rapid, and her head fell back

against his shoulder. He pressed his face against the side of her head, moving his lips over her ear, letting her hear and feel his own excited breath, dipping his tongue into her ear, and pulling her lobe between his teeth.

She lifted the pressure from his right hand until her palm barely grazed it, the skin on his knuckles tingling, the hairs rising, and then she gently guided his hand down, down, down until it rested over the vee between her legs. She wore a light cotton blouse, and thin summer capri pants, the fabric no barrier to their exchange of heat and friction. Once there, she stilled, leaving him to take the next step.

He groaned and murmured words of praise and delight into her ear, rubbing her mound, and slipping his fingers between her legs. She was hot, and he could feel her seeping moisture through the fabric of her pants. "*Mio Dio, Bella.* You are hot. You are so sexy." She squirmed against his hand in response.

A moment later, not satisfied with stroking her, he pushed her forward and laid her gently on the floor, cradling her head in his hand, feeling his way. He kept his eyes closed, and assumed she did the same. Then he knelt over her, straddling her. He would not remove any clothing. As much as he felt himself swollen and throbbing with wanting her, he would do nothing for himself tonight, other than give her pleasure. He thought only of Clio.

Bending over her, Guillermo slid his lips and tongue down her cheek and neck, pulling aside the collar of her blouse to kiss and lick and suck at the delicate skin of her collar bone, feeling the gooseflesh rise over the soft mounds of her breasts. Then he smoothed the fabric down and opened his mouth, covering the crest of her breast, exhaling his heated breath over her. She arched her back, moaning, and thrust her breast closer. He pulled at her taut nipple, suckling her through the fabric until it was wet and translucent, biting her while massaging and pinching the other. When she was squirming under him, he switched breasts and did the same until her breathing hitched and quickened.

He grunted, involuntarily thrusting against her, pressing his erection on her leg, clenching his jaw, trembling, waiting a moment to regain control while his heart pounded in his ears. He forced the images of him tearing off her clothes from his mind. This was for Clio, only Clio. *Stronzo*, this was taking all the self-mastery he had, and then some. Sweat dripped into his eyes, and he wiped his brow with the back of his hand. He wanted to fuck her so madly, he was wild with need.

He slid his chest down between her legs, pulling the hem of her blouse out of her waistband, slipping his fingertips under the edge to gently stroke the silken quivering skin of her stomach. She shivered and moaned, and he pressed his face against her breasts and ground his erection into the floor.

"*Cazzo IO TI voglio così male*, Clio," he murmured, panting. "You are so gorgeous, so hot, so fucking sexy. There is no one like you. I want you. I need you." Then he slid further down, and placed his open mouth over her core, biting down on her and growling, taking a deep breath and exhaling, slowly enveloping her in his moist hot breath until a keening sound rose up out of her.

"Aahh, Memmo," she moaned, twisting and thrusting up to meet him. "Memmo. I... I... aahh."

At last he opened his eyes. He had to watch. He could not stop himself. Her head was thrown back, her eyes closed, and her beautiful, blood-engorged lips parted and panting. She looked just like Santa Theresa in her ecstasy from her office wall.

His pulse thundering in his cock and in his head, heat flooding his body, sweat soaking his shirt, Guillermo brought one hand down while he continued to knead and pinch her breast with the other, and began to rub her through her pants, feeling the shape of her, unable to penetrate her as instinct screamed for him to do, but touching her forward and back, round and round her clit, faster and faster, until she writhed and screamed her release, her back arching off the floor.

Suddenly she convulsed as a sob tore from her throat, and tears seeped from her tightly closed eyes, like blood from a stone.

He froze, muscles locked, his cock pressed hard to the floor, gritting his vibrating teeth, his head buzzing. *Cazzo*, he'd have blue balls to pay for this, but it would be worth it. It would be worth it. That such passion should be bottled up was criminal. *Mio Dio*, she was magnificent, and his heart swelled with love for her.

"*Brava, Bella. Brava.*"

She slumped to the floor, limp and shaking and he immediately rose up and wrapped himself around her like a shroud, kissing her neck and her face, kissing her mouth, sucking hungrily on her full lips. "*Ti amo, cara. Tu sei un dono del cielo. Sono abbagliato da te. Ti adoro. Grazie.*"

"*Memmo,*" she whimpered, her chin quivering. "*What about you?*"

"Never mind me. I am so very happy. You have given me a great gift, *Bella*. Your pleasure is my pleasure." He pulled her up into his lap again, holding her tight, placing a hundred tiny kisses over her face. "I give to you and you return the gift to me by letting go, by surrendering control, by giving yourself to me and accepting my gift of love. This is beautiful, no? We make a beautiful memory to drive away the pain. There is no shame, only beauty, only ecstasy, *mia cara*."

Guillermo was deeply disturbed by Clio's father's call, despite his attempts to make light of it.

Even though he'd inferred many things about her family, it wasn't until he'd heard the man's voice, his tone, his manner, his condescending words that he began to understand the family environment that Clio had grown up with. The man was self-important, imperious, and rigid. Guillermo's hands tightened on the handle bars of his Ducati. He burned to confront the bastard. He wished he'd seen his pompous face. Dr. McBeal made Guillermo's own father seem like a benign bureaucrat by comparison. At least Guillermo understood that his own father was simply a weak man who had done what he thought was best for his family, his heritage, and his estate, however ill-judged, even though he was largely ineffectual.

Once Clio had told him the story of her youthful indiscretion and cruel humiliation by her father, the pieces of the puzzle slipped into place. At least he now understood how the man had kept her under his thumb all these years. The question was, had Guillermo's experiment freed her from those bonds? Was one pseudo lovemaking encounter enough to undo the habit of so many years of repression?

Remembering her passion, he shuddered, a river of fire flooding through him, making his already aching balls throb. Dear God he hoped so.

Guillermo roared along the road toward the nursing home on the outskirts of Firenze where Nonno had lived these past ten years. Despite Jacopo's neglect or evasiveness or whatever it was, Guillermo had been feeling a growing need to visit the old man, even though it would accomplish nothing. Nonno was a touchstone for him. Despite the fact that Nonno rarely recognized him, and sat in his geri-chair drooling and mumbling, it anchored Guillermo and helped him regain perspective.

He pulled into the lot and parked his bike near the door, tugging off his helmet.

At the front desk, the younger nurse was on duty, and she smiled at him in recognition. "*Buon giorno*, Senior d' Aldobrandin."

Of all the family, Guillermo was certain he was the only one who visited regularly. No one spoke of it, but even Pia, the dutiful one, was too busy with her own family to come out here very often. They found it difficult, and perhaps pointless, to sit and talk to an old man lost to dementia.

Guillermo knew his way around. He strode down the wide linoleum corridor towards Nonno's wing, pausing at the common room to quickly scan for him. Sometimes it was hard to tell them apart. A slightly mis-tuned radio announcer droned on about some conflict in the upper parliament.

He continued to Nonno's room, and there he was, slumped in his chair, facing out the window at the garden, his thinning white hair just visible over the high back. Nonno had been a tall, slender man, similar in build to Jacopo and Papa. In every other respect, he'd been quite different. Charming, warm-hearted, fun-loving, romantic. It was from Nonno that Guillermo had learned his love of history, of art and architecture, of music, food and women. He was a dreamer. An idealist.

Guillermo strode forward and stepped in front of him, bending to kiss his sagging cheeks. "Nonno. *Buon giorno. Como stai?*"

"*Eh? Gia gia gia gia. Chi è?*" His watery pale blue eyes peered at Guillermo intently, questioning, confused.

Guillermo sighed. Too bad. Not a good day. He should know better than to hope. He pulled up a stiff-backed chair and sat down next to Nonno, taking his papery stiff hand.

"It's me, Memmo, Nonno. How've you been, eh? Have they been keeping you busy?"

"*Gia gia gia.*" A bit of spittle overflowed Nonno's thin lips and made its way down his creased face in a rivulet.

"*Si.* I know how it is. It's been a crazy time for me, too."

"*Si, si.*"

Guillermo pondered the fact that though Nonno and his inmates remembered nothing specific about their lives, they still somehow retained the social niceties. They always knew when it was their turn to say something. The give and take. Which tone of voice was appropriate to the occasion. He stroked and patted the old man's hand, feeling wistful.

Sighing deeply, he continued talking, knowing the sound of his voice was a comfort. "I saw Pia and Bianca just last week. They miss you."

"Pia? Pia, Pia. *Bella ragazza.*"

"*Si*, she's even more beautiful now. Grown up now, with two children of her own."

"*Si, si, si.*" Nonno threw back his head and gave a wheezing belly laugh, a response to some pleasurable thought that only he could know.

Guillermo dropped his head, closing his eyes. "Oh, Nonno. I know they'll be alright. I'll take care of Bianca of course, and eventually she'll get her act together."

"*Finita scuola?*"

Guillermo's head shot up. "*Scusi?*"

Nonno lifted a hand and wiped his damp chin with the back of it. "Is she done with school now? Bibi?"

Tentatively, Guillermo raised his eyes to Nonno's. They were clear and sharp, and peered intently at Guillermo's own. "Ye-es. She was studying digital communication."

"Digital... what does that entail, exactly?"

Guillermo grinned. He'd rolled a seven. "You've got me, Nonno. Some new-fangled mumbo-jumbo. Computers and internet and... I-don't-know-what."

Nonno laughed again, and Guillermo felt his own laughter bubble up. "Welcome back, *caro*."

"Have I been away?"

Guillermo nodded, hot salty tears flooding his mouth and throat, stinging his eyes. "*Si*," he choked out. "I missed you." He stood and leaned in, kissing Nonno's cheeks again.

Nonno squeezed his hand. "What troubles you, *figlio?*"

Guillermo sniffed back his tears. What harm, when he would forget by dinner time?

He drew a deep breath. "It's the villa. I'm afraid we're going to lose it."

Nonno went rigid. "Eh? What's that you say?"

Guillermo rocked back and forth. "It's Jacopo, and his politics." He thought about that. "No, that's not fair. It's just that it costs too much, and we don't have the money to keep it up. It's old and–"

"Of course it's *old*. That's why it's priceless, Memmo. Just think about it." The old man still had fire.

Guillermo thought about it. He could hardly think of anything else these days, except for Clio. His heart tripped.

"I met a girl."

Nonno's head swiveled toward him, his white wiry brows twitching. "What's special about this one, Casanova?"

Guillermo laughed, then sobered. "You know, I can't quite put my finger on it." He swallowed. "She's beautiful, of course."

"A dark vivacious beauty, like Gemma."

"No. A Titian beauty. With eyes like the Ligurian sea. With hidden passion."

"Mmm. Mmmhmm." Nonno nodded sagely. "Your grandmother was a redhead. From the north?"

"She's not even Italian, Nonno. She's American and Canadian. A scholar and an artist."

"Ah. That's just what you need, my boy."

Guillermo smiled at the old man. He could hardly believe his good fortune. It was a blessing, a gift, to have this conversation, as though the past –wasted– ten years had never happened. Guillermo had had moments like this before, though not so many in recent years. But still, so rare.

"Are you comfortable, Nonno? Do you have any pains anywhere?"

"Eh, no. I'm fine."

Guillermo gazed into his sharp pale eyes, so wise. This was what he missed the most. The decaying frail body was unimportant. But when Nonno was absent, he missed that keen intelligent knowing gaze. It gave him comfort, anchored and oriented him in the world like nothing else could. Where did he go, he wondered? He felt himself tearing up again, his chin quivering.

"Something's bothering you, Memmo. Tell me."

"Jacopo is selling the estate, Nonno. *We* are selling it."

Nonno's face hardened, his gaze intensified. "No."

"There's so much debt." It wasn't important to tell him why. "We can't take care of it. We can't keep it."

Nonno jutted his chin forward and worked his jaw, his teeth, making a sucking noise. "It's an old house on a rundown farm. Who wants it but d'Aldobrandin? What is the point of selling it?"

"You'd be surprised how much it is worth. Enough to pay off the debts and more."

Nonno shook his head. "You must do something else. Anything else. Give up everything."

Guillermo thought. He thought about his apartment, his car, his bike, his savings. "It's not enough." And what would be the point?

"Farm it. We never tried hard enough to farm it."

"I'm not a farmer, Nonno. I'm an architect. None of us are farmers anymore."

"Hmmph."

They sat in silence for a few minutes, and Guillermo was convinced that Nonno had slipped back into the fog of his past, or wherever he went when he went away.

"The villa is our legacy, Memmo. We are the Contes d' Aldobrandin. What are we without our legacy?"

"Hmm." Guillermo nodded sadly. "That's what she says. The girl. Clio."

"Clio?" He chuckled. "Ironic, no?"

Guillermo snorted softly. "*Si.*"

"Will you marry her?"

"Phht. I just met her. That's not for me, anyway."

"Pah. Of course it is. What does she say?"

"She has ideas. Innovative ideas. Grants, leases, rentals. I was skeptical, at first. But…"

"Tell me."

Guillermo summarized their plan, explaining the various sources of funding for renovations and operations, the different functions that would make the villa and estate their home. Nonno seemed to take it all in. Guillermo also explained about Mad Richie and his offer, his grand renovation plans and Guillermo's duplicitous role in them.

"Do it. You must do it. You cannot allow that man to tear the villa apart. That is an abomination."

"There are many details to work out yet. The universities we are negotiating with want to know everything, and we don't have answers yet."

"You will find a way. This Clio sounds very smart and determined."

"She is that."

"That is why you love her."

Guillermo's heart beat a little faster. "Maybe."

"A woman who valued the villa, and could contribute to it's preservation, would be a good partner for you, *si?*"

"Ah..." How could Guillermo explain to Nonno that he was trying to set up this institute, and go back to his old life in Florence? His *current* life, though his routines had been so disrupted lately he could barely recall what they had been. Yet one of the pressing problems he and Clio needed to solve was the issue of directorship. She had hinted that this would be a job for a family member, but Guillermo could not see Jacopo in that role. He would be hopeless. Nor Pia. Without saying so directly, he'd imagined that they would hire someone from outside, someone qualified.

For the first time he wondered if Clio herself would like the job. What else would she do once her Ph.D. was complete? She didn't want her father's well-meaning but controlling arrangements for her career, especially if that meant taking some junior teaching post in Ohio or some small town university. As a historian specializing in Renaissance art, with a long academic pedigree, she would be qualified to run the show, even though she'd be green. She had connections. She was certainly organized. It seemed perfect. But what if she didn't want to? He leaned forward, swiping his sweating palms on his knees.

"This is such a complex plan, Nonno. Every piece has to be in place. The risk of failure is—"

"Did I not teach you to be a risk-taker? A problem-solver? What was that for, if not for times like this?"

Guillermo breathed slowly in and out. In and out. If Clio stayed close by, if she decided teaching and directing a research institute would be a good career move for her, would he like that? Something flipped over in his stomach, fluttered and shot down his arms, up his spine to the base of his skull, tingling like a small cosmic eruption. Yes, he decided, yes he would.

A nurse in pink paused in the doorway. "It's time for your milkshake, Conte. Do you want it?"

"Eh? No. Go away. Leave us. Go away. I'm talking to my grandson."

Guillermo met her eye. She raised her brows and gave him a wry smile, holding up the canned drink. Guillermo stood up, strode to the door and took it from her. When he turned back to Nonno, he was slumped over in his chair.

"Nonno?" Guillermo spun him around, peered at his face. He was staring, glassy-eyed, into space, and a string of spit hung out of the slack corner of his mouth.

"Nurse! Nurse! Come back!"

CHAPTER 22

A few evenings later, Guillermo and Clio were back at the villa for another weekend, to collaborate, take photos and measurements, and write their letters and proposals. Deadlines were looming; they both needed additional information that could only be gathered at the villa, and in between, Clio would work on her thesis.

Clio sat across from him at one of the library tables, laptop to laptop, walls of old books at their backs, robed scholars peering down on them from above. Except for the technology, and the glasses of half-drunk wine at their elbows, it reminded Guillermo of the days when he'd sat here with Jacopo and Pia, doing school work. The same warm sense of camaraderie, the same feeling of belonging.

"Has the hospital called?"

Guillermo looked up. Clio's clear, turquoise eyes met his, filled with sympathy and concern. His chest grew tight. She was so earnest, so committed to this cause, so caring. He hardly understood why, but he felt himself drawn to her, trusting her. Sure, she loved Renaissance art and history, and she wanted to help save his villa, but she shouldn't be doing this at all. She had other, more pressing concerns, though he didn't agree with the way she bowed to her father's will. He hoped that would be at an end.

They'd spent an awful lot of time together lately, and it was getting harder and harder for him to maintain his self-control. Especially since this increased intimacy had seemed to make her more comfortable with him. After their encounter at her apartment, she'd reverted to being reserved, even more shy. But step by step, day by day, she had let down her guard, softened. She was easier with him, friendly, even affectionate.

He daren't let himself hope that she was coming to care for him. She continued to keep him at arm's length, forever teasing him about his "Latin ways." Despite her moment of release, he still couldn't tell if she *wanted* him, not that way. Not the way that he so badly wanted her.

What could he say or do to persuade her that she was not just another conquest? That something had shifted in him, and he was really –was he?– really falling in love with her. To prove it, he held himself back, resisted the temptation to touch her. Martina would laugh. Certainly his sisters would. He wanted her so much; he would do anything to keep her near. He didn't know what else to do. He could not bear to frighten her away.

"Guillermo?"

"*Scusi?*"

"Have you heard from the hospital? About your Nonno?"

"Not since this morning. There was no change." At least Nonno's latest stroke had not been fatal. He felt a tight pain at the back of his throat. Undoubtedly the stress of his news had done Nonno some upset, and he felt his gut squeeze with guilt, even though he knew it made no difference. There had been a moment...

"But they're sure it was another stroke?"

He nodded, shrugging. "This has been happening periodically since the big one. They explained it to us. He'll just keep having these little strokes until finally..." He couldn't say it. Of course one day Nonno would die. Please God let it not be now. Even though he was back in some semi-vegetative state for the time being, Guillermo needed him. Needed to know he was there, cheering them on. Guillermo was even more determined to succeed now. For Nonno. For his family. And for Clio. Only via this scheme could he dream of convincing her to stay. Only then did he feel he might persuade her to take him seriously, and be part of his life.

His heart staggered in his chest, rolled and then squeezed until he couldn't draw breath. *Is that what I want? Truly?*

Clio's fingers clacked away at her keyboard, weaving some persuasive arguments that Guillermo could not even imagine, while he worked on drawings. He had two sets now. Not only did Mad Richie expect to see final design drawings very soon, along with preliminary pricing, but the various government restoration grants and partner universities all had need of plans showing how space would be allocated. Where would offices and classrooms and seminar rooms be located? Which rooms would provide accommodation for graduate students and visiting faculty? All afternoon, Guillermo had jumped up to check measurements and evaluate spaces, racing upstairs and down, pacing around and visualizing spatial relationships.

The thought of his ancestral home being used by students of design and history, who would love and value it, somehow didn't bother him nearly as much as Richie's decadent plans. Reluctantly, he would go back to putting the finishing touches on Richie's media room and recording studio, and the new ensuite bathrooms that were more numerous than statues, as well as the new pool and cabana.

He tried to be objective, as though he really were putting these ideas forward to a client. They had to be clever, tasteful and convincing, but he was second-guessing every decision, every detail. If he were the slightest bit glib or heavy-handed with his designs, Richie would sense something was up. He couldn't suggest something that would be offensive if this scheme really went ahead.

Guillermo had to give the guy credit, he really did care. Richie wanted what he wanted, but he didn't mean to destroy the villa in the process. He wanted something first rate. Guillermo liked him and wanted to do right by him. But at the same time, when Guillermo wore his architect's hat, it galled him that he was holding back. He couldn't be his usual bold and creative self. He wasn't able to serve his client's needs to the best of his ability, because of his devotion to his ancestral home and traditions, and because in his heart this renovation would never happen. Could never happen. He was torn in so many directions, it was a wonder he could design a thing.

"I can't do this," he muttered. He grabbed clumps of his hair, shaking his head, his jaw clenched tight.

Clio stopped typing, hands in the air. "What?"

"I am a *bidonista*, deceiving Richie this way. He doesn't deserve it."

"I know. I feel guilty, too. But what choice do we have? We can't withdraw from the sale agreement until every alternative is locked in place. And he forced your hand."

He loved it when she said 'we.' It gave him hope. Warmth swirled in his groin, and his heart squeezed. She didn't know what that did to him, or what vague ill-formed hopes floated at the back of his mind. "To tell the truth, I'm also a bit worried that he'll sue. For breaching the terms of the contract when we unveil this. That's all we need. Lawyer's bills and damages."

Clio sighed. "If only he would stumble upon some other villa, and fall in love with it instead. Then he'd go away of his own accord and leave us alone."

He stared at her, the bottom half of her face hidden, only her lovely aquamarine eyes and freckled nose floating over the screen. She'd spoken dreamily, barely aware of what she had suggested. A bubble of hopefulness buoyed him, lifting his chest, like a burst of pure oxygen. An amazed smile stretched his mouth. Her fox-red brows rose in question. "What now?"

He blinked. Blinked again, his mind racing. Saliva swamped his mouth, and he swallowed. Was it possible? Why hadn't he thought of this before? "You are brilliant, *Bella!*" He stood up, rounded the table and hauled her up, crushing her in his arms, lifting her off the floor and spinning. He laughed.

The air rushed out of her lungs with a faint cry of astonishment. "Wha–?"

He badly wanted to kiss her, but set her down and away from him. He picked up his phone and scrolled to Andreas Fitucci's number, clicking while Clio stood, her expression bewildered.

"*Senior d'Aldobrandin. What can I do for you?*"

"Andreas. I've been thinking. What other properties have you shown Richie, or might you have shown him, if he hadn't settled on ours?"

"*Uh, but, aren't we–*"

"Just hypothetically. I'm curious about the competition, if you know what I mean?"

Clio's eyes widened.

"*Well there were several. Most of which he didn't like at all. But I had a few options that might have done, with a little fixing up.*"

"Aha. Perfetto. Could I... Ah, could you send them to me? Photos, floor plans, any information you have on file?" His pulse raced with excitement, ideas and images already forming in his mind's eye. His pulse thundered, driving adrenaline racing through his veins like a drug, making him feel more awake, more alive. It was like when he rode or ran, the risk, the speed, the thrill was exhilarating.

"*Er. I, uh...*"

"I'll explain everything later. Right now it's just an idea in my head. Don't worry. You'll do just fine."

"*I'm afraid to ask, but... tutti bene. I'll send you an email.*"

"Grazie." He hung up and beamed at Clio. "Clio! I've been underestimating my own talents, *Bella*. Listen to this. What if we found another property that, with a little help from me, could temp Richie away? Something so fabulous he'd thank me for it?"

Understanding dawned, her face opening with delight. "I'd say you were the brilliant one, Guillermo d' Aldobrandin."

He belly laughed. "You haven't seen anything yet." And then he couldn't help himself, he did kiss her. Most surprising of all, she kissed him back.

Clio clung to Guillermo like a limpet to a stone, her mouth on his, her body pressing urgently. She didn't know if it was this latest insight of his, added to his charm, his beauty, his steadfastness, his many talents, just the feather that tipped the scales of her mounting desire, or simply that the moment was right, and her will had finally dissolved. She hadn't been able to think of anything but this since the night Father had called, the night Memmo had unlocked her desire. The thought of being with him filled her with a fizzing joyful feeling, and she wanted more of it. She wanted him, and she wanted him now.

His arms, hesitant at first as though shocked by her response, came around her, gripping handfuls of her shirt, cupping her bottom with a groan, threading into her hair, pulling it loose from its ties as he returned her hungry kiss. Her body lit on fire at his rough touch, the way his hot mouth took possession of hers, the sound that came from his throat, as though he were in pain.

He pulled away slowly, his face tense, a muscle twitching in his jaw. "Clio, what... I'm sorry, *Bella*...I, oh, ugh..."

He leaned back, released her and pinched the bridge of his nose, looking down. For a fleeting moment, she worried that she'd misjudged, that he didn't really want her, even though she knew he desired her, and had done so since they'd first met. Hadn't she been swatting his hands away, scorning his charming compliments, pushing space between them, for weeks? What was he doing now?

Her eyes followed his downward. They were still pressed hipbone to hipbone, close enough to feel each other's radiating heat. She could feel how hard he was. He throbbed against her. Or was that her own blood pulsing between her legs? They both breathed audibly. Her head swum.

He definitely was hot for her, so what...?

"Oh. Is it Marcella and Martino?" She released her death grip on him, slid down his body and glanced to the door, her heart fluttering with nerves. Cool air stole between their heated bodies, and she felt the tug of regret, like a lost opportunity, slipping away, a bright effervescent moment, like the memory of a lovely song that skips through your mind, but then stutters and skids away, and you can't even remember its name, you can't reach it. "Of course. We couldn't–" Her eyes dropped to his chest, her face flooding with heat, embarrassed at her lack of discretion.

"Clio..." Guillermo's voice was choked, and she looked up, met his eyes. "It's not that."

She frowned, puzzled. Why were they even talking?

"They are away. I gave them the weekend off."

Her eyebrows rose. It was true. She hadn't seen them all day. "Oh?"

"No. Not because I thought..." He swallowed. "I *thought* we'd be working. We have so much to do I thought that it would be safe. That I wouldn't be tempt... well, that at least I would be able to control myself. But I didn't expect you to..."

"I'm sorr..." Clio almost apologized, and then realized, she wasn't sorry. He *did* want her, but thought she would not want him. That she would push him away again. A mischievous smile stole across her lips, and she dropped her chin, glancing up at him. "You mean that we are alone in the villa?"

He stopped talking, his features arrested, quizzical. "*Si.*"

Tilting her head up, she met his eyes, her smile widening naughtily.

"Clio?"

"*Si?*"

For an endless moment, Guillermo gazed down at her, his blue eyes darkening with understanding, lust flaring his nostrils.

"What do you have in mind?"

She stepped away from him, her pulse skipping, dropping her voice to a seductive whisper. "Well... I was thinking, since we *are* alone, and there is no one to see us... well, that, for example, if I were feeling a bit warm, and wanted to... undo a button or two on my shirt. That would be alright?" She lightly touched the buttons at the top of her shirt, toying with the top one, slowly slipping it free.

Guillermo's mouth opened, but he didn't speak. His eyes, though they were locked on her fingers, seemed clouded, almost to be seeing something else, something in his imagination. "*Gesu,* Clio." He swallowed, his Adam's apple sliding up and down his bronzed neck.

She stopped moving. Tilted her head to one side. Doubt fluttered through her heart, a little shadow of insecurity. "You don't want...?"

"Aa-ahh. I want. Yes, I want. You." His hand slid down and pressed his groin, and he squirmed, adjusting his twitching erection in his pants. "*Bella.*"

"*Benissimo.*" A jolt of heat shot through her at his gesture as images of his tanned, toned body flashed through her mind, sending fissures of fire through her veins, to her core, pooling between her legs. Suddenly she needed to be close to him, skin on skin. What had she been waiting for? She continued to unfasten her buttons, while he stood like a statue, wooden, stunned, his breath rasping, watching her every movement. He swallowed slowly, with difficulty.

She turned away, slipped her shirt off of her shoulders, glanced back at him, taunting. She felt like a sixties movie star, a coy but wild Jane Fonda to Robert Redford in Barefoot in the Park, their roles suddenly reversed. She dropped her eyes, feeling her face flush with heat. A nervous laugh bubbled to her lips at the thought. She, Clio, was trying to temp the reluctant, work-obsessed Guillermo into letting go. *I've lost my mind. What am I doing?*

She was having fun. Perhaps for the first time in her life, she felt free to have fun, to let go. Her improbable, astonishing partnership with Guillermo had opened a door for her, allowed her to see, to feel, that she had worth, that she could contribute something of herself that came naturally, and, amazingly, be appreciated for it. Be admired. For herself. For her mind of course, her clever contribution to solving his problem, but also for her body and soul. She could see it in his eyes. Bright haunting blue, shimmering beacons focusing on her like an obsessed artist on his work, leaving no doubt in her mind that he found her desirable, had forgotten his work entirely, that there was nothing shameful in this.

At the thought, a tremor shook her, and she felt a tingling sensation dash across her skin, her stomach suddenly twisting with nausea. A small voice whispered in her head, *Oh, no, I'm afraid, I'm afraid.* She took her lip between her teeth, uncertain.

His response was to lick his lips and groan, his eyes on her mouth. He was rigid and shaking, a sheen of sweat visible on his upper lip. His obvious desire made her feel brave and reckless. Not like someone else, but more truly herself, for the first time in her life– or at least since she was fifteen. She felt freed from a dark enclosure. A shadowed pressing place that had held her in so long it had almost become part of her.

But yet there was always this part, bright, fluttering, striving. As though she was stepping forward from dark wings onto centre stage to take her bow, the spotlights now shone on her, and the appreciative eyes of the audience were now on her, warming her. She had a bit of stage fright, but the allure was so compelling.

Biting her lip, she let her shirt fall open and turned to face him, lifting her hands to her hair, pulling it free of its tie, raking her fingers through the tangles to shake it out and pull it forward like a veil over her partially exposed breasts. Only his obvious delight tamped down her habitual reticence at letting her wild locks loose, thrusting her breasts toward his admiring gaze. She slid closer, letting her hips sway, keeping her eyes locked on his, which dropped to her breasts, then up, then down again, his expression pained.

With a stifled roar, he closed the distance between them, gripping her sides in his strong hands, pulling her towards him. He bent his head to her neck, devouring her ear, her jaw, her cheek with his hot mouth. Then, with one hand cradling the back of her neck, the other sliding down her spine to the small of her back, lifting her up and hard against his groin, he pulled her to him as his mouth came down over hers. She let her head fall back, her mouth opening to his probing tongue, meeting him half way.

Yes. This is what I want.

He kissed his way across her collarbones to her chest, kissing and licking the mounds of her breasts, muttering a stream of incomprehensible Italian words, his tone disbelieving, as his hands slid up to cup her breasts, his thumbs pausing to circle over her tightening nipples. His touch triggered her senses, her skin tingling and rising up to meet his grazing palms, a shiver traveling up her arms and down her back, as much a memory of the other night as a response to this moment. She clenched the muscles in her butt and legs, and a tremor shook her. "Memmo!" Her knees felt weak, and she fell against him, feeling his hardness press against her soft belly as his arms locked around her.

He kissed her again and again, muttering endearments. There was no question, love sounded tremendously better in Italian, and she ate it up, ready to let go. She felt him tense up. He steadied her, lifting his head, panting. "Clio. Do you know what you're doing? Have you been drinking too much wine or something? Because I can't..." His voice broke. "I can't stop this time."

She smiled up at him. "I'm not drunk. Except on you. I can't resist you anymore. I know exactly what I'm doing. And I don't want you to stop."

That was all the reassurance he needed. Suddenly he'd torn off his own shirt and hers and tossed them away. He pulled her down onto the rug, and they were rolling over and over, his hard thigh pressing the hot need between her legs, his delicious weight on top of her. She traced the lean muscles of his stomach, his rippling ribs, combing her fingers through the dark hair that dusted his chest.

He paused, gasping. "Do you want... should we go upstairs? Find a more comfortable–?"

"No. Let's not. This feels naughtier." *Who is this crazy, uninhibited woman? I don't recognize myself.* But, in fact, Clio did. Guillermo had seen through her shell, and loved what he saw, and given her permission to be herself, to be real. And she wanted that so badly.

She stroked a hand across the old carpet beneath them. It was worn thin with the years, and would offer no comfort, but she loved this room, the wood paneling, the book-lined walls, the painted vault of the ceiling far above. If Clio had dreamt of a perfect place to make love to Guillermo for the first time, she couldn't have come up with a better plan. Old libraries had been both her great passion, and her prison. But this room was her favorite in the villa, and Guillermo's too.

He laughed and gently peeled the rest of her clothes from her limbs, sliding sensuous kisses over her arms, her ribs, her naked breasts. He caressed and kissed her thighs with a sigh, murmuring words of love and admiration that made Clio feel like a heavenly queen. She helped him unfasten his pants and kick them off, and caught her breath as his Latin beauty was finally fully exposed, his erection springing free. Tawny sun-kissed skin. Firm, lean legs, his hair tickling hers as their legs slid together, feet tangling, stroking. His skillful, sensitive fingertips traced her curves and dips, touched every place, every point, with a confidence and knowledge that she knew came of much experience, but she put it from her mind, knowing only that it was she who was the beneficiary tonight, and reveling in it.

She tried to return the favor, tried not to feel self-conscious and clumsy, skimming her cool hands over his wide shoulders and sinewy back, sliding down to caress the amazing firm curve of his ass as he pressed his thick silky erection against her, the pressure and suspense building inside her, thrumming. He slipped a hand between their bodies, sliding his long fingers over her mound, into her groove, circling and pressing her so gently, and dipping into her wet, welcoming centre. A shuddering sigh escaped her, and his luscious mouth captured it, kissing her with such devotion, such attention and sensual immersion, Clio was certain that was enough, that she would orgasm again just from the sensation of his delicious tongue stroking her mouth, his fingers inside her wet core. His kisses made all prior kisses fade from her memory, becoming ash.

Raising his hand, he slipped his wet fingers into his mouth, his eyes closing, his dark lashes brushing sensually against his cheeks. Then he slid down, sprinkling kisses along her neck, nipples, ribs and belly. *If he kisses me like that, again, I'll disintegrate. I'll surely die.*

But it was a good kind of death, and she realized she wanted it. She wanted him, and she wasn't afraid anymore.

Her body trembled uncontrollably, the burn intense now, and her need for release mounted urgently, drawing hungry moans and desperate whimpers from her throat. He knew better than she did, as she knew he would, this body of hers.

"*Sei tutto ciò che voglio. Hai conquistato il mio cuore.*"

Her heart swelled with delight, hoping that were true, and pushed away the thought of all those other women he had known. He could have anyone, yet he was here with her. But once he'd taken her, would the draw be so strong? "Perhaps for this moment," she mumbled, thinking that he would not say such things in a calmer moment, but nevertheless they were lovely to hear. He made her feel special, desirable, beautiful. She felt beloved.

Anything he chose to say to her, to do to her, she would welcome, and think herself blessed.

He reached for his discarded trousers, and the next thing she knew, he had sheathed himself, and was poised at her entry, hovering, waiting for her to acknowledge him. His eyes burned with intensity, holding hers. Questioning.

Do I want this? Will I regret it?

The answer that came to her was a resounding *yes*. No matter what happened. Even if he became bored with her and moved on. This was her rebirth, and she wanted it to be with Guillermo.

She told him with her eyes, and nodded wordlessly, and she felt his thick silky hardness push slowly inside her, stretching her, while he shuddered with self-control, and she drew in a gasping breath and held it. She felt his cock throb twice, and trembling, clenched her inner muscles to welcome him. Ahh. At last.

"*Non. Per sempre*, Clio, *Bella. Per sempre.*" Always.

Clio wouldn't argue. This moment would last forever in her memory, and that was good enough.

Guillermo advanced slowly, so slowly, until he was buried to the hilt inside her, filling her, and pressed his pelvis hard and hot against hers, holding, trembling with controlled passion, waiting until she twisted, moaned, arched up to meet him, throwing her head back, her eyes rolling up. A helpless groan welled deep in her chest, a plea, begging for completion. "Memmo!"

Then he withdrew until just the head of his cock teased her, stroking her, kissing her, touching her everywhere at once, and so exactly the way she wanted to be touched, driving her insane. He knew her. He was everything she needed, and more, and she arched up to meet him and take him in again, shuddering. He filled her again, and withdrew again, each silken stroke stoking her fire, lifting her higher, her heart pounding madly, and in a very few slow, deep, trembling powerful thrusts, they were both slick with sweat and quaking.

He kissed her, plunging his tongue fully into her mouth, and pulled back.

"Look at me, *Bella*. Don't take your eyes away. Be with me now." She met his eyes, and in their depths, cerulean blue shadowed by desire, she saw something she had never seen before, certainly not with the innocent Hektor on the dark beach. She rose up outside herself, outside of him and their joined bodies. They were joined together in ways far beyond the corporal, somewhere cosmic and in that moment she believed his heart was hers and they would be one forever and always.

He drove himself once more, deeply into her, and went rigid, a roar tearing from him, rocking her and merging with the physical sound that she became as she turned inside out. And then they burst into a million tiny sparkling fragments, like stars in the dome of the Tuscan sky.

CHAPTER 23

"I'm sorry 'bout this, Mista D. My financial advisors been after me to give dem some numbers to work with. Course the money's there, but they need to jiggle thangs around, make arrangements. Until they is a final design, we can't get those contractors estimates to the bank."

Richie was back in Florence for a few days, having been collaborating in London for the past weeks, and insisted on a progress report. He was anxious to see the latest design drawings, and Guillermo knew he was expecting it to be essentially complete. It was, he knew, less than his usual stellar work.

"Not a problem, Richie. We're nearly there." Guillermo was sweating. The back of his neck tingled, and he rubbed it anxiously. He needed to ask Richie for more time, and somehow make it seem reasonable.

He bounced on the balls of his feet, standing before the projection screen, fingering the remote control for his laptop. At least he'd been able to get a rough digital model thrown together over the weekend. Lay clients were typically pretty impressed with what they could do with computer animated 3-D model flyarounds. They didn't have a clue how easy the new software applications made this kind of imagery. Thankfully. It might buy him some time. Or at least make it seem like he'd been using his time well.

He darted a glance toward Richie, reclining easily at the meeting room table. Guillermo was embarrassed, and felt the squeeze of guilt in his chest. After this amount of time, he would have been much further along, had he been working on just one scheme. But between Richie's version of the villa, the Instituto's version, the alternative villa design and the rest of his project load, Guillermo had been working flat out, and still not keeping up. If Richie found out how he'd been spending his time, in direct opposition to his needs and repeated urgings for speed, Guillermo would surely be looking at a lawsuit. Not to mention what his family would do if they found out about his treachery.

His thoughts muddled, he tried to pick up the thread. "So here we are, on the East wing upper level..." He advanced the flythrough, as though they were taking a virtual walk through the house. "The new elevator core runs through here." He knew he'd faked it, but Richie wouldn't see that. Only the contractors would notice that it conflicted with existing mechanical and structural systems. "These are the bedrooms on both sides of the hallway, and in between, we've made accommodation for new office... er, I mean bathrooms." He swallowed. His pulse was racing, and his breath accelerated. Stress. This was exactly what he'd spent his adult life avoiding. This kind of all-consuming pressure to perform, to measure up, to tackle insurmountable obstacles. The kind of stress that killed his father, and was still in the slow process of killing his grandfather.

What am I doing? Didn't I vow that I wouldn't go down this road? How did I end up here?

Guillermo wondered if each of his ancestors had been caught in similarly tangled webs of their own design, just as he had, in some desperate attempt to save the villa. And failed. And been too embarrassed to tell anyone about their failed, ridiculous schemes.

And had to carry on, on the cusp of financial ruin, only to pass along their burdens to the next generation.

But then there was Clio. A blast of remembered heat rushed through his body, his teeth vibrating with aftershocks. He still couldn't believe it.

"Mista D? You alright, bruvva?"

Guillermo started, remembering where he was. He cleared his throat, laughed, and said. "Yeah, sorry, Richie. My mind wandered. I've got a deadline on another couple of projects coming up, and I'm trying to juggle a few other design problems at the same time." He laughed again, realizing he sounded idiotic, and shook his head. *Stronzo*. Clients never wanted to hear that you had projects other than theirs. There was nothing for it but to focus his mind on one thing at a time. And do his best.

He completed the virtual tour, and sat down.

"Of course this is still basically conceptual design, Richie. What I really need, before we have something that can be reliably priced, is to spend some time working out the mechanical and electrical requirements. Rooms are just rooms. You can call them what you want. But the degree of modernization you require, without unduly changing the historic character of the spaces, requires some finessing. I had to go back out to the villa again, and I have been..." It was a stretch of the truth, but it would help his case "...Uh, I need to meet again with a couple of engineers, and get more input from them on these issues. I should be able to do that in the next week or so, and run a couple of scenarios past them. They've been unavailable until now."

"We is running' outta time, Mista D. It's almos' the end of the month. How long you–?"

Guillermo's gut clenched. He exhaled. He couldn't do it by the deadline. "Well, that's just it, Richie. I don't think the end of the month is going to do it for us. I was really hoping you'd be able to give us a couple of extra weeks. I'm afraid it means getting Andreas involved and annotating and initialing a few of those sale documents to extend the deadlines. But I'd really hate to send you to the bank with incomplete information."

Richie chewed his lip, scowling, while Guillermo continued to sweat, glancing at his cellular phone for the time, for messages, for any excuse to call the meeting short.

He could use a drink. "Would you like a *caffe*?"

"Hm? No." Richie shook his head, his neck chains clinking. He sucked his teeth. "I guess I don't got much choice, here, Mista D. I'm not totally feeling the vibe, yet. So I see you need mo' time to find yo' spark. I get dat. We is both artists, an' I respect you. I trust you, Mista D. I got no choice but to defer to your judgement."

Guillermo released a breath. He didn't deserve this man's trust.

"But the timing is bad fo' me. I gotta head back over the water for some meetin's in da States, yo? It's actually gonna be mo' like three weeks before I can get back here."

Guillermo's eyes locked on Richie, his body stiff. Three weeks would be even better. More than he could reasonably have hoped for. *Per favore.*

"We want to get this right, Richie. I want to do my best for you." He felt pain in his chest, as though his lies were bands that cinched around his ribs, like the girth of a saddle, and with each lie, they squeezed his heart and lungs tighter, increasing his burden.

Richie's head bobbed. "Yeah, I got dat. Dat's cool."

"Should I call Andreas?"

Richie stood up. "Nah. I take care of it. You jes' get yo skinny white ass in ova'drive, yeah?"

Guillermo stood up, offered his hand for a knuckle bump. "*Certamente.*"

Clio drew a deep breath and held it, listening to Dr. Bensen ramble on. She scrunched up her face, trying to release some tension, and let go of her breath. "Excuse me, Dr. Bensen. Of course I do understand how important it is that you approve the director of the academic programs. But the fact of the matter is, there are many complicated approvals involved in saving the villa, and setting up the not-for-profit foundation, and these have to be taken care of or there will be no institute. And so–"

He cut her off. "Why don't *you* submit an application, Ms. Sinclair McBeal?"

"I'm flattered, sir, but I haven't even written my thesis yet, nor defended it or graduated, never mind my lack of administrative experience. Besides..." Clio couldn't even think about the why-nots. "...we need someone right now or we can't complete the other applications." She didn't seem to be able to get him to understand that there wasn't time to follow the standard recruitment procedures. Advertising internationally for an academic with the right qualifications, who then would satisfy Bensen's personal criteria, would take time. Months, possibly. More time than they had.

"What if they were not the same person?"

He stopped talking. Finally she'd managed to get his attention.

"What if we had an academic director? And took our time recruiting the right person? Later." Her voice sounded stained to her ears. "But...but in the meantime, we appoint a managing director for the foundation. I know they can be combined. But since there are so many components to the scheme, perhaps that would be better anyway."

It was a great solution. It put away the problem of convincing the universities to give the job to Guillermo, by no one's measure an academic, even though she knew he was the only one to oversee the whole operation. Despite the fact that she hadn't had the courage to broach the subject with him, and in her heart knew he would refuse, would, in fact find it a ludicrous suggestion.

"And who might fill that position?"

"I have someone in mind, but, it's just an idea at this point." *I must talk to him about it. Tonight, when he comes over. I can't put it off any longer.*

She rose from her chair and took a step away, pacing. Bensen had to agree or this wasn't going to work. She turned and paced back to her desk, turned again. Please, please.

"It will require more money, Ms. Sinclair McBeal. I'm not convinced the trust and tuition would allow for that kind of extravagance. Normally we try to find someone with combined experience–"

"Who would of course draw a much larger salary, Professor."

"Mmm. Point taken."

Was that tacit agreement? "And of course there will be other, non-academic, sources of income. The institute is only one part, a major part, of course, but only one part of the operation."

"Yes, but still. But still."

She played her last card. It was premature. There was no guarantee this one would even come through. "We've applied for an additional grant, from the Ministry for Enhancement of Cultural Heritage with the Italian government. It's too early to say yet, but if we are successful, that will add another two to three hundred thousand dollars to our trust. That should help, don't you think?"

"It would help, of course. Well, I'll think about it, Ms. Sinclair-McBeal. I think perhaps you may be right."

"Thank you, Professor."

She hung up and turned to take her seat.

She gasped. The hulking shape of Father filled the doorway of her office.

A great fluttering feeling filled her belly, and her hands flapped around, shuffling papers into piles. "Father!" In her mind was only the thought that she must hide any evidence of her work on the estate. Papers slid, and she couldn't see what was what. She tidied everything and shoved it into a file, certain she had shuffled villa papers in with thesis papers. A good metaphor for the state of her brain these days. "You're here. I... I... you didn't call."

"I attempted to call. You are quite difficult to reach, it seems."

She swallowed, hesitated, lurched toward him. She put her

arms around his broad middle, and felt his stiff arms enclose her and pat her on the back. It only took a millisecond, and that was enough of that. She stepped back. "You flew in today? Just now?"

He raised his brows and pursed his lips, reminding her how he loathed senseless nattering and erratic behavior, two things she seemed to be doing in spades this afternoon.

"You're staying at the–?"

"The usual." The Hotel Albani, of course, with its tasteful Florentine decor and exquisite, obsequious service. He cleared his throat and stepped into her office, his critical gaze casting around. She wasn't sure if he was judging the general state of chaos and clutter, or just looking for a place to sit down.

"Here. Take Jonathan's chair. He's away today." She pulled it out for him, and he scrutinized it, nostrils flaring, before carefully lowering his bulk down into it.

He stared at her, and she realized he was waiting.

She stood, gripping her elbows, smiling tightly at him. *God, I wish he weren't here. What am I going to do now? How can I get anything done?*

"Who was that? What trust were you speaking of, just now?" Father asked.

Her stomach clenched. She tapped her lips with the fingers of one hand. "I beg your pardon?"

"As I came in, you were on the telephone. You were talking to someone about a trust."

"Yes?" Oh, shit. "Um." What the hell could she say? "I... uh, have been... assisting a local... charity, with... some minor fundraising." She pursed her lips and shrugged.

Father's bushy faded orange brows dropped lower and Clio felt a familiar wash of shame. Just like that, he had the power to make her feel like an idiot. Irresponsible. Careless. Of questionable virtue. All at once. "Do you think that is a wise use of your time, under the circumstances?"

Her legs wobbled, and she slumped into her chair, drawing

breath through her nose. "It's a little thing. A bit of advice. Insignificant." She waved away the distraction. "It's taken no time at all." *I knew he was due. Why didn't I prepare?*

"Hmmph."

"So-o..."

"Are you quite well, Clio? You seem scatterbrained today. Are you going to make me ask to see your outline? That is why I came."

"Ah." She'd thought for sure Dr. Jovi would have already sent it to him long ago. She thought they kept no secrets. "Yes. Yes, of course." She scanned her messy desk. Lovely. That would impress Father. She had to find it. "I'll just print a clean copy for you, shall I?"

He blinked slowly. So patient. Sometimes that was as close to agreement as he got. She sat and opened the file on her laptop, quickly scanning it to make sure she hadn't made any stupid annotations, and sent it to her printer. They sat, not speaking, as the printer whirred to life, and the sounds of several pages clicked, hummed and shushed through the machine. Clio rose, straightened the pages and handed them to him. He leaned back and began to read.

Clio released the breath she'd been holding. She tugged at her clothing, smoothing her frizzy hair. *I'm so disheveled. He must think I've slept in my clothes.* Then she sat again, her back rigid, folding her hands on her desktop. "How long are you staying? This time?" She tried to make her voice conversational. She tried to quell her nerves. She tried to imagine him gone again and everything back on track before long. If only.

"A day or two. We can go to dinner shortly, and discuss it."

"Dinner?" she squeaked. She was to meet Guillermo later, at her place.

Father's eyes lifted, resting on her face.

"I had plans for this evening, Father."

He waited.

"Er, I was to meet a friend later. But– I'll... call and cancel." She forced a smile. "It's so nice to see you."

"Nonsense. Have her join us. I like to know how you live here, on your own. I'd like to meet your friends. I'm buying dinner, after all."

Clio froze. "Um. Father. It's a... he."

The muscles of his face hardly moved, and yet they did, his eyes narrowing slightly, the bristly hairs of his brow, his white mustache, his beard, rotating a tiny bit, like heat-sensing antennae. Just enough to show her what he thought of that. A touch of annoyance. A bit of incredulity. A smidgeon of scorn. A measure of curiosity.

"Is it this fellow..." he gestured with his thumb to the other workstation. "Jon...Jonathan, or whatever he's called. Isn't he a fairy?"

Clio pressed her lips together. "That is neither relevant nor any of our business, Father. And no, I'm not referring to Jonathan."

"Is this a... a boy... friend of yours?"

She sighed. Not now. Why now? She'd just made such a monumental choice, everything since the weekend with Guillermo was new, and raw, and tentative between them. She didn't know what it meant, or how it made her feel. How could they endure Father's scrutiny? "No. Not really. Just an interesting guy I met. An architect."

"Very well. Call him now and tell him to meet us at Restaurant Bernini, at my hotel, at five."

Clio's mind raced. Her stomach twisted in fear. Was there someone else she could call, instead of Guillermo, to make this problem go away? Who would lie for her, and be able to fake their way through this ordeal without causing her undue problems? There was no one else. She almost laughed. Really, if anyone could rise to the occasion and feign credibility, it was actually the charming, smooth-talking Guillermo. And she had to call him, regardless.

So much for asking him about the directorship tonight. It would have to wait for another day. And time was slipping away.

She picked up her cell phone and speed-dialed his number.

"Guillermo?"

"*Bella. Sei il sole della mia vita.*"

She sighed. Romantic nonsense, but it made her insides swim dangerously. Since last weekend, everything had changed between them, and yet she was just as concerned. She tried her best to keep that part of their relationship separate from their work. It was hard. "*Si.* Well let's see if you mean it. I have a big favor to ask. I hope you don't mind."

"*Per te farei di tutto!*"

Anything? Well, we'll see about that.

"I have to change our plans for tonight. My father has arrived unexpectedly from Athens."

"*Stronzo.*" He paused. "Is he there with you now?"

"*Si.* And rather than disrupt our plans, he wishes for you to join us for dinner."

"You told him what we are doing?" Guillermo's voice croaked.

"No, no. Nothing like that. It's just social. He wants to meet my friends, that's all."

"Aha. So... what? Should I bring others?"

"Maybe. No, I don't think so. Just the three of us. More intimate."

"What is it we are... you know?"

"Well, we'll have to figure that out, eh?" Clio looked at Father, smiling. "No need to be shy. Just be yourself."

"Heh? Oh, I see."

"Can you meet us at the Restaurant Bernini, in the Hotel Albani? Via Fiume 12, at 5 o'clock?"

"Do I have any choice?" He chuckled.

"No, I'm afraid not."

CHAPTER 24

Catching Clio's meaning, Guillermo thought that his best strategy might be to play the buffoon. He couldn't be sure what Clio had told her father, or why she would agree to include him in this dinner with her father, but this way he could perhaps avoid digging any deep holes that either he, or later she, would be unable to get out of.

But to be on the safe side, he hid behind a potted lemon tree in the corridor waiting for them to arrive. He leaned against the wall, straightened his tie again and chastised himself for being nervous. This wasn't like him at all. He had nothing to worry about. He could handle himself with anyone, even the formidable Dr. McBeal.

It was Clio he was worried about. He remembered how she'd shrunk during the Skype call with her father. Her color and spark had withered. His chest ached for her, and he wanted only to relieve the oppressive binds caging her passionate and creative spirit. Which was why he'd resorted to silliness the night he called. To lift her up, and to remind her that there was a big wide world outside of the one so strictly inscribed by her rigid family.

That was the main argument for playing a similar role tonight.

However, he worried it would not work with Dr. McBeal sitting across from them in the flesh. Clio would feel too heavy to elevate. And then there was his own relationship with the man. He might not know it, but if Guillermo's wishes came true, they would have to see more of each other in the future. What sort of first impression did Guillermo want to make?

He gritted his teeth, straightened, glanced to the door, peeked at a clock on the wall, and scanned the room once more to make sure he hadn't missed their entry. He sighed. Then suddenly jerked back, his pulse thudding, peering at the entry. It was them.

Guillermo watched Clio's father stride in, speak with the maitre d', puffed up like a king. Clio, in his shadow, looked like a frightened rabbit. Her eyes darted back and forth, and her posture was hunched, as though being smaller could somehow lessen the pain of this encounter.

What should I do? How should I play this? What would help Clio the most?

Then, just as the maitre d' was about to lead them into the dining room, Clio excused herself and turned toward him. He caught her eye, jerked his chin, and turned down the hall toward the toilets, knowing she would follow. A second later, he was able to pull her into his arms.

"Memmo! Why are you hiding here?"

"Waiting for you, Bella." He pressed his lips to hers, reveling in her softness, and the way she swayed and melted at his touch, despite her distress. "Mmmm." He released her, but kept one arm loosely draped around her. "Well? What shall we do?"

She looked up at him, chagrinned. "I have to pee. I was really hoping you'd feel inspired. I don't know." She was pale, her brow creased.

"Calm down. It will be alright. The main thing is to get our story straight. How do we know each other? Are we dating–?"

"No."

He tilted his head by way of query, unable to hold back a smile.

"Not that there's anything wrong with you, aside from being Italian." She smiled to soften the blow. "It's just that he *really* won't approve of me wasting time on anything social, let alone dating, when I'm so pressed for time to meet my deadline. Isn't there something else we could–?"

"Tell him we're engaged." *Gesu*! Where did that come from?

"God, no. Be serious."

He withdrew his embrace and leaned back, crossing his arms. It was unexpected, but it wasn't that far-fetched. Was it?

"Memmo. Seriously." Clio swatted at him. "It has to be something that seems… like… defensible."

"Why cannot we have met the way we did? He knows about your accident."

"We need a reason to continue seeing each other."

There were so many reasons, not least of which was his decided penchant for kissing her, and touching her, and the slight dizziness he felt in her company. Images of their lovemaking crowded his mind, making it difficult for him to think of anything else. Ah, Clio. Unbelievable that she had turned the tables on him. She was magnificent, beautiful, passionate. "*Senza di te la vita è un inferno.*"

She rolled her eyes, and he grinned. "*My* life will be hell if I don't join Father, *pronto*." She never believed his endearments were sincerely felt. If she only knew.

Guillermo blinked rapidly while he considered. He cast his gaze up at the ceiling. Aha! "I've got it. I will be me, of course–"

"Very helpful."

"Just wait. We met at a rural church, *si*? I am restoring it, consulting with the diocese, and you were there for your research. While we were both taking pictures and sketching, we talked a little, discovered common interests, and became acquaintances."

Clio pursed her lips, considering. "That's not bad."

"Am I brilliant?"

"Yes, you are." She rose up on her toes to kiss him quickly.

"Okay. That will do." They agreed on a church and a date, in fact the same one she had visited the day they met.

"We get together from time to time for a drink or a meal to talk about Renaissance architecture, that's all. You can be as clever as you like. Impress us both." One of her delicate rusty brows rose up, challenging him.

They shared a warm smile. He'd do just that.

A few hours later, Clio and Guillermo returned to her apartment, after Guillermo had gallantly offered to see her home, assuring the protective father that she would be safe. *But not, he reflected, from me.*

The moment the door closed, he pulled her into his arms. "I have been dying for your kisses all evening. I thought he would never get tired of talking."

"It's because you played your part too well. If you were not so erudite about history and architecture, I'm sure Father would have dismissed you earlier. But you kept him engaged." She hesitated, blinking. "He liked you."

"That is what you call liking? He grilled me like a candidate on Apprentice." Guillermo thought he'd successfully hidden how intimidated he'd been by the imposing man. His skin had shrunk under the shrewd, icy blue gaze, framed by copious sharp lines carved into his flaccid, habitually frowning face. The man even had the faded orange hair of that American fellow, though Clio's father was a bearded, and bushy-browed Scot.

She chuckled. "He treats everyone like they're defending their thesis. It's just the way he is. But you impressed him. I can tell."

"Hmph. I felt like he was testing me." Guillermo stood a little taller, raising his chin, winking at her. "So now I deserve *scopare* his daughter, *si*?" He ground his groin into her. It killed him not to touch her all evening, and to hold back his expressions of admiration and desire that he was now, finally permitted. "Do you think he suspects about us?"

Clio made a face. "Oh, no. That would never occur to him."

He lifted his brows in doubt. His hands slipped down to cup her delicious bottom, and pulled her hips into his. "*Grrr.*"

"Slow down, cowboy. We've got work to do."

He grumbled in protest, nuzzling her neck, planting kisses behind her ear, nibbling and murmuring of his desire. "No work. Play." He let his palm graze her breast, stroking it until he felt her nipple harden in his hand, and felt her shiver and swoon a little, and he squeezed her *chiappa,* pressing into her heat, feeling himself stir to life.

"*Memmo.*" She pulled away, her palms soft on his chest, and he bent to press a kiss to her forehead. "We have to write that letter to the Cultural Ministry, so you can sign it tonight. And there is something else I wish to discuss with you."

He drew back, pensive. She sounded so serious. "Have I done something to upset you? You're not regretting–"

"Not at all." She took the opportunity to slip out of his embrace and saunter to the living room, sitting down in front of her piles of paper and files. He let his gaze rest on her soft curves and long legs, smiling. Her perfect *sedere,* which he never tired of admiring, clothed or not. *I would like to get it* nuda, *at the moment.* "I spoke with Dr. Bensen this afternoon," she said.

"*Si?*"

She patted the sofa beside her. "Sit down."

He sidled over, not sure he wanted to know why she was being so stern. He veered toward the kitchen. "Do you want some wine?"

"No, no, *grazie.* I've had enough." She shuffled papers, searching.

He poured himself a glass of the red from the bottle sitting out on her counter. "Can I make you some tea?"

"*Memmo.*"

He grimaced. "Okay. I'm coming." He perched next to her. *What have I done to make her so somber?* Did he say something out of place at dinner with her father? Did he suspect their romantic involvement? When would he have had a chance to say anything to her? Or was Guillermo pushing too hard, too fast with their new-found intimacy. He could hold himself back. "What is it?"

Clio swallowed and averted her gaze. He watched her lick her lips, and licked his own, tasting wine. He leaned in, inhaling her fruit and floral scent, wanting more. Wanting the taste of her. "Dr. Bensen was balking at the appointment of an academic director without due diligence. This is a major investment for them, and they want to make sure they've considered all the suitable candidates before selecting someone."

He frowned, taking a sip of wine, and nodded. "Continue."

"Well that takes time. More than we have. And the government wants to know who will be in charge before they approve licensing or release funds. So it's a Catch-22."

"Hmm. I see." But she would have already solved the problem, this he knew from experience. "And...?"

Clio filled her lungs and turned to meet his eyes. She was so earnest, so grave, so lovely. He had to reign in his thoughts, which very quickly slipped into a slide show of her bare skin, her rosy lips ripe for his kisses, her fiery hair spread out across the pillow. His fingers itched to touch her. He reached out and grazed her bare arm with his fingertips, relishing the gooseflesh that rose up in response. A corresponding shiver danced across his neck, sending a spiral of heat down to his groin.

"Are you listening?"

They shared a small smile, and he saw a twinkle in her eyes, like the sparkle of sunlight on the sea. She already knew him too well. He dropped his chin and pressed his lips together to suppress a grin. "*Si, cara.*"

She shook her head, her eyes crinkling. "I made a proposal to Dr. Bensen that would solve the problem of timing, and, I believe, be a better solution in the long term... which is to split the directorship between academic programs and running of the foundation. This way the ads can go out for the academic director and..." She spiraled her hand. "Whatever, whenever. In the meantime we can move forward with establishing the foundation, accessing grants and saving the villa."

She'd lost him. He scowled slightly. Had he missed something?

"Memmo, it has to be you."

"*Scuzi?*" A tremor shook him.

"You know it."

"Do I?" His voice was wooden. Suddenly instead of sex, he felt a profound urge to go for a long, fast ride.

Clio's hands came up and framed his face. Her eyes pierced his, as though by trapping him there, she could prevent him from escaping. His breath wouldn't move, and he forced it out, in shallow puffs, trying to kick start a deep breath that would feed oxygen to his brain, to help him figure out what this meant, and what he should do. She couldn't be serious. She knew he loved his family estate, but he couldn't sacrifice himself for it. They'd talked about this!

An engine revved in the street below, followed by a muffled shout, and the tinkling of a glass bottle tumbling along the cobbles. He raised a hand to rub the back of his neck, to quell the twitching, crawling sensation that had invaded his body like a rash. He was flushed, and his neck was moist.

"Can you hear me?"

He realized she'd continued speaking, and he hadn't heard. "Uh..."

"I thought this all along, and I knew you would have difficulty with it, so I... I prevaricated. I suspected there would be issues over qualification of the academic director. But you must see, Memmo. The director of the foundation *must* be a member of your family. How else can we ensure the estate is managed according to the family's wishes, and at the same time incorporate the private holdings, the farms, and the supporting business interests?"

He shook his head, but when he attempted to meet her earnest gaze, his eyes wouldn't settle on them, and slid around her face and the wall behind her head, erratically, evasively. He leaned back, pulling at her hands. He needed to think. He didn't want to disappoint her, but this...his head shook from side to side, caged by the frame of her palms.

She continued to hold his cheeks gently but firmly. "I know what you're feeling, even if you don't. I know you, Memmo. You can do this." She pulled his face toward hers, and tipped her forehead to his, touching brow to brow. Her warm sweet breath caressed his face. He felt his heart squeeze and twist painfully. Ah, Clio. *Il mio cuore è solo tua.* My heart is yours. *Per te farei di tutto,* anything, anything, but not this. I can't do this.

He lifted his chin to bring their lips together, and she kissed him, deeply and passionately. His arms encircled her and pulled her softness into his embrace. Instantly, desire flared between them. His pulse kicked up. She swung one knee over him, and straddled his lap. He felt blood rush to his groin, and he grew hard. Clio, too, was aroused. Her arms wrapped his neck, her heated core pressing against him. Her breath came quickly, and she whimpered into his throat as their tongues tangled.

Guillermo grunted, slipped his arms under her, and stood up, lifting her, only one single thing in his mind driving away his conflicted thoughts. Need. He needed to claim her, so that no matter what happened, she would always be his. So that no matter what passed between them, no matter what difficulties the future brought, she would know how much he wanted her for his own. He strode urgently to her bedroom and set her down on the bed, lowering himself on top of her, their mouths still joined, beginning to strip away their clothing. "Clio, *Bella, cara. Il mio cuore è solo tua.*" He murmured endearments between kisses as he bared more of her smooth skin, caressing her lightly with his fingertips, and tasting her, running his hot tongue over the gooseflesh that rose in the wake of his quaking touch. She arched up to meet him. "*Ti voglio. Ti desidero.*"

When he entered her, he at last opened his eyes and met hers, the blue of the sky merging with the blue of the sea. *Look here, cara. Look inside me now, and tell me what you see. Ti voglio, ti voglio, ti voglio.* Don't take this away from me. *Per favor, Dio, don't take this woman away from me.*

Their lovemaking was fervent. Guillermo was driven to possess her, and without the words he could not find, and couldn't utter, show her how he felt about her. At the same time, to revel in her beauty and her passion, as though it were the last time.

Afterward, they lay entwined, her head resting on his damp chest, their breathing settling back to normal.

"I'm confused."

He raised his head an inch to look at her. "About what?"

"Does that mean yes?"

A long breath escaped him slowly, and he felt her tense. It couldn't be avoided any longer. "I have my career to consider, *Bella*. What am I supposed to do about that?"

She shrugged one shoulder against him. "I thought maybe you could do both. Probably the foundation would take a lot of time and energy in the beginning. Only you can figure that out. But in time…"

He hitched himself up on an elbow and sought her eyes. "Clio. My beautiful dreamer. You know saving the villa and this project are as important to me as life itself. I wouldn't be doing what I am doing if it were not. But am I to give up everything? The entire life I have built for myself? My reputation? My income? The design work I love?"

She shrank away from him. "Who else but you?"

He reached out his hand, palm up. "There will be someone who cares. We will find someone to do it."

Clio pushed up and rose above him, her elbows braced on his chest, and met his eyes. "Who else? Some stranger?"

"*Bella*." He reached for her arms, pulling gently, hoping to return to the blissful intimacy of a moment ago. "You could do it better than I."

Clio leapt from the bed, pulling the sheet off to wrap around herself, backing away, glaring at him. "There is no one better qualified than you. No one who will care more than you do."

He found himself sprawled on the bed alone, naked, flaccid, and suddenly felt exposed and awkward, his stomach sinking. *Stronzo.*

"Think about this, Memmo. This foundation will exist in lieu of the traditional family estate that was managed by your brother, your Papa, your Nonno." She measured her points with hard rhythmic strokes of her hand through the air. "The family will hold title, but the bulk of the assets will be held in the foundation. So the future security of the estate will depend entirely upon a well-run foundation. All the maintenance decisions, restoration and protection of the building, many of its valuable artifacts, all the estate businesses, including financial decisions about the institute, will be in the hands of this person. Who would you trust with it?"

He squeezed his eyes shut, trying to tamp down his frustration. He'd been working three jobs. He was already exhausted and felt as old as dust. After all he'd done for her, she wanted still more. "You don't understand, Clio."

She dipped her chin, her eyes burning into his, narrowed with frustration. Her nostrils flared. Didn't she? "Really?"

He spun his legs off the edge of the bed and sat up, scowling at the carpet and the paisley patterned quilt that had slid to the floor during their spirited lovemaking, stroking and pulling at his brows. He could feel the anger radiating off of her, hear her labored breathing. He refused to be forced into doing this. Frame it differently though she might, this was exactly the job he had always avoided. Basically the same set of responsibilities that had destroyed all the men of his family for generations. It went against everything he believed in, everything that he was. He stood and approached her, with trepidation, and tipped her chin up with his fingertips. "*Per favore, Bella*, try to understand my position. Don't push me on this."

She stiffened and pulled away from his touch. "It's not just about you and your preferences. The villa *needs* you. Your family needs you."

He dropped his hands to his sides, his fists gripping, cracking. Out of respect for her, and because he couldn't afford not to, he said, "I will think it over. I don't know what else to say right now. That will have to do, Clio."

She pressed her lips together, and her eyes welled. "You can't run away this time." Her chin wobbled.

Don't you dare weep. Damned women! She wouldn't manipulate him into doing what he couldn't do. He searched the room for his discarded clothing and began to dress, his movements jerky. *Where are my socks?* "I can't say yes. Not like this. So don't try to–"

"You are running away again."

Their eyes met, both equally cold and hard. "I am not running. I'm making a choice. I'm doing what is right for me."

"You said you would think it over. But you've already made up your mind, haven't you?"

He ground his teeth as he buttoned his shirt. He was sweating, and the shirt stuck to his flushed skin already. *Where is my fucking sock?* He flipped the fallen quilt up, tossing it down again. *Fuck it!* Pacing to the living room, he threw his laptop into its case, leaving the papers strewn about for Clio to sort.

"All our work will be for nothing!"

He shot a hard look at her. Tears were running down her cheeks. She'd followed him, but stood, draped in the sheet, her shoulders bare, the fabric twisted around her legs and pooled out on the floor like a train, looking for all the world like a statue of Grecian goddess. Or her namesake muse. His throat felt sore and tight. His chest ached.

Stronzo. He strode to the door and jammed his feet into his shoes, the leather binding on his bare heel. His limbs were heavy and clumsy. He fought to grind his foot into his loafer. It seemed to take a ridiculously long time, yet she stood, and did not speak until he turned to leave.

"Memmo!"

The door slammed behind him as he thumped down the stairs and into the street.

CHAPTER 25

The letter to the ministry was written and printed, lacking only a signature. It burned a hole in the file that sat on Clio's desk while her calls to Memmo remained unanswered. Her stomach roiled with nausea while she waited, hoped, prayed that he would call her back. Fruitlessly.

Clio had sacrificed and risked too much to quit now. She couldn't give up on the villa. Time was running out. She had no other options. What did he expect her to do?

She had considered contacting Jacopo. He was the eldest. He was currently in charge of the family estate. It seemed logical. But Clio had met him only the once, and very briefly. And if Guillermo was hiding this from anyone, Clio knew it was Jacopo. She'd picked up the phone more than once, but overcome with heart palpitations and fluttering in her stomach, she'd nearly fainted with fear.

So she had called Pia and asked her to meet in the city. She and Pia had connected that first weekend at Villa Cittadini, and she'd been such a warm and generous hostess. It offset some of her nerves.

Pia was happy to do it, in fact had planned to be here today anyway, to meet with a friend, she said. Clio hurried to meet her at a *caffe* on via Pellicceria, a street of fashionable shops between the Ponte Vecchio and the Cathedral, not sure why she would want them to suffer the crowds of tourists or the inflated prices in that part of the city. She would rather have had a quiet place to share what she needed to say.

Pia waited at a table at the rear of the caffe. She greeted Clio warmly, embracing her and kissing her cheeks.

"I'm so happy to see you, Clio. Bibi told me that she'd seen you at the villa, but I haven't heard anything of you since then." She bent to rearrange several large bags and baskets at her feet, and Clio thought she caught the edge of a hidden grin. The liar.

A waiter took their order for *caffe*, and she used the distraction to surreptitiously study Pia's face. Clio felt that she was sincere in wishing she'd had the opportunity to get together again before now, but she would swear there was more to it, and wondered what Bianca had said about her humiliating night of indiscretion. Too much, probably. Not that Bianca knew the whole story. She felt her face heat with shame, remembering.

"Have you seen Guillermo?" Pia asked, straightening. It seemed disingenuous. Surely she knew something. Probably she was in touch with Marcella.

"Yes, quite a bit actually."

"Oh? Really?"

Clio smothered an uncomfortable smile, glancing at her hands. There was no reason for Guillermo's family to know about their affair, if they didn't already, despite the need to confide in them about the project. This seemed like as good an opening as she was likely to get.

Clio drew a deep breath and began her story of the past month's activities, interrupted only by Pia's gasps and exclamations of, "You can't be serious!" and "I can't believe Guillermo would do this and not tell me!"

"Well, it began in such a frenzy in the wake of the real estate deal. Everyone was so upset. And I know Guillermo wanted to make sure it was real before getting anyone's hopes up."

"And he's been working on all these different design options. Without telling Andreas, or Jacopo?"

"Yes, I believe so, although Andreas may have suspicions, since we solicited his help to identify alternate properties. I've been handing most of the paperwork- correspondence, application forms, proposals, phone calls. And he's been dealing with Richie and the bank. We meet regularly to discuss and plan, sign documents, and whatnot." Images of their passionate lovemaking, whatnot indeed, flashed in Clio's mind's eye, sending a shiver down her neck and arms, and making her blink and swallow. She refused to dwell on their last painful parting.

Pia sat back, silent, studying Clio's face. "What has happened? Why are you telling me now? And why you, and not Memmo?"

Clio lifted her coffee to take a large gulp. She dragged her tongue around her lips, stalling, trying to find the right words. "We, uh...we had a difference of opinion."

Pia frowned, her gaze shrewd. "And?"

Clio drew a deep breath. "I need a signature. A member of the family. It's very important, and must be dealt with immediately. And Guillermo won't return my calls. I haven't seen him for three days."

Pia's eyes narrowed further. "I gather three days is a long time for you to not see him?"

Clio nodded slowly. "Rather."

"I see. And you want me to call Guillermo? Or-"

Clio shook his head. "No, no. He won't talk to me. I need you to sign the letter on behalf of the family, to keep the gears turning."

"Can't you resolve-?"

"He refuses to consider my proposal that he be director of the foundation."

"Oh?"

"You wouldn't consider acting as director, would you?"

Pia's eyes widened. "I'm flattered. I think. But that is absurd. Even if I were willing, my talents, er, don't lie in that area. In fact I've got my hands rather full of my own new venture."

Clio's heart sank. Though of course she didn't think Pia would be receptive to the idea. "Well, we'll find someone. Maybe even Jacopo. But I haven't had the courage to contact him. I hardly know him. And I'm pretty sure Guillermo dreads the blow up that will inevitably happen when he finds out we've done all of this behind his back."

Pia nodded. "Of course I'll sign the letter. Though you realize this is only a stop gap measure. You and Guillermo will eventually have to resolve your differences, and you'll have to bring Jacopo into it soon."

Clio's shoulders drooped, and she hung her head. "It may be all for nothing, in any case," she mumbled.

"Well don't you give up yet, Clio. I'm excited that this is happening, even if the odds are slim. I have been quite depressed about losing the villa, and feeling very sad that there seemed to be nothing we could do about it. I'll sign the letter of course. But I really ought to understand what is involved. Can you fill me in? Or give me something to read when I get home?"

"*Si.* Sure."

"And... even though I'm quite overwhelmed myself right now, I want to help. Tell me what I can do to help."

Clio dropped her head into her hands, raking her fingers through her bound curls. Her rings became tangled, and she dislodged strands as she tugged her hands free. "Ugh. Bloody mop." She stared at her empty hands, laughing mirthlessly, sounding a little crazy to her own ears. "There are so many pieces to it." She shook her head, overwhelmed.

"Are you still fretting about this?" Pia reached out and smoothed her frizzed hair, gently tugging on an escaped curl, and shook her head. "I'm going to take you to my hairdresser."

"Why?"

Pia smiled. "Angelo will know what to do. A little strategic layering, some deep conditioner and the right styling products and you'll be transformed."

Clio snorted and shook her head. "Yeah."

"Break it down for me."

At Clio's blank look, she clarified. "Tell me about the villa. What have you and Memmo been doing?"

Clio tried to clear her thoughts. She rattled off the components to the plan, the many faceted items on her to-do list. "I know Memmo's been talking with the banks, and I'm no expert at business, but I know our outline of finances is sketchy in many areas. He is able to quantify and estimate all the building costs, of course. And I have a reasonable notion of the costs of running academic programs, hosting conferences, that kind of thing. But we have gaps. Our business plan includes supplemental activities that would support the institute, but have the potential to earn income for the estate. Hospitality services, holiday rentals, special events, accommodations and food, that sort of thing. But between us, Memmo and I have no experience and few particulars to fill in the blanks."

Pia straightened. "Food? Houseguests? Parties?" She laughed. "Now that's something I do know about."

Clio frowned. "You do?"

Pia shook her head in disbelief. "Of course. That's my specialty. In fact, I have a secret of my own."

"What?" Clio's mind raced, trying to make sense in what Pia was saying.

Pia reached forward and took Clio's hands between her own. "I would hesitate to share this with you, Clio, if you weren't so obviously deeply involved in our family affairs already."

Clio nodded, leaning in.

"As you already know, Paulo and I have invested our fortunes in the restoration of the vineyards and the Cittadini label. What no one knows is how hard it is. Paulo is making great strides with the wine-making, but the lead time is so long. Longer than we expected. And despite Paulo's connections, it's taking too long to develop markets for our product. I'm confident we'll be alright in the long term." She hesitated. "If we survive that long." She met Clio's eyes. "So you see, I'm getting squeezed from both sides."

Clio's mouth opened, but she couldn't think of an appropriate response. Poor Pia. And now Clio had dumped another beehive of trouble into her lap. It was bad enough that she thought she was losing her family home. Now this. "I'm so sorry."

Pia's face was alight. "Don't be sorry. Don't you see? This is exactly what I need. I have a plan."

She most definitely didn't see.

"Not only can I help you develop that part of the business plan, but I can make it my business."

Clio stared.

"I can see you don't understand." Pia began to explain how her solution to the Cittadini family finances was to start a business of her own– specialty foodstuffs. She retrieved an assortment of jars and bottles and boxes from her bags to show Clio. Clio examined them as Pia spoke– sauces, antipasto, jams, biscuits, herbed oils and flavored vinegars, all beautifully packaged, with a charming trendy label decorating each one. *Alimentari Fattoria/Cucina Cittadini.*

"Bibi designed the logo and labels for me. Aren't they lovely?"

Clio was amazed. "This is what you've been doing?"

"*Si.* I've been very busy. That is why I am here. I brought samples to show my friend, who owns this caffe, and several others in town. I've been making the rounds, not just here in Florence, but Sienna, San Gimignano, Arezzo, Pisa, trying to get orders. It turns out I have a lot of friends." She laughed.

"But you're already so busy, Pia. What more can you take on?"

"That's just it." Pia grabbed Clio's arm. "I'll roll the whole thing together. I'll calculate the numbers you need while I'm expanding my own business plan. The foods I make will be served at your

Instituto, provided at wholesale prices of course. And I'll also manage the hospitality side of things, and with Bibi's help, market the conference, vacation and wedding rentals and such, too. I'll earn a salary, which will help Paulo and I with our bills, and both estates will profit."

Clio's body tingled, she felt breathless and dizzy, almost euphoric, as though an angel of God had visited her himself, and delivered the most astonishing news, reassuring her that all would be well.

"This was meant to be."

"Show me this letter you need signed," Pia said. "Let's get started!"

~

"This just arrived by courier," Ignacio said, pushing into Guillermo's office with a letter in one hand, a *caffe* in the other."

"Eh?" Guillermo looked up, raking his hands through his hair.

"You are such a mess, *Capo*. Look at you. Have you been sleeping at all? How can you keep track of what you are doing?" Guillermo accepted the *caffe* and gratefully took a huge swallow, the hot liquid searing and temporarily soothing his empty stomach. *When did I eat last?*

He looked around him at the piles of sketches and prints. He grunted. "Isn't that what I pay you for, Ig?"

"If I knew what the hell you were doing, maybe." Ig handed the letter to Guillermo and started sifting through the papers, pulling his glasses from his curly dark hair and planting them on his long nose. "I can't tell one project from the other."

"Hmph. Neither can I some days. In fact there is so much overlap I may have mixed them up." He waved a hand over the mess, his gaze bouncing over his many drawings. "I am drawing one thing, and get an idea for another scheme, and sketch over it, and then realize it's the wrong permutation, the wrong..." He set down the coffee and ripped open the envelope with his letter opener. "Who's this from?" He scanned it. "Oh, *Stronzo*. No."

"What is it?"

Guillermo scraped a hand over his chin, grimacing. "Um. More problems. The Heritage Ministry." He wished he could just ask Jacopo for help with the government approvals, but that was off limits. This had to be above board. Shuffling through the papers on his desk, in search of the banking files, a profound longing to have Clio here with him washed over him like a tidal wave, sucking him under, making him feel feeble. She'd know where he put it. He rolled his shoulders, twisting his neck, trying to dislodge a knot of tension that had taken up permanent residence.

He stood up. "Where the hell is it?"

"Guillermo? Can I help?"

"Ah... A blue folder..."

Ignacio began to sort and stack the papers, helping him search. Together, they bent over the table, rummaging. His flailing hand almost knocked over the coffee. Ignacio reach out and caught it just as it wobbled. "*Attento!*"

Stronzo. That's all he needed was coffee all over his drawings and files.

His hands trembled, and he curled them into fists. Keeping track of the letters that came his way without her to vet them was adding stress to his already overwhelmed life.

He turned and paced away from the table, an edgy frisson pulling at his nerves like a cord that was unravelling, soon to snap. He turned back, scowling and faced the chaos of papers and facts again. How had Clio kept everything, including him, so organized, purposeful and calm? How did she make it seem so easy? They were actually having fun. It had been a grand adventure. Now he felt as though his life were fraying at the edges. If he couldn't even do this, how did she imagine he could head a foundation?

This was exactly why he didn't want this fucking responsibility in the first place. This was precisely what he'd built his streamlined, pleasurable life to avoid. Couldn't she see that? Her demands were killing him. They would kill him, as surely as they killed his father.

Calm down. It was ridiculous trying to carry on without communicating with her. But he'd have to deal with this alone. It wasn't her problem. He knew that. It was his own fault. He was so angry and frustrated and confused, he'd been avoiding her, fearing he'd say something regrettable. Or perhaps fearing that she wouldn't want him anymore. It made him feel sick with stress, and something more, a heaviness that felt more like grieving. *Dio,* he missed her. His heart ached with longing for her, so much it felt like physical pain, as though in the past month, while they'd spent time together almost daily, and made love often, she had become a part of him. A part that was now throbbing, like a missing limb.

"Is this it?"

Guillermo snapped out of his reverie and looked up at Ignacio. He held the blue folder out. "Eh. *Grazie.* This is a disaster. I have to go to the bank and talk to *Senior Belloggi.*" He rolled down his sleeves and buttoned them, straightened his tie, grabbed his jacket and yanked it on. "Maybe while I'm gone you can sort this stuff out. It would make it easier on me if there was some order. Just leave a pile of stuff you can't figure out. You know what I'm doing."

"*Bene.* I'll try."

Guillermo quickly dialed Clio's number as he left the office. He'd been childish. He needed to know what she knew, and what had happened over the past week. And she needed to know that their application for heritage designation was threatened. They'd thought it was in the bag. But now the Ministry insisted their non-profit status be in place first, which was dependent upon the financials, which were not yet complete.

She didn't answer her office phone or her cellular. *Diavolo!*

Although he was pretty sure she didn't have the answers either, he wished they could talk it over. He'd have to do some quick thinking. Now they were caught between the bank and the government, each needing reassurance of the viability of their business plan. The government needed to know they could cover their operating expenses. The bank required confirmation of their non-profit status before approving a business loan. And he knew that all the tax advantages they were counting on required heritage designation. The bureaucracy was incredible, each entity passing responsibility on to another, round and round. Without Clio to stay on top of it all, and make sense of it, he wasn't sure what to do first.

He called the bank on his way there. They wanted to see more detailed financial figures, proof of solvency. He'd have to improvise. Or beg.

An hour later, he was on his way back to the office, his frustration and worry tripled. The damned loans officer, *Belloggi*, was immovable. If they couldn't flesh out the business plan with several different options, and demonstrate sufficient income to balance the expenses, the bank wouldn't confirm the final loans. The operating budget must align with the foundation trust's earnings and expenses, on the conservative side. Everything would fall apart without this approval. His head hurt.

Ah, Clio, where are you when I need you most?

He hunched his shoulders as he strode along the street, hands shoved in his pockets, mumbling to himself, though he knew he looked like a madman. He was sweating. He'd missed breakfast and lunch, but had no appetite.

What could he do about Clio? He knew what she wanted, but he was still resistant.

This latest problem could be fixed by sourcing and proving additional sources of revenue, which was always part of the plan, though a vague one. They were so close to making this work. He wanted to be rid of Richie and all that duplicity. He was tired of juggling so many balls. And he'd be willing to give up a lot. He was committed to giving up everything for the villa- except his freedom. That he couldn't do. And yet... without Clio, everything was coming apart in his mind. He couldn't do any of it alone.

What was he saying? He didn't know himself anymore. Was Clio so important to him that he could no longer function without her in his life? His pulse hammered at the question. A sudden awareness of emptiness, in his stomach, in his chest, fluttered through him. His body knew the answer.

He loved her. Really loved her. This woman was the one he'd been searching for, waiting for, though he didn't know it. But he couldn't surrender his soul, even for love. Papa was wildly, foolishly in love with Mama, but it didn't spare him.

Perhaps he could do it without Clio, but only with his family's full knowledge, approval and support. If he dared to confide in them. He felt terribly alone.

Before he made it back to his office, his phone dinged and vibrated in his pocket, and he stopped on a street corner and pulled it out, along with a handkerchief to mop his damp brow. *Diavolo,* it was hot today.

Huh. Speak of the devil. It was a text from Bibi.

Where r u? Need to talk. Pronto. Urgent. BB

He didn't have time for Bibi's histrionics. What the hell did she want now?

CHAPTER 26

Since Bibi wanted to meet him for lunch, and he knew he needed to eat before he fell down, he agreed to meet her at the Gucci Cafe in the Piazza della Signoria, across from the Fontana del Nettuno and Palazzo Vecchio, despite the crowds that perpetually loitered there. It was nearby, and on his way. She sounded distraught, and wanted to talk about the sale of the villa, she said. He prayed she wasn't going to have a *crollo nervoso* now. It was far too late for that, and he wasn't about to tell Bibi, of all his siblings, what he'd been doing behind the scenes. She was difficult to manage without adding chili to the sauce.

"Wow. You look like shit," she said when he approached. "So what the hell is going on? Why are you not talking to Clio?" she demanded, once they'd chosen a table under an umbrella on the edge of the open piazza.

"What?" Guillermo exclaimed, his hands on the back of her chair. He hadn't even sat down yet. What was she talking about? He was fairly certain nobody knew how involved he and Clio had become. "Why would you ask that?"

She stared at him, deadpanned.

Avoiding her gaze, he turned to survey the piazza. The sun was blistering today, and the volume of tourists was significant. It was past the lunch hour, and most of the foreigners had eaten. While some lingered over cold beverages at the cafe tables, many instead strolled listlessly by with their cameras and shopping bags, dawdled in the shade, clustered around the logia and squinting at the replica of David.

"I know you've been working together for weeks."

The rhythm of murmured foreign tongues carried to them, unintelligible, with the odd shout carrying on the air, filling the silence. He sat, pulling his tie loose, and mopping his brow and neck with his handkerchief. Working together? What had she heard?

"I don't know what you mean, Bibi." He kept his voice flat and soothing. As soon as he was able to calm her down, he had to head back to the office and get to work on the financials. Speaking of Clio, he would have to call her. Hopefully she would accept his call.

Bibi tutted. "Pia called me. I want to know why you haven't talked to me about any of this."

"There's nothing for you to know. I have to satisfy Mad Richie with a design for the renovations to the villa and then that's it. The deal closes, we pack up and we move on. What are you doing to move on, Bibi?" He thrummed his fingers on the table top.

"Don't jerk me around, Memmo."

He sighed and shook his head.

Her phone binged and she held a thin aggressive palm in his face while she read and responded to a text, her gold bangles jingling.

Gesu. "There's nothing for you to do. And no point dwelling on it. Why don't you look for a job?" There's an idea. "If you're done with school for now. Move on. Get a life."

She set her phone down and rolled her eyes. "You're such an asshole. You have no idea what I do."

He pursed his lips and waited. A waiter came to take their order. Bibi ordered a salad Caprese. He thought a moment, his hand on his queasy stomach. "Just bread, *per favor. Olio.* And some broth."

The waiter looked at him like he was insane. "Eh. On such a hot day you want *Broda?*"

"*Si. Broda.* Oh, and a Campari with ice." He waived him away. Nothing else would stay down.

"You really do look ill." She shook her head, narrowing her eyes at him. "I know something's going on, Memmo. I talked to Pia. And I want to be involved. You don't know what I can do."

He couldn't deal with her whining right now. And fortunately whatever she was talking about, it was fiction, since Pia knew nothing either. He sighed. Humour her. "What can you do, baby sister? Tell me."

"What do you need?"

He laughed. "A miracle."

"Memmo. Tell me exactly what you need."

"I need to get back to my office. I have a million things to deal with. I'm in the middle of a crisis and what I don't need is to waste time listening to your whining."

She sat back slowly, placing her hand against her chin. "Am I whining?"

He sat back, too, and looked at her. Her eyes, bright blue like his own, bore into his, clear and keen. She wasn't, actually. She was in a tetchy mood. That much was normal. But she seemed calmer and more focused than he'd seen her since Mama died. Suddenly a knot of fear formed in his already feeble gut. "Are you sick? Is Pia sick?"

Her phone pinged again, and again she paused their conversation to read and respond to a text.

He ground his teeth, glaring at her while she typed. "You know, that's a perfect example. You want to be included. You want to be treated like an adult, and then you behave like a sullen teenager. Can't you just be here and now? Do you always have to be chatting with your friends? How can you expect anyone to take you seriously?"

"You always assume the worst of me, Memmo. I had another appointment. I'm just dealing with it. Okay?"

He pulled back at her abrupt retort. "*Si. Scusi.*"

"Listen to me." Bibi set her phone down and leaned in. "I know what you and Clio have been doing."

He almost missed it, his mind already back at the office, wringing out the possibilities for the business plan. Clio had outlined a number of support functions, many tied to the resident students and summer conference activities. But there was more. And he knew they hadn't had time to get cost estimates. He wondered who he could call... And Bibi's words hit him like a fist in the gut. She knew about their affair? "What?"

"Pia told me about the plan. And now you've got her involved managing and organizing food services and hospitality and event planning. Why can't I do my part, Memmo? We all must contribute to saving the villa."

"P-Pia's doing–" He coughed, clearing his throat. This wasn't what he expected to hear. "She's doing what? What did she tell you? When did you talk to her?"

Bianca smiled mysteriously. "You'll find out soon enough." He scowled at her, his mouth dropping open. What the hell was going on? She continued. "That's the amazing thing. Pia has been working on her new business for the past month, making all sorts of condiments and preserves, taking them around." Bibi waved a hand around the piazza, indicative of nothing that Guillermo could see. "I put together her package. Well first she just asked me to design a new logo for her company–"

"Her company?"

She continued as though he hadn't interrupted. "–then one thing led to another, and I was designing packaging for her products, and the website, ads. That sort of thing. It's a great first gig for me. Who would have thought that–""

"What company? What do you know about all that?"

She shook her head. "Do you know what I studied?"

"Um. Digital... er..." He scratched his neck. "Something to do with computers. Online stuff. I thought maybe *html* or some web stuff. But I kind of thought you'd dropped out."

"Yeah. Some web stuff. *Ma chi diavolo significa?*" She rolled her eyes again. "Memmo, I have a dual certificate in web design and graphic design. I've been in school full time for two years. What do you think I've been doing?" She pushed her face close to his with a frustrated glare, her hands open, palms up, shaking. "You are so self-absorbed. I can't believe it!"

Guillermo sat back, frowning, and scraped a hand over his beard. This wasn't making any sense. And he didn't have time to deal with it now. But how had he missed the fact that Bibi actually had graduated? And had these skills? It seemed to him she was always partying with her friends, or whining about being bored or needing money. How did this happen?

He sighed. "*Bene.* Slow down and explain. I'm sorry I'm so out of touch. I've been very preoccupied, as you know, and I haven't really got time for this right now. Uh, why does Pia need all this? I don't understand. And how did she get involved in the villa business?" As if he couldn't figure out who was responsible for that. But how? His mind reeled with questions.

Bibi picked up her fork and dug into her salad, shoving a bocconcini slice topped with a basil leaf into her mouth and chewing while she talked. The sharp scent of basil met his nostrils, along with the tang of balsamic vinegar. "Well, I think Pia should tell you that herself. You're not the only one with secrets, you know."

"Bianca. Tell me."

Bibi glanced at her phone. "She'll be here any minute. Hold onto your panties."

He took a deep breath and released it, attempting to stay calm. Was this a trick? Had they planned this meeting together? "Okay, so tell me about yourself. What can you do besides logos and packages? What's this about a web site?"

Bianca chewed on and on, shrugging. When she'd swallowed, she said, "Whatever is needed. I design websites, advertising campaigns, corporate identities, any kind of graphic design." She shrugged again. "Why don't you tell me what you need and I'll tell you how I can help?"

"Huh." Guillermo could hardly gather his thoughts. He was so preoccupied with the question of Bibi's certificates, Pia's business and what Clio had done. And the fact that everyone seemed to know his plans, and were working together. "What I need right now are numbers. The short version is we're caught in a catch-22 between the government and the bank. The Heritage Ministry has decided there are too many old properties that have been designated only to be run into the ground, because the restrictions imposed limit the interest of new private owners." He ripped a hunk of bread and dipped it into his broth, sucking out the juices. It was already tepid, but it soothed the gnawing pain in his stomach. "So their new rules require that any person or organization proposing to preserve a property prove they have the financial viability."

Bianca nodded, her gaze on him intent and serious, but her eyes darted past his shoulder more than once, scanning the piazza, making him feel on-edge. He rolled his shoulders to loosen the tension, and the tickle of nerves that ran up and down his spine like melting ice.

"We require heritage designation before we can be granted non-profit status. And we need the non-profit status to qualify for the tax breaks to make our numbers work. And until the numbers work, the bank won't give us final approval on our development and business loans." He pursed his lips, thinking. "That pretty much sums it up. It's an endless loop, unless we add something."

"I can't do too much about any of that, but I think you'll be pleased with what Pia has to say."

"You insist on torturing me."

"It won't be long now." She placed a hand on his sleeve. "But once you hear what Pia's going to do, you'll see how I can help. Both this Instituto and the Foundation will need an image, right? They'll need a presence, customers, and ongoing publicity and fundraising for the trust. I can do that. And all the hospitality functions, like accommodations, will need websites and programs for bookings and such." She windmilled a hand.

Guillermo nodded. These were things that he hadn't even begun to think about. But Bibi was right. Getting the approvals and the funding to go forward were only the beginning. It was a huge responsibility, and an ongoing commitment. The bread and broth in his stomach curdled, cramping. Once there was an institute and foundation, all of this theory would have to be put into practice. Someone had to run it. Someone who knew what the hell they were doing. Someone other than him.

He was impressed. "You're actually making sense, Bibs. You're thinking about this like a business, and your ideas will help that business actually function and be successful. But do you really want to be involved in the long term?"

Bibi gaped at him. "Are you kidding me? Of course I do. This is our home. Why wouldn't I?" She made a quizzical face. "I thought you did, too. Don't you?"

Guillermo swallowed. His shirt suddenly felt impossibly tight in the stifling heat. He took another long draught of his Campari. Maybe he should broach the subject of the foundation directorship with his sisters, asking them if they thought Jacopo would accept the role. Perhaps with their help–

"Memmo? I thought–"

"*Buon giorno, mio cari!*" Pia's voice cut into their exchange, and in an instant she was there, all flowing skirts, flying scarves, her arms draped with multiple bags like a *vagabondo*.

Guillermo shot out of his chair, feeling a disconcerting relief at the interruption. "*Mio Dio*, Pia. You startled me." He placed his hands on her shoulders and they exchanged kisses.

Pia took some time settling her bags on the ground at her side in a whirlwind of movement and chatter, and in a moment the waiter was there, and she was ordering a drink. At last she turned to him, taking his hand between hers, squeezing. A broad smile stretched her face. His stomach leapt and dipped and surged again like an ocean wave, and he offered a watery smile in return, waiting.

"Don't look so frightened, *fratello*." Pia laughed. "This is exciting!"

"What is this about a business, Pia?"

He perched on the edge of his chair, sipping on his Campari while she filled him in. Clio had approached her for the signature he had failed to provide, and mentally he kicked himself. Of course that's why she'd been calling. He was so busy feeling sorry for himself he'd compromised their timeline by neglecting his duties. *Oh, Clio. What have we unleashed here?*

Pia backtracked to explain how she and Paulo were struggling to make ends meet, and how she'd decided to take an active role, and realize a personal dream at the same time. He'd had no idea she wanted to make condiments for sale. Or at least, when she'd aired her wistful desires, he, along with everyone else, hadn't taken her seriously. He scowled. It seems he'd underestimated both of his sisters. And here they were, prepared to work, and offering to help save the villa. A job that he thought only he could do, and even then, reluctantly. Now it only remained for Jacopo to get involved, and it would be a family affair. As it should have been all along. Hmph. As if that were likely to happen. Isn't that what he'd complained to Jacopo about at the start?

Giddy laughter fizzed deep inside him, as though the hard brick of tension that had resided there this past week had suddenly melted into a churning miasma. Half joy, half terror.

Pia pulled samples out of her bags to show him, and he was amazed. They were beautiful, not just the glistening, colorful food itself, but the containers and their tasteful, modern labels, designed, apparently, by Bibi. In a flash, he realized how talented they each were in their own ways.

"I am speechless, *mia sorelle*."

"Oh, I just had an idea how I can help." Bibi bounced in her seat, bubbling with excitement. "You know how you said your main problem right now is convincing everyone to approve the plans, *si*?"

He nodded.

"Well I think maybe we need to present more than dry spreadsheets and floor plans. I know you do beautiful drawings, but I sense you've been focusing more on the money."

"True. Go on."

"What if I threw together a website quickly, with some photos and your drawings, of course, but also I could write some copy with Pia's help, about how the pieces will function. Something dynamic. You know, really sell it. Kind of like we would be selling it to customers eventually. If we give it a little spin, then we will engage their imagination, and that may make them more willing to take a risk."

Before he could respond, Pia cut in. "That's a wonderful idea, Bibi. I'll work with you on that. But Clio and I have already calculated some estimates for the bank, of the operating costs and projected income, and I think you'll be surprised at how good it all looks. We need to go over it with you, particularly about the outbuildings, and how we can retrofit them as vacation cottages, but it can be ready in a day or so."

Pia and Bibi were bright with enthusiasm, their eyes sparkling, and Guillermo felt he'd caught their buzz, like an electric current being passed from hand to hand. The voices and birdsong of the piazza around them fell away, and time slowed, as he listened to their jumbled words, ideas flying back and forth.

Bibi bent her head to Pia's, speaking earnestly, while she clutched her hand. How they had changed. Mama and Papa would be proud. "We could do the interiors. That would be so fun. I know

Memmo's probably got it covered, but I've always wanted to redo some of those rooms."

"There won't be that much–" he attempted to interject. Money. Some of the buzz deflated.

"*Sapere*! Especially the bedroom– Oh, here she comes." Pia jumped out of her chair, stopping the conversation dead. They all turned to follow the direction of her gaze.

A Pre-Raphaelite goddess strode across the piazza toward them framed by a sunlit cloud of bouncing red curls, like a bonfire. She was a runway model from Milan, tall and flamboyant. She looked cool and breezy, defying the stifling July heat in a gauzy pale green blouse and loose fitting linen pants. A silky ribbon fluttered in the breeze, cast out behind her like a kite. Vivid, passionate, feminine. When had she transformed into such a beauty?

Her step faltered when she saw him, and their eyes met, skipped, locked before she glanced away. Dare he think he saw pleasure there? Hope? Attraction? Clio's cheeks bloomed with a rosy hue, she smiled shyly, and Guillermo's heart leapt against his ribcage like one of the resident pigeons from the piazza, beating its wings, taking flight. Ah, *Bella*. He'd only seen her hair loose and wild like that when they made love. It was his own private indulgence, and even she couldn't know how much he adored it. His groin tightened at the memory. *Dio*, I've missed you. *Mio* Clio.

She stood between his sisters, poised to sit, and though they clamored and fussed over her haircut, he couldn't hear their words. The blood roared in his ears like a torrential river, swollen with the flood of his desire. He licked his lips, and his fingers tingled with the urge to reach across the table and pull her to him, to caress every inch of her skin, hold her tight, and bury his face in the soft mass of her wondrous scented hair. *Amore mia. Senza di te la vita è un inferno.*

There followed an awkward silence. Guillermo could only stare, and rub the sweat from the back of his neck, pictures playing in his brain. No words came immediately to mind. Bibi snickered, and Pia cleared her throat, while Clio continued to gaze expectantly at him. He flushed with sudden heat. His mouth was as dry as limestone and he swallowed. This had never happened to him before. If there was one thing Guillermo could always count on, it was his savvy ease with women. But this was not any woman. The more he thought about the right thing to say, and how to say it, the less he could find any words, and the more his stomach hardened with dread.

He recovered himself, taking a long drink. His sisters must not suspect what a blubbering fool love had made of him. And Clio would not appreciate his making their private affair a public one. Drawing on years of experience as a lady-charmer, he forced his slack face into the semblance of a welcoming smile.

"*Ciao, Bella*. How incredibly *bellissimo* you look today. I have missed you." He leapt from his chair and circled the table, lifting her hand to his lips, applying just the right amount of pressure to be flirtatious and portray a confidence he utterly lacked. The feel of her skin on his sent a shock through him. "Have you eaten lunch?" He waved at the waiter. "*Scuzi. Ehi, cameriere.* What would you like to eat, Clio? A salad?"

"No, *grazie*. I ate lun–"

"You must have a drink. So tell us about your week. I hear you met with Pia. I'm so surprised to hear of your plans."

"Well, I–"

"*Mi dispiace di* the letter. It completely slipped my mind. Of course you needed a signature. My sincere apologies for being unavailable. I was swamped with work at the office this past week. I hardly took note of the time." He was blathering like the idiot he was, but couldn't seem to stop.

"Memmo." Pia tried to interrupt.

"Oh, you've got it bad, *fratello*," Bianca mumbled.

"I, er–" Clio stuttered, while the waiter arrived, and Guillermo ordered a cold sparkling water for her.

"I'm so relieved you are resourceful and thought to call Pia.

That's why we have gotten this far, eh? You are so clever. And now look what happened. A surprise bonus."

"I wanted to talk to you—"

"*Si, si. Scusami.* You can tell me now."

Clio's voice rose over his, brittle and uncharacteristically impatient. "I will if you let me!"

He released his breath.

Three pairs of female eyes bore into him, expectant, annoyed. What a *pazzo*. His face tingled with heat that had nothing to do with the afternoon sun, and everything to do with being in the presence of this woman, who for some reason completely unraveled him. She pushed him and pulled him in the most uncomfortable directions. He squeezed his eyes shut.

"Memmo." Clio's voice was soft.

He drew in a deep breath and released it, suddenly overcome with exhaustion. He could feel the weight of generations hanging like iron shackles on his arms and legs, on his lungs, and on his spirit. This entire day was not going according to plan. He opened his eyes. Her eyes were glazed, and she had trapped her rosy lips between her teeth. He was such an ass. He wanted to give her anything she asked for. He wanted to promise her the moon and the stars. He wanted to say whatever was necessary to have her back in his arms. If only he could.

He stood. "Are you going back to l'Accademia? May I walk with you?"

She sniffed and nodded stiffly.

As she rose and they strolled away, he did not fail to notice the meaningful eye contact exchanged by his sisters.

∽

Clio and Guillermo ambled slowly across the Piazza della Signoria, at first not speaking, the sound of their shoes scuffing softly on the pavement. The afternoon sun sank lower, skipping along the cobbles through narrow gaps between buildings, but the city shimmered, radiating gentle accumulated heat like a limestone oven, after the bread had been baked.

Clio let the heat soak into her bare arms, waiting for Guillermo to begin. She wasn't sure what, precisely, was on his mind. She had, in her defense, tried to reach him many times before going to Pia. It was impossible to tell whether he was angry. It hurt, not being with him, not touching, not sharing their ideas every day.

"You have a talent for this," he said at last, pausing.

She glanced sideways at him. "For what?"

He gestured vaguely. "Problem solving. Organizing. Recruiting people and inspiring them."

She gestured back across the piazza, where his sisters still sat at the cafe, pretending not to be watching their exchange in fascination. "It was not my idea to get Pia involved in this. I only–"

He turned slightly toward her, both palms raised. "I'm not criticizing, *Bella*. I'm impressed, that's all. Under your stewardship, everything seems to fall into place. Problems are solved. Obstacles removed. People beguiled."

She remained silent. His voice was strange. Tight and contained. Strained. She felt she was being scolded, for something, despite his words to the contrary. She kept her eyes averted from his face, despite her longing to gaze at him.

She hugged her arms, feeling a chill that contradicted the late afternoon sun. "I don't know what you want from me, Memmo. I'm just carrying on with our plan the best I can. I happen to think it's wonderful that Pia's plans align with your needs. And now Bianca has these talents she can contribute. I actually think this is for the best. To include your family. Perhaps you should have trusted them from the beginning."

"Did I say I was unhappy?"

She thought about it, her eyes assessing his face. "No. But you sound unhappy."

"Hmph." His gaze drifted back toward his sisters, his expression pensive. He was unhappy, alright.

"Well?"

They began walking again in silence, and she waited, her muscles tense. As they approached the fountain of Neptune, the cooling air chilled her heated skin, lifting gooseflesh. She stepped into the sun and rubbed her arms, tugging on her short sleeves.

"Your hair is very, very beautiful. I'm glad you decided to wear it down."

She dipped her chin to hide the flush she felt creep up her cheeks. "It was Pia's idea to cut it. She's very persuasive."

"I adore it." He reached out and picked out a curling strand and caressed it between his fingers.

She nodded. She knew he loved her hair down. He often said so, and made a big fuss of touching it, burying his face in it when they made love. Another shiver shook her, and her stomach felt leaden.

"I miss you, *Bella*," he whispered. "This week has been hell without you."

Their steps faltered and they stopped, standing side by side, contemplating the fountain statuary, then turning to face each other. Guillermo reached tentatively for her arms, rubbing them with his warm palms. She gazed at his tie, licked her lips, feeling shy.

With one finger, he lifted her chin, and she was forced to meet his eyes. Their deep blue depths shimmered with emotion, heat and longing, and she knew he was going to kiss her. "Memmo–"

Then his mouth came down and covered hers, so gently at first. A feather light kiss. Another one. Then his lips pressed more firmly, and his tongue darted out, requesting entry.

Clio's heart rate accelerated, and her skin tingled at his familiar touch. At last their mouths fused as they were used to, all their mutual desire and love flowing between them, as his hands wove into her loose hair and tangled there, holding her head reverently.

"*Bella*," he said on a sigh as they broke apart. "I need you so badly."

Something shifted in her chest, a sharp pang of emotion. Her hands were resting on his chest, and he still held her in the circle of his arms. Her breathing had quickened with just one kiss. She wanted him body and soul, ached for him. It made her dizzy.

She wanted to ask why he'd avoided her calls, then. But she knew the answer. She just didn't know what to do about it now. Had he changed his mind? Was he considering the directorship?

She swallowed. "Have you... I mean, what are we going to do?"

Guillermo's chest rose with an indrawn breath. Then he hitched his shoulders slightly, and his chin twitched. "I thought about approaching Jacopo. Asking him to be director." His gaze darted sideways.

"Jacopo?" *No, no! Not that.* She dropped her head. Beneath their feet was a plaque marking the spot where Savanarola was hung.

"Especially after today, with Pia and Bianca so involved. Perhaps he could do it." Guillermo shook his head.

"You don't believe it."

"No."

Clio waited.

He turned and took a few steps away. Slowly. Clio followed.

They made their way out of the piazza and walked up Via dei Cerchi, toward the Piazza del Duomo, in the direction of Ricasoli. They both knew the route well. For several blocks they walked in silence, side-by-side, not touching.

"This is really your project, you know, Clio."

"It's not. It's ours, together. But I am only trying to help you. Help your family."

They paused again, in the vast shadow of the Duomo.

"I could not have done this without you. This past week has shown me. I don't know what I'm doing. I have no vision and no understanding of these processes. I'm an architect, *Bella*. A designer. What do I know of this? This is your world, all these academic programs and conferences. The students, and the artwork. The government grants and special licenses. I don't–"

"Guillermo that's not true. This is not different from the kinds of things you do, with your heritage preservation, and juggling client demands and government regulations. Plus you know about the building itself. How to keep it safe and make improvements. Also its history and significance."

"For me it's just my home. The house I grew up in. Nothing more significant than that. That does not qualify me to–"

"That's a lie. You know it. If anyone has appreciated the villa and loved it beyond its immediate value to the family, it's you. I know it. I've seen you. Heard you speak of it. And I've heard Marcella say how involved you were growing up."

He grimaced and raked his hands through his dark hair.

"I want to ask you something, Clio."

Her heart lurched.

"I don't want you to leave, *Bella*. I want you to stay."

She held her breath. Was he asking her to be with him?

"I don't think this institute will come together without your ongoing involvement."

The physical shock of his words struck her like a blow. She held her spine stiffly, her breath shallow.

"I think that *you* should be director." He held up a palm toward her, warding off her protests. "I know you think someone in the family should direct the foundation. Pia and Bianca will be involved now, and they will be a great help. But there's nobody better suited to be director. This job was made for you. It would use your training, and your talents. And our original plan was for a single director, wasn't it? You could do both, *Bella*."

No. He didn't want her for herself. Only to do the job he couldn't bring himself to do. The coward. She pressed her lips together. It was flattering, but it hurt like a knife to the heart.

"I am better off staying focused on my architectural practice. I have already achieved considerable success for my age. It would be foolish to abandon that." He shrugged. "And I would be close by. I would be involved, of course. We could be together, *Bella*. I want you to stay here, not go back to America. Your heart is here."

Her chest tightened. If he only knew. Did he want her for the foundation or for himself? She didn't know the answer. And she daren't ask.

Shaking her head, she said, "Guillermo, I'm not qualified either. I have no experience. I don't even have my Ph.D. and at this point I may never have it. You know the academic director has to meet at least that requirement."

"So *get* your degree, already."

She flinched, and her chin trembled. She brought a hand to her tight throat. That hurt. How could he say that? Her voice emerged in a choked whisper. "That's not fair. I'd be finished by now if it weren't for you and the villa."

"I never asked for your help. We wouldn't even be doing this if it weren't for you."

She fought the hot tears that pushed at her burning eyes. How could he be so cruel? She shook it off, pushing away the emotion that threatened to overwhelm her. "In any case, I have a career path already planned out. I have to put my efforts toward completing my degree. There is a job waiting for me in Ohio."

His face darkened, and his nostrils flared. "You don't want that stupid job."

She lifted her chin. "Who says I don't?"

"You don't. That's your father's idea. You don't have to do what he tells you to do, Clio. You're a grown woman. You must live your own life."

"That *is* my life, Guillermo. Why should I alter my plans and give up my career when you won't consider doing it for your own home?" She flapped her hands. "This is your villa. Your family estate. Your history we're trying to save. What is it to me?"

He seemed to deflate, his shoulders drooping, his eyes suddenly suffused with sadness. "Don't say that. I know you care. It's your destiny, Clio. My Clio, Muse of History. You came to me and this happened all at once for a reason." He reached out a hand to touch her shoulder.

She shoved his hand away roughly. "Don't touch me."

"*Bella*."

She stalked away, and he followed.

"Don't you see? You're my angel. You were sent to me so we could save the villa from destruction, but also this is your salvation. Your escape from the stifling cage of a life your father built."

"Oh, how convenient for you. That's sentimental crap. Don't tell me how to live my life, Guillermo d'Aldobrandin. You don't know me. You don't know what I want, or what I dream of." *I dream of you, Memmo. I want you. I want you to want me.* But he wasn't capable of that. Guillermo was incapable of facing responsibility or commitment. He was the boy who cut and ran when things got uncomfortable. He certainly wouldn't be interested in committing to a life shared with her. He was selfish and cowardly. Why did she expect anything else? He was who he was, and she was a fool to think he had changed.

She turned to him, determined, her hands on her hips. "I'm going back to my own life. If I work hard now, there may be a chance Dr. Jovi and Father will let me complete my degree."

"Don't abandon me. What will happen to our scheme?"

"Without a director, it's doomed to failure anyway."

He scowled. "I'll ask Jacopo then."

"You said he can't do it. And you will not do it. You don't care enough to make the personal sacrifice to save your family's estate."

He stiffened, his eyes pulling tight, the light going out of them. "I will not give up my career, no. It's not for me."

"Well if you won't, why the hell should I? I'm sorry to have wasted your time." Clio felt her heart shatter into a trillion tiny fragments.

"*Beh, in tal caso.* I guess that's it." His voice was clipped, cold.

She sniffed and nodded stiffly, crossing her arms. "Fine."

They glared at each other, her fury, disappointment and hurt mirrored in his eyes.

"*Arrivederci*, then, Clio." He moved to leave.

She spun on her heel and stormed off, back to her office, back to her own miserable life, and she didn't look back to see if he was doing the same, or if he stood watching her. It was too late for that.

∼

He stood watching her stalk away, disappearing into the crowds of tourists at the entrance to the Duomo. The hot and cold flash of anger drained away, leaving only a tight ache in the back of his throat, as though all the emotion that had zinged back and forth between them, all the words, both spoken and unexpressed, had balled up and wedged there, making it impossible to swallow.

What the hell had just happened? Everything was shattered, out of control. He felt as if a sudden explosion had flown in his face and embedded his entire body and soul with shards of sharp glass or shrapnel. Numbly, he looked down at his hands, almost expecting to see blood.

What went wrong? He thought everything was going well - the scheme, his sisters' involvement, his relationship with Clio. She'd left him with the sense that he was disappointing her? But how? Why? What did she want from him that he hadn't given? Why did she insist that only *he* be director? He'd never gotten this deeply involved with a woman. Never felt so vulnerable, so out of control. He felt betrayed. And he hadn't seen it coming.

A sharp tight pain pierced his chest, and he grabbed a fistful of his shirt and squeezed, pressing at the spot that made his breath catch. Was that really it? Could she throw away everything they had shared so easily? Did he mean nothing to her? The piazza tilted and seemed to fall away under his feet. Someone jostled him as they walked past. He wobbled and staggered.

If this was what rejection felt like, it was devastating. He felt a rush of shame at all the women he had used so cavalierly. He'd told himself they didn't care anymore than he did, but he knew it was a convenient lie.

His lungs felt flat, as though a great stone had been set down on his chest, crushing the air out of him. The whole thing seems to deflate - lose its buoyancy, its joy, its very significance - if she was not there with him making it happen. Not just the villa project, but his whole elaborate, fake, empty life. He'd lost the will to go on.

He fell back against a bollard, out of the way of the foot traffic, allowing the stream of pedestrians to move past him in a river of faceless bodies, their mingled voices a dull rumble.

What was she doing to him? He raked his hands through his hair. He'd never felt this way before. Like... like such a failure. A *pazzo*.

Why should he feel this way? The answer pummeled him, and he refused to look directly at it. It loomed beside him, like a bully, nudging his shoulder, and he turned away, jerking his arm out of reach, grunting. His body heated, and he broke out into a sweat that radiated outward from his centre, pulsing.

He was a successful man, the envy of all. Agitated, he stood upright and paced, his eyes cast down at the cobbles. He was always successful at whatever venture he set his mind and heart to. *I make the choices. I make the decisions. I'm a man of action.* And yet. The truth relentlessly stared him in the face.

He had always avoided judgement by running away. He knew it. His family had called him on it, as had Clio, and he'd chosen to ignore them. But this time, he felt like both the problem and the solution were out of his hands, out of his control. *What am I supposed to do?*

His hands curled into fists of frustration, and he pounded his thighs until they throbbed. A roar built in his throat, the scream of a madman, and he held it in, afraid of the looks the passing crowd would give him, though it burned in his chest like a ball of fire.

Would he see the truth in their eyes? He was impotent. Powerless. Worthless.

No. No, no, no! He spun on his heel and paced in the other direction, ignoring the bumped elbows and curious glances of passersby.

I have to do something. I will solve it. I can't let my family down. His family's home and legacy were at stake. They depended on him - he knew this. They always had depended on him to hold everything together. How could he not see this? And yet they were still critical of him - as though he'd disappointed them at the same time. What did they need him to do now? To carry on.

This project was the only thing he had to keep Clio with him. A bitter laugh escaped, drawing stares. Hadn't that been the reason he'd begun this charade? To please her and lure her because she didn't want him? And now, he didn't want to lose her. But she was gone. And he was left holding the proverbial bag. But it wasn't just a ruse. It was real. The realest thing he'd ever faced. And his self respect rode on the outcome.

Could he carry on without her? Could he shoulder this responsibility himself?

He muttered, gnashing his teeth. He felt like he'd lost control of his life. He squinted at the brightness of the vivid blue sky behind the monumental silhouette of the Duomo. God's house. He lifted up his arms. *What am I to do? What do you want me to do?* He turned around and walked, his pace picking up as the need to move overtook him, burning through his veins like rocket fuel. Unable to suppress the urge any longer, he burst forward, running.

If only he could save the villa, then he could still offer Clio the job of academic director. It was perfect for her. It would give her options, independence, freedom. He could help her, too. If he could prove his worth to her, maybe she would stay with him after all.

He laughed bitterly. Since when did his self esteem hinge on being a hero?

He never had problems before. *I make the choices. I make the deci-*

sions. I'm a man of action. Solved problems or walked away. If he didn't like his odds, he didn't get involved. It was that simple. He chose the projects he could master. Played only the games he knew he could win. Chose which women to dally with and walked away, never risking his heart. He always maintained *bella figura,* and came out smelling like a rose. He was in control. This was always a point of pride.

What a load of *merda.*

He ran until his chest hurt and he was breathless, and realized he'd run through the back lanes right back to the Piazza della Signoria. How much time had passed? He felt like he'd been to hell and back. Across the *piazza,* his sisters still sat at the cafe, their heads together. He slowed and walked toward them, breathing heavily, his heart hammering in his chest.

This kind of thing never happened to him. He was under water, at a loss, out of control. He had no one to turn to. He had to save himself, as well as everyone else. This time he really had to be a hero. And he'd never felt less capable, less in control, less heroic.

All he could think about was Clio. He wanted Clio with him, and seeing her walk away from him so definitively ripped him apart somewhere deep inside, somewhere he hadn't felt anything in a long time, hurt him so much he thought he might never heal. Clio.

He stopped in the middle of the piazza, looking at his sisters, not really seeing them. His vision blurred, and he dug the heels of his hands into his eyes. He gasped for breath, his pulse slowing gradually.

He stood at the edge of a precipice. He stood at a cusp. Everything before, and everything after this moment, would be different.

He'd been lying to himself. He was not content with his life. *He* was not who or what he'd thought. He was so much less. Incomplete. He needed so much more. A whole family, like they used to have, a welcoming home, full of beauty and history, a profound love to share, like he'd had –so fleetingly– with Clio. Maybe someday, his own children, to nurture and teach, to carry on the traditions and the legacy of his great family. And... maybe, perhaps, he was capable of more, too. If everyone else thought he could do these things, then maybe he could. Maybe it was worth the risk of failure. Maybe he just had to try.

He walked towards them. They looked up, saw him.

He could see it in their eyes - worry, sympathy, disappointment, hope.

He walked up to them, stood before them, and lifted his hands, palm up, to each side. A question. Or a surrender? He choked, his throat burning, his eyes hot. The image of his sisters' faces blurred.

Pia leapt from her chair and wrapped her arms around him, squeezing. "There, there, Memmo, *caro*. You really love her, don't you? Shhh. Everything will be alright, you'll see." He shut his eyes, felt moisture on his lashes, thickness in his throat. He opened his eyes, sucked in a ragged breath. Bibi stared at him, her face slack, her gaze sharp.

"*Stronzo*. You're a mess."

CHAPTER 27

"What the fuck have you done?"

Jacopo sat rigidly at his desk, staring at his blotter. A dark expression clouded his face, its lines etched into the immovable stone of his lean cheeks.

"Did Pia tell you? Or was it Bibi?" Guillermo hunched his shoulders and leaned back, stretching his face into a facsimile of a smile. His stomach rolled over, the bitter taste of bile burning his throat.

He had raced to Jacopo's parliamentary office suite, his heart pounding in time with the soles of his shoes on the polished marble, after receiving the curt message: "Get your ass over to my office, *pronto!*" Guillermo reminded himself that it was easier to ask forgiveness than permission.

Jacopo's eyes lifted to meet Guillermo's and waved a hand dismissively. "So you admit to sneaking around behind my back. Am I the only one who didn't know this was going on?"

Guillermo conceded silently. "I wouldn't call it sneaking, exactly. It was–"

"This has to stop. Immediately!"

Guillermo swallowed and stepped forward. "Listen. Let me expl–"

"It's probably too late, but at the very least that must happen. My staff are running interference with the press and the ethics committee right now." He sighed. "Though I'm not sure there's any point."

"Ethics? What has this got to do with…" A light went on in his head. "Oh, *stronzo*!"

Jacopo nodded. "So you are behind this application for heritage designation. For our own house!" He glared. "My enemies will enjoy adding this to my list of crimes."

"They can't possibly think that you're behind this. My name's on it. I was about to tell you."

"It's a bit late now, don't you think?"

"I'm sorry, Lapo."

Jacopo winced, and his voice softened, breaking. "You could have told me you were doing it, even if you didn't want me involved. There's protocol for this type of thing. It's being blindsided I resent. You know what I'm dealing with up here."

"That's the other reason I didn't tell you. We're so close to making this work. But the application to your ministry is essential to ensure that we qualify for grants and tax breaks. I *wanted* you to be completely uninvolved. I know how closely the heritage designation and grants tread on your territory. I didn't want anyone getting the wrong end of the stick. I didn't even want you to see it."

"Well someone got hold of it anyway and has the wrong idea. It's Brunello, of course. He confronted me with it. He's already sent it on to the ethics committee, eager to take me down. Now what am I going to do?"

Guillermo winced at the sound of Jacopo's old enemy's name. "Fight it. You did no wrong."

"Easier said than done, Memmo. It looks bad. Really bad. Even I think so." Jacopo slammed his palms down on the desktop. "You've finished me. I might as well have quit and gone to prison the first time."

"That can't be true. You had nothing to do with it."

"Tell that to the ethics committee. Tell it to the reporters. They are all happy to believe the worst of me." Jacopo raked his hands into his hair, loosening a strand that flopped over his forehead as he hung his head.

He looked for a moment like the boy he had been, before the burden of adulthood stole his carefree spirit. They had always been different, but he was a good big brother, responsible but fun, silly, adventurous. "I'm sorry, Lapo. I'll fix it somehow, I promise. Maybe I could talk to the press. They like me well enough."

"I'm sorry, Lapo. I'll fix it somehow, I promise. Maybe I could talk to the press. They like me well enough."

"I don't know if I'm angrier at the threat to my reputation or that you're compromising the sale of the villa and my only financial bailout. No matter how you look at this, I'm screwed. I can't believe you kept it from me. Why?"

"Do you not recall our last conversation? You challenged me. What else was I supposed to do?"

"Nothing. We all understood what your job was. Keep the buyer happy. That's all."

"I understand your position, Lapo. But when Clio presented the case to me, I felt we had to try. You dared me, after all, to find a way. How could I let it go without making the effort? You know what's a stake!"

"Clio. Clio?" Jacopo threw up his hands. "How does this woman factor into our family troubles?" Jacopo had met Clio only the once, but Guillermo supposed his sisters had filled him in on their personal relationship. Perhaps not.

"It was... she was a big help. I couldn't have...wouldn't have done it without her."

Jacopo scowled and peered darkly at Guillermo for a long moment. "I thought we had everything sorted out."

Guillermo firmed his jaw.

Jacopo's face was flushed red. "Wait until Valentina hears of this." He laughed without humour.

This was a disaster, not only for Jacopo's career, but also for the project. Both were doomed. They'd never get their application approved amidst this scandal. Worst case scenario, they would lose everything they'd worked so hard for. "But you're innocent of any wrongdoing!"

"It's too late, Memmo. There's no hope."

"We'll fix it somehow. I'll talk to them. I'll write letters."

"I'm sure that will clear everything up, you being my brother," Jacopo deadpanned.

"There must be some way. Maybe you could put it forward as a public initiative, argue the benefits."

"Not likely, without credibility. I can't be seen to be patronizing my own family and our assets." Jacopo slumped in his chair, his eyes shadowed with worry. "I don't think my career will survive another scandal, Memmo. I think you have to withdraw the application. If even that will save me now. You have to give it up."

"I can't." Guillermo stood taller, his muscles tensing, and felt his hands draw into fists. "I won't give up now, Lapo. We've got the first viable plan to save the estate that anyone has ever proposed. This could be the sustainable solution we've been lacking for generations. We are so close to making it happen. You have to agree to let it play out. I want to do this, if you'll agree."

Jacopo exhaled, long and slow, kneading his forehead with his hand. "Tell me everything. Let's see what we can come up with."

Guillermo summed up the situation. "The short version is, now we're in a catch-22 between the government and the bank."

"And now you'll have what you need, as long as you get your heritage designation approved."

"Yes. The girls made the difference. Pia and Bibi weren't involved, at first. But now that they are, they're committed. They're excited about it, about having a role to play."

"I'm glad. It feels right." Jacopo's eyes shone. "I wish... I don't suppose your withdrawing the application will save my ass now, anyway. That would take a miracle. But I'm afraid the application is going to be tainted. It'll be caught up in whatever investigation occurs now. I can't see a way around that. I also can't see how I can help, with my hands tied."

"Would you consider putting your name forward as the foundation's director?"

"Me?"

Guillermo shrugged. "Who else? Clio feels it ought to be a member of our family."

"I can see that. But aside from the obvious conflict of interest, I would be a handicap, surely–"

"You might need a new job." Guillermo shrugged.

That earned him a hard look. "You're the logical choice."

Guillermo groaned. It was a conspiracy. "No. I have my career. And that's not my kind of thing anyway."

Jacopo snorted. "It is if you want it to be. Think about it. You've always been the one most interested in the villa and its history. You're qualified to be its caretaker, both in terms of its cultural value and its technical..." Jacopo waved a hand. "Heh. More than I am, certainly."

Guillermo ran a hand through his hair, staring at a national flag on the wall. "For a while I thought Clio could do it. But she's better suited to run the academic program, and even then.... she refuses to discuss it. She's fed up with me." He squeezed his eyes shut. How was he ever going to win her back?

"What's going on?"

Guillermo drew in a long breath, puffed out his cheeks and exhaled. "Everything was going so well. But we're at loggerheads over the directorship issue. I want her involved. I need her help. I'm afraid..." He rubbed the back of his neck, trying to order his scattered thoughts. He couldn't see how to make her happy without becoming director himself. That was what she wanted.

Jacopo leaned forward. "Is this... are you actually serious about this woman?"

Serious. What did that even mean? He rubbed his chest with the heel of his hand, trying to ease the tightness there. Saving the villa seemed an impossible challenge. One he'd never be able to face alone.

Alone.

Even though he had his family with him now. Somehow he needed Clio to make it happen. Guillermo had never found himself in this situation before. He had never enjoyed being with a woman more. He knew that. She understood him and pushed him in ways no one had ever–

"Memmo? Did you hear me?"

"Mmhmm. I was thinking about Clio."

"Well. What do you know?"

Their eyes met. "What?"

"My little brother's in love."

Guillermo continued rubbing his ribs, working at the tightness that made it hard to draw a full breath. "Am I? Is that what this ache is?"

A sly grin slid across Jacopo's face, and he chuckled silently. "I'm afraid so."

"I want her back, Lapo."

"I can't believe I'm saying this, but, let's get her back. And maybe Valentina while we're at it."

Guillermo smiled. "Or go down trying." He sighed. "But what can be done?"

"The problem is one of perception primarily, as far as I can see," Jacopo said.

"We can come up with something, as long as we work together." He inhaled, standing straighter. "You've been shouldering the burden by yourself for too long. And I hate what it's done to you. I would have done anything to avoid the same fate. But I believe we are stronger if we work together, and share the load. We can do this."

Their eyes met, assessing each other. "You've changed. I can see you digging in," Jacopo said.

It was true. Something had shifted in him. He felt taller, and stronger, if a little older. He smiled wryly at his brother. "Someone's got to."

"Anything for the love of a good woman."

∽

"Look who has come to see you, Clio." Dr. Jovi hunched just outside the open doorway of her office, his hands clasped together.

Guillermo? Clio sat up straighter, throwing off the cobwebs that clung to her groggy brain.

The long hours at her computer writing were numbing. She had just one goal now, to finish writing her thesis so she could get out of here and move on with her life, whatever that might turn out to be. Now that Pia and Bibi were helping Guillermo finalize the numbers for the business plan, she knew he would be alright, that he didn't need her help anymore, and she had forced herself to focus on her thesis, but concentrating was torture.

Dr. Jovi's eyes sparkled. His jowls flushed. But no, he wouldn't be so excited to announce Guillermo, about whom he continued to express skepticism and concern. At least until a week ago, when Memmo had stopped coming by after their fight.

A sigh escaped her. Of course it wasn't Memmo. She had told him she didn't want to see him, didn't want to help him. Lies, yes, but he couldn't know that. And even if he did suspect how much she cared for the villa—for him—there was still the small matter of his Italian pride. *What have I done? Why am I choosing to inflict this pain on myself?*

"Clio?"

She looked up. Dr. Jovi was still standing there.

"Father?"

"*Si!* The *Dottores* have arrived. Right on schedule."

Both of them? "Where are they?" Maybe she could slip out. Buy herself some time. Or just disappear forever. "I-I'm not exactly prepared, Dr. Jovi. You know that."

He scratched his long nose with a hooked finger. "It's not your final defense, Clio." He smiled. "Think of it as a dress rehearsal."

Except she hadn't even learned her lines yet. Presenting to her parents was worse than presenting to her advisory board. Far worse. Far less forgiving. The old traitor could have put them off if he'd had the courage to stand up to her father. But then she was one to talk. She shot out of her chair, grabbed her handbag and took one large stride toward the door before skidding to a stop.

Father loomed in front of Dr. Jovi, completely obscuring the old man. Shit. Shit, shit, shit! "Father."

"Clio." He stepped toward her and squeezed her shoulders between his large palms, leaning in for a kiss. His perpetually squinting blue eyes assessed her. She squirmed, feeling like a lowly undergraduate under his critical gaze.

She stretched up to peck his bearded cheek and pulled away. "You surprised me. I was just heading out. My goodness." She turned back to her desk, dropped her bag there and rummaged around in it, looking for nothing short of excuses. "Did I hear Dr. Jovi say Mother was with you?" She faced him again, her heart racing.

"Yes, she–"

"Why don't we go out for a coffee? Is Mum at the hotel? Let's go there."

"Ah, Clio. I was hoping to sit–"

She lunged forward and scooped a hand through his arm. "There's loads of time, Dad. Let's go. Dr. Jovi, would you like to join us?"

His face brightened, then fell. "*Certamente*, ah, but no. I-a have a student-a coming in shortly."

"Oh. Well." It might have been easier to break the news to Father with her advisor present. Not that he would defend her, but he had a gentling effect on Father. She wasn't going to do it without Mother, though.

Clio managed to make small talk and get Father to talk about his own work, never very difficult, en route to the Hotel Albani. Once there, she got a table in the restaurant and prodded Father into going upstairs to fetch her mother, who was lying down. Her stomach churned. What was she going to say? How was she going to say it? How would they react?

Her parents appeared at the restaurant door. He, large and imposing, Mother, rigid and pale, as though she had one of her migraines. Clio felt detached, as though she were viewing her parents in the abstract for the first time, the way someone else, a stranger, would see them.

The moment of truth had arrived. Clio felt dizzy. She knew her shallow breathing was depriving her brain of oxygen, and contributing to the sharp shooting pains in her side. This wasn't going to help her pull her arguments together coherently, so she tried to slow and deepen her breaths, expanding her ribcage and calming her pulse.

She stood to embrace and kiss her mother, who carried an air of distraction, as usual. "Are you well, Mum? Do you have a headache?"

"Oh, no, Clio. I'm in the middle of writing a paper. I have a—" She shook her head as if to clear away the unsolved problem or the half-written sentence.

Ah. That was Mother. Never entirely in the moment.

Father ordered a carafe of wine, and while they waited, she felt them scrutinizing her.

"You've either gained weight or lost it, I can't tell," Mother said. "But you look healthy, dear. Your complexion is bright. And I rather like your hair loose like that."

Father grunted, his eyes scanning over her, as though he hadn't noticed the changes until Mother mentioned them.

Clio forced a smile. "Really? Good." Surprising. A week ago she might have attributed it to the frequent and amazing sex. But not now. She felt Guillermo's absence from her life like a gaping void. Like a wound. Like a cold ashen hearth. Forlorn.

The waiter served the wine, and Clio grabbed hers and tossed it back with a desperate thirst. Father raised an assessing brow and refilled her glass.

"I was expecting you could run through your defense presentation for us, Clio. Between Mother and I, we could pick up any weak points and advise you. It always helps to practice a little before the big day."

Clio drained another glass, set it down and licked her lips. The soft buzz from the wine took the edge off her dread.

She cleared her throat.

"Father." She swallowed, gathering her nerve. "Mother?" She knew there was no sympathy to be found from either parent. And no point postponing the inevitable. "The fact is, I'm not ready. I'm… *almost* ready. But I won't be able to defend on Tuesday as scheduled. Dr. Jovi knows. I'm not sure why he didn't tell you before you flew over. I'm sorry to waste your time." She pressed her lips together, waiting.

Mother averted her eyes, pressing her manicured fingertips to her temple, pruning her mouth with a sucking motion, and focusing on some distant object. That was her way of expressing her dissatisfaction. Detachment. Even more detachment than usual. It was only really accomplishment that got a rise out of her. Anything less simply couldn't be processed. Clio could hold up her prizes and awards in exchange for love and affection. Attention. Approval. Or not.

The skin of Father's large nose was stretched taut, altering its shape, making it broader and more flared. A look she knew well. Through his compressed nostrils, his slow, deep, even breathing was emphatic. Clio always focused on his nose, for some reason. A fleshy island in a sea of judgment. Maybe it was to avoid the downturned corners of his proud mouth, or the shattered feeling his cold, flinty eyes inflicted on her. Like a thousand sharp knives slicing, slicing all over, leaving her feeling shredded and bleeding. And he hadn't even spoken yet.

"What have you got to say in your defense?"

It was a question she'd heard a thousand million times. She must defend herself before the judge. A vibration, a kind of resonance, slowly built up from the center of Clio, rising, and filling her. It became audible to her, at first a hum, building to a dull roar. She lifted her eyes to her father's cold gaze. And she felt... still. Stillness in the midst of a storm of emotion. "I don't have to defend myself to you."

The outline of her father seemed to waver. As though a projected image had suddenly flickered, or the surface upon which it was projected had rippled, causing a distortion of the solid, familiar image she had expected to see.

"I beg your pardon?"

Mother sat upright, suddenly alert. Her head tipped to one side, like a skinny bird that had just noticed an odd colourful bit of fluff. A tiny red flag.

"I'm twenty-eight years old. Whether I succeed or fail at my doctoral thesis should be entirely my own concern."

"Who do you think has paid for this education of yours, young lady?"

Clio narrowed her eyes, trying to reconcile the disconcerting, conflicting images of her parents. The way they appeared in her mind, with the people who sat before her. She knew they loved her, in their own rigid, narrow way. Everything she'd ever had was given to her by them. "You of course, Father. And I'm grateful. Although I wonder if... if maybe..."

"What?"

She swallowed. "I'm not sure you've done me any favors by choreographing my life so...so completely."

Father sucked in a breath, his mouth downturned, his eyes bulging. "Well I never..."

"Clio you don't mean what you're saying." Mother's sharp eyes were fully on her now. "We've given you every advantage."

Father bristled. "This is some kind of rebellion so close to your deadline. You're feeling stressed, obviously, but I don't see the need to be disrespectful. I expect better of you, Clio."

"Father. Most people my age are fully independent. They've long ago embarked on careers, families, lives of their own. Why do you persist in micro-managing me?"

A long moment of silence passed, during which they stared at each other, as if seeing each other for the first time.

"You're going to deliver the final draft of your thesis? You plan to defend?"

Clio shrugged. Some demon urge prevented her from agreeing with him. She lifted her chin and met his icy blue eyes. "I don't know what I'm going to do next."

Father's face filled with blood, reddening like a thermometer building pressure, going taut. "This is not to be born. I can't believe it. I'm fed up with you."

"I need more time, Father. I need to finish this thesis on my own terms. I need a little time to gather my thoughts, that's all."

"You need. What makes you think you can have everything just the way you like it, missy?" He tossed back his wine and pushed his chair back. "More time? Ha! We've given you extra time already, Clio. I'm fed up. You never took your academic career seriously. We've lost faith in you. I don't know what else to do. I don't know how to impress upon you the importance–"

"Father! You don't need to do anything. That's my–"

"You're twenty-seven years old and never lived on your own. Never had a permanent job. You think you can make it on your own? Fine. You take care of yourself from now on. You're cut off." He stood up.

"Donald," Mother murmured. "Perhaps, you're being too hasty."

"No! I'm through with her." He straightened his large frame, looming, and glared down at Clio. "How do you like that?"

Clio sat back, expecting to feel devastation. But she wasn't as crushed as she thought she might be. Strangely, she felt as though a great weight had been lifted from her shoulders. She felt as though the steel bands of a cage had broken open, and suddenly she could see the sky. She felt as though she were floating upward, as if she were one of those angels drifting heavenward, glowing, ecstatic, secure in the knowledge that all was as it was meant to be. She wanted to giggle.

Instead, a steely determination and a strange detachment from her father's wrath, and her mother's pinched disappointment, filled her. Or rather, washed over her, like a halo of light, or an epiphany of recognition, leaving her feeling very warm all over.

"You know, I'm really alright with that, Father," she said, suppressing the smile that pulled at her lips.

He drew back. "You'll be cut off. You'll have to earn your own keep. And I can't guarantee that position will be held for you at Ohio if you ever manage to graduate."

Clio blinked. He really didn't understand at all. "Oh. How will I live without that?"

"This is hardly the time for sarcasm, Clio."

"I never wanted to go to Ohio, Father! You never even asked me if I wanted that position." Clio thrust out her chin.

His icy blue eyes bulged, and his arrogant mouth seemed frozen into its downturned scowl of disapproval.

"I'm finished with you."

"So you said."

The color drained from Mother's pinched face. She shook her head back and forth, back and forth. "Oh, Clio. A wasted opportunity. If you abandon your career now, you'll lose all the advantage of our reputations. Moreover, your failure will reflect poorly on us. Our only child. People expect such great things from you."

Clio glanced from Father to Mother and back again. And she felt... nothing. Nothing at all. She was numb. A powerful heaviness pulled down her limbs, weakening her so that she couldn't move a muscle. What had just happened? Perhaps it was inevitable, the conflict she felt with her parents had been bound to explode one day. But she couldn't help but feel a profound disappointment. She had never been the daughter they wanted her to be. And they had never been the family she yearned for. What *would* she do now?

She realized in that moment that she felt more for Guillermo and his family's home than she did about her thesis, or about pleasing her parents. In the past month, she'd felt more committed, more passionate, more alive than she had at any point in her university career. For the first time in her life she had taken on a cause of her own choosing. And it was about bloody time.

True, she loved her thesis. It had taken a few false starts, but she'd finally stumbled upon an idea that she believed in. Something she could champion and carry through. But it was the research itself that propelled her forward, rather than completing the thesis and getting the degree. About what came afterward, she felt nothing. About Doctor Clio Sinclair McBeal and her illustrious academic career, following in the footsteps of her accomplished parents, she felt nothing. That was not her future.

"I suppose you'll want me to withdraw from the program."

Father's face contorted even further, his eyes pinching to narrow slits in a field of crow's feet, like cracks in a dry lakebed. "What's the point in staying if you don't intend to finish?"

"I didn't say that. I just want to do it in my own time, on my own terms."

"Well I can't pay another Euro to keep you. You can't expect Jovi to hold your position open any longer while you dawdle. You've been taking up space for far too long, and he's kept you on only as a favor to me."

"Well, that is good to know. However, it doesn't matter. I've been talking to another academic, at… Perugia. Someone who supports my research." Clio's neck felt like twisted steel, it was so taut and cramped. She lifted her shoulders to ease the cramping.

"What?" Mother said. "Who?"

"You planned this?"

"You always taught me to have a backup plan, Father." A shudder shot through her from top to bottom, rattling her. It was a bald-faced lie, but it could be true. She knew people. She pressed her elbows tightly to her sides to quell the tremors, and gripped the edge of the table until her fingertips turned white.

"You talked to them? And kept this from me?"

Clio jigged one shoulder up. "I don't want your help anymore, Father. I'll manage my career and my life on my own."

He pushed his chair out of the way with a jerk, his breathing raspy. "We'll be leaving then." Mother shadowed him, looking a little stunned. She had her own opinions, not necessarily in alignment with Father's, but he seldom left her an opportunity to express them.

"Clio," she hissed. "Oh, Clio, please. A little more effort–" Her face folded up and she turned away, her eyes casting after Father.

Oh, hell. This is it, then. Her breath failed her, but she squeezed out, "Fine. I'm happy for you to go." She watched them walk away, all the hope that one day they'd see her for her true self and love her unconditionally shriveling and shrinking into a small, hard pellet in the pit of her stomach.

She did want her Ph. D. Of course she did. But she needed more time. She'd think about that later. First, she realized, she'd need a job right away to support herself for the first time in her life. She had only her stipend and a little savings. Not very much. A tremor of excitement shook her. It wasn't how she'd envisioned it, but here it was: independence. At last.

I have to live my own life. I don't want to be shunted around like a puppet, sent to Ohio just because Father owed some old crony a favour, or maybe the other way around.

She waited for the sensation of shame at the next thought that skipped through her mind. But it didn't come. She realized what she'd always wanted, the reason she'd allowed herself to be manipulated and controlled all her life. She simply wanted to be loved and accepted. She wanted to be valued for herself, and to belong somewhere. Somewhere she didn't have to continually prove her worth with accomplishments and kudos.

Only one person had ever made her feel that way. She swallowed the sob that tore at her throat, and tilted her face up to the ceiling, as tears welled and overflowed onto her cheeks.

The truth is, I want to be with Guillermo more than... more than I want a PhD or Father's approval. Even though he doesn't want me for himself.

CHAPTER 28

"Memmo! *Telefono per te!*"

Stronzo. Guillermo huffed out his breath and set down his tools. "*Momento*, Marcella." Why did the phone always ring when you were at the top of a ladder?

He worked his way down, his thoughts torn between the caller, and the problems he'd discovered under the cap flashing of the portico parapet wall. Hopefully it was that contractor from Montechiello calling back already.

Yesterday, when he'd driven down for the weekend to check a few details on the villa, he hadn't anticipated the mid-summer thunderstorm that followed him out to the country. Though unexpected, it was not atypical for the late July season, since the weather had been exceptionally hot and humid the past week, temperatures hitting a high of thirty-seven degrees Celsius yesterday. Rain already fell in the city as he drove south, fat warm drops sending up clouds of dust from the dry cobbles, dark clouds rolling over the hills in pursuit.

It was a good thing he was here during the downpour. The sudden flood of water during the hot dry season, when wood and stucco were shriveled and sere, made the building envelope especially vulnerable to leaks, breaks in seals and cracks in membranes. Fortunately, he'd been standing in the large salon when the water started seeping through the frescoed ceiling, and he'd been able to respond quickly by dragging huge tarps out of the garage and covering the vulnerable areas.

It was over as soon as it began. A couple of hours of hard rain, dust and steam rising into the hot dry air, and it was done. Now it remained for him to assess the damage, and analyze the source of the problem, which entailed removing the metal cap flashing and poking around in the membrane. So far, it was clear that the whole assembly was at the end of its lifespan and needed replacing, even though the failure was confined to a small area at present, as far as he knew. It added another significant expense to the budget. It couldn't be ignored.

"*Grazie*, Marcella." He dusted his hands on his trousers and took the phone from Marcella. "*Pronto. Sono* Guillermo."

"Memmo."

"Lapo! *Cosa c'è?*"

"I don't know. I'm not sure our plan will work. They're on me like wolves, *fratello*. The next session of parliament starts Thursday. I applied to the Speaker for a special place on the agenda, but he says he cannot accommodate me this time."

Guillermo's chest tightened, his pulse drumming against his ribs. They needed the element of surprise, but they also needed sufficient time. "Did you tell him what you plan?"

"No. Of course not. I can't give myself away. It would defeat the purpose."

Of course. A moment of silence passed between them.

"What time are you up?"

Silence.

"Lapo?" This had to work. There was no other way.

"What are you suggesting?"

"Do it anyway. *È necessario fare ostruzionismo.*"

Jacopo's voice was low, murmuring, as though someone else in the room might overhear. "No. It would cause a riot. I don't dare."

"You must Lapo! What hope is there if you don't?"

"I don't know Memmo. I'll have to see how it goes."

"If they won't give you time, you have to take what you need."

"I can't do that."

"You can. Write it out and read it if you must."

"No. I'm in too much shit already."

"You're in so much shit a little more won't even stick."

Jacopo groaned. "Even if I try, I'm not sure I want anyone watching. It's bad enough going live. What if–?"

"What if what? Be serious. The whole point of this is to get attention. I've spoken to people already. The press who are sympathetic will be there."

Jacopo moaned.

"Don't back out now. *Per favore*. We have to do this, Lapo."

"It can't possibly succeed."

"It's our last chance. And we get points for trying. Remember that, *fratello*."

Jacopo sighed. "I can't promise."

Guillermo jiggled his foot on the marble and gritted his teeth. "If I could do it myself, Lapo, I would. But this is something only you can do. Even if it means you can no longer be a politician. It will be okay. It's the right thing to do. The rest we can figure out, together. We'll be okay."

He planted his feet wide, his gaze locked on the marble staircase leading up from the entry foyer. In his mind's eye, he could still see Mama there, descending, on any given day, her dark curls shining, her smile broad and warm. He could envision Papa emerging from the doorway of the study over there, his eyes on her, his brow lifting in understated appreciation of her beauty. The hall still echoed with the sounds of his family throughout the seasons and the years. "They're depending on us." He didn't know if he meant the living or the dead.

Lapo said nothing. He understood.

Yes, it could blow up in their faces. But at least they were trying. And they were in it together. Pia and Paulo and Bianca had to be watching. And Valentina. And... Clio. His gut twisted like a knot of rope. He'd never been so certain of anything.

Guillermo set his jaw. "Come on, Lapo. The stakes have never been higher, *fratello*. Of course there will be an uproar. But we'll surely lose everything if we *don't* act!"

Jacopo grunted. "I don't know. I just don't know if I can do it. If I get an opportunity to raise the matter, it will be around seven. That's the best estimate I can give you, assuming nothing unexpected comes up before me. Gotta go. *Ciao*." He hung up.

As Guillermo hit '*end*' a sudden crash reverberated through the house.

"*Stronzo!*"

Marcella reappeared, twisting a tea towel between her brown hands. "*Cos'è successo?*"

"I don't know."

Martino's voice, garbled, carried to them. "*Signore* Memmo! Come quickly!"

Guillermo raced to the salon.

The air was thick with swirling fine plaster dust billowing towards them in a white wave, obscuring everything, including Martino's whereabouts.

"*Maria madre di Gesù.*"

Guillermo fought his way through the dust, coughing and squinting. He stumbled over a chunk of rubble as he approached the far corner of the room, and he waved his arms to clear the air enough to see. Peering upward at the vaults, he could see a dark section had cracked and fallen away, like missing puzzle pieces. Martino stood under it, caked in white plaster like a garden statue, an expression of panic frozen on his creased old face.

"Oh, *Signore*," Guillermo whispered. He needed to get tarps and scaffolding up there immediately. "I'm driving to Montechiello. Don't touch anything!"

∽

Clio wondered if her father would stop payments on her new Fiat500 now that he'd virtually disowned her. The insurance had paid for the replacement, but they still had a way to go on the original loan. If she were proud, she'd give it back anyway, on principle. But she was also practical. Trains were fine, but there were many places one could not go without a car.

She pulled into the gravel courtyard at Villa Cielo Incantato, her stomach tight, and her heart thumping nervously against her ribs. Guillermo's assistant had told her he'd come down here yesterday to finish up some work. She hadn't seen him for over a week. If she didn't speak with him right away, she would surely lose courage.

She hated fighting with him. Despite their fundamental disagreement about management of the villa's new entities, she didn't want to fight. It felt wrong. And she missed him. She needed to talk to him about the blow up with her parents. No one else would understand.

If only she could feel his comforting arms around her, see the situation with his characteristic *joie de vivre* and sense of the absurd, she knew everything would be alright. But maybe he didn't see himself in that role in her life. But it didn't matter. In any case, she had to go away. She had to find temporary employment so she could resume her thesis, once she found a new advisor at a different university. And he would be left alone to deal with the villa.

She needed to explain about her thesis, and apologize for baling, but also, she wanted to thank him. She would not be embarking on this new adventure if not for him and the work they'd done together, without the courage and self-knowledge his friendship had given her. She imagined he would be pleased that she was taking control of her life. She hoped so.

A fluttering against the azure sky drew her attention as she stepped out of the car, and she squinted up against the glare of the hot summer sun. There was a huge green tarp draped over the side of the portico on the *piano nobile*, hanging partway down the wall to the ground, ropes stretched from its corners this way and that like a tall ship's sails collapsed. Its edge fluttered in the breeze. A long ladder leaned against the side of the building. *What is that about?*

She looked around, expecting to see Martino engaged in some routine maintenance. Painting perhaps. But no one was outside. The front door stood open.

"*Buon giorno!*"

She paused in the doorway, letting her eyes adjust to the dimmer interior light, listening for voices or movement. She heard scraping sounds from the large salon and turned.

Marcella appeared in the doorway. "Clio! *È che voi?*"

"*Ciao, Marcella!*"

Marcella swooped in and embraced her. "*Scuzi, scuzi. IO sono sporco.*"

Behind Marcella, the salon was in chaos. Plaster dust covered everything, and Martino was in the process of sweeping it into piles, stirring up clouds. Marcella released her and stepped back with her hands up. "Ah, I got dust on your clothes." She held rags and a duster in her hands, and several of the paintings, busts and statues were draped with sheets. There was no sign of Guillermo after all.

"What is going on here? *Cosa è successo?*"

"Ay-ay," Marcella moaned and twisted her rag in her hands. "*Un disastro!* A sudden rain two days ago leaked into the roof. And now this!"

"*Oh, mio Dio!* Do the family know?"

"*Si, si.*" Marcella led her across the foyer to the kitchen. "Come. I make for you a *caffe*. I need to rest a bit."

Clio sat at the kitchen table while Marcella washed her hands and made them each a *caffe latte.*

"When did it happen? What is being done?" She lifted the cup to her mouth and sipped the foamy *crema* from the surface.

"Just this morning. Memmo was looking at the roof when–"

"He's here?" She set her *caffe* down on its saucer with a clatter, coffee sloshing over the rim.

Marcella shook her head. "He has gone to Montechiello to find the contractor. He's very worried about the fresco."

Clio's breath hitched. "Is it damaged? I didn't notice."

"It's not too bad yet. Just a corner. Not yet the *figura.*"

"Yet?" Clio's heart kicked. "He thinks more will come down?"

Marcella shrugged, and her dark eyes met Clio's as she crossed herself.

Clio inhaled deeply.

Marcella wrapped both hands around her cup and drank.

"Is Guillermo very upset?"

Marcella nodded. "He wants to prop it up. He needs help. But the contractor did not answer his phone."

"He's coming back?"

"*Si.* He did not take anything, just tore out of the driveway like the hounds of hell pursued him."

Their eyes met. Clio offered a wistful smile. That was Guillermo - always running. Always in motion.

"It will be alright. My Memmo will fix it. He always does."

Warmth enveloped Clio. She was suddenly overwhelmed by a feeling of safety and gratitude, as though she were cocooned in love. Her chest expanded and filled with it. It was a feeling she wanted to hold close to her and keep with her forever. Not being part of its rebirth would be a great loss.

"*Grazie*, Marcella."

"*Per che cosa?*"

"For taking such good care of this beautiful villa for so long. You really love it, don't you?"

"It is my only home." She shrugged with a resigned air. "But yes, it is more than that. They are my family, too."

A moment of silent understanding expanded out into the quiet warm atmosphere of the kitchen, a place so welcoming and secure Clio felt as though she too had grown up and spent her life there in its embrace.

"*Desidero ringraziare voi, anche, cara mia.*"

"Thank me? For what?"

"For bringing my boy back to me. I never saw him before, until you arrived. He was always running– running away. Now he is here all the time, singing, and he has stopped running." Marcella's wrinkled face folded up, and she lifted her apron to cover her face. Her shoulders shook.

Clio reached out and cupped a hand over Marcella's bony shoulder. Her voice came out in a whisper. "He loves you, Marcella. You know that, as much as he loves this place. He's been busy with his career and his life, of course. But he, I think, has felt frustration in the past… and fear."

Marcella nodded. "He loves you too, Clio. As much as you love him." She paused. "Don't look so surprised. You feel it. Even though *he* may not yet be ready to acknowledge it."

Clio's head shook back and forth minutely. She knew it was not true. But did she hope it was true?

Clio cleared her throat. "I have to get going, Marcella. I need to get back to the city." The kitchen felt suddenly hot and stuffy.

"What? You just arrived. You aren't going to wait for Memmo? He'll be back soon."

All the more reason for her to leave immediately.

Clio stood up and carried her coffee cup to the kitchen sink, her spoon clattering noisily to the tile floor before she bent to retrieve it, almost upsetting her cup in the process. She lurched to stabilize it, and set it down clumsily. "Ah, no. I really have to go."

"But what did you come for if not–?"

She paced back to the table and picked up her bag, almost upsetting its contents on the floor, cursing softly under her breath.

She couldn't tell him she was leaving now. He had enough problems. She would write a letter.

"It was nothing important. That was before I learned of the fresco. He has enough to deal with." And she was determined to leave before he returned. She wasn't sure she could face him, and needed time alone to think.

CHAPTER 29

Guillermo raced to Montecchiello, praying the construction workers he knew that were closest were available to quickly stabilize the ceiling. He'd left a message, but tried again, dialing them on his cellular phone as he drove.

He desperately needed to get this situation under control. Although he'd minimized the amount of water that got in, there was no knowing what it had already dislodged, or the extent of the damage that had occurred.

No answer. *Stronzo*!

A sharp pain pinched in his chest, and he tapped his ribs with the edge of his phone, trying to loosen the tension, dislodge the pain. He grimaced. Maybe he was having a heart attack. He wouldn't be surprised if this was it. That's what had killed Papa. His time had finally come.

It would serve him right if his heart gave out and he drove off the road right now. If he'd paid better attention to maintenance of the villa over the past few years, instead of burying his head in the sand, he would have caught this decay before now. Jacopo couldn't be relied upon for this. Guillermo *knew* about these things. This was his business, his profession. Isn't this why he'd studied architecture in the first place? How could he be so negligent? Now the priceless fresco was falling apart and it was too late!

His second attempt to get through resulted in a busy signal. At least someone was there.

"Aargh!" He tucked his phone into the console and switched hands on the steering wheel. He'd be in Montecchiello in another fifteen minutes. It didn't matter.

He worried his brow, tugging and tugging, while he chewed his chapped lips. Catching sight of his reflection in the rear view mirror startled him. His hair was disheveled and streaked with plaster dust. His eyes rimmed with dark smudges from stress and lack of sleep. The wild, frantic look in his eyes terrified him. He was a wreck. What had become of him this summer? He'd gone from being relaxed, well-groomed, successful, totally in control of his life, to this. A madman. A raving lunatic.

All he could do was grip the steering wheel tighter and press on the gas pedal, taking each twist in the road tighter and faster in his effort to get there quickly.

He needed to solve this latest technical problem, but this was just the last in a long series of crises that had piled up, and not even the most challenging one. So many things to take care of. So many people to care for. Guillermo felt the load on his shoulders like the weight of the whole world, crushing him.

Jacopo and his bungled political career, all tangled up with his failing marriage to Valentina. Pia and Paulo with their financial worries, and now Pia counting on the new foundation to kick-start her business and supplement their income. Bianca and her fledgling design practice, so excited to help out and get her start in life. Marcella and Martino, anxious about losing their home of thirty-five years, the only home they'd ever known, in the twilight of their lives. He felt responsible for them all.

Acid burned his throat as the pain in his chest pulsed again. He pulled in deep, ragged breaths, trying to calm himself.

And Nonno, wasting away in that nursing home, his life spent trying to rescue the villa and family from ruin. Expecting that this generation –that he, Guillermo– would carry on the good fight. Nonno, who he loved more than anyone. Nonno who had nurtured and inspired him, guided and taught him, loved him for himself, while Papa molded Jacopo in his own image. And for what? How could they let the estate be lost to the family after so much sacrifice? *I can't. I just can't.*

But now there was the foundation and institute, the plans and applications, the directorship issue, and Clio. Now there was Clio. Clio who needed to break free from her controlling parents and create a life for herself. Brilliant, beautiful, passionate Clio, who would make the best director of a Renaissance art institute. And with whom he'd fallen hopelessly in love.

For all his running away from stress and responsibility his entire adult life, this was the first time that he really felt it. He raked a hand through his hair, his eyes burning, and he blinked and blinked away the tears that welled up. *I don't know if I can do this. I just don't know.*

His phone rang, making him jump. He grabbed it. "*Pronto*!"

"Senior d' Aldobrandin? It's Luca Tomassi, in Montechiello. You left a message."

"*Si, si.* Are you at your office? I'm just around the corner. I need to talk to you right now."

"*Si.* I'll be here."

Guillermo hit 'end', and jumped again when the phone rang in his hand. He assumed it was the contractor calling again. "*Si.* Luca?"

"Uh, no. It's Richie, my man."

Stronzo. What next? Had he somehow found out about the roof failure? How could he? Guillermo forced a smile into his voice. "Richie. How are you doing?" And then there was Richie. He'd forgotten to add Mad Masta Richie to the list of people to whom he owed something. People he had to take care of.

"Can we meet? I need to talk to you." His voice had an edge Guillermo didn't care for.

"I'm-a little busy at the moment-a, Richie. What can I do for you, man?" More stress. This was going to kill him. Wait until Richie found out about the leak and the collapsing ceiling. He wouldn't want the villa at all. It would be the perfect opportunity for him to pull out of the deal and leave them on the brink of bankruptcy.

Which would be fine, if everything with Jacopo and the bank went well. But if it didn't... if it didn't, he'd need a new Plan B. And Richie, like it or not, was still their Plan B.

He steered through the centre of Montecchiello and pulled into the parking area in front of Tomassi Contracting's office. Luca stood in the doorway waiting for him, and he raised a hand in greeting.

"I'm-a just going into a meeting, Richie. Can I call-a you back in a bit?"

"Oh, right. Well, see, Mista D. I won't take much of your time, but listen. We need to wrap up this deal, bro, and fast."

"I know the closing-a date is approaching, and I want to talk-a to you about that-a." Now would be a good time to convince Richie to delay the close. With everything going on, a couple more weeks to sort it all out would be ideal. He could use the design as an excuse to stall him. And then he'd be able to get both options finalized, as well as determine the outcome of Jacopo's plan.

"Yeah, yeah. Can we meet tomorrow? I need to see your final drawings, man. Everybody's on my back. The bank. My agent. My wife. Jesus. The stress is gonna kill me. I gotta be happy with the plans before we sign off. You told me it all would be settled last week."

Guillermo felt a bubble of hysterical laughter pressing on his chest. Richie was feeling stressed? He blew air out through puffed cheeks. "Sure, sure, Richie. I'm-a not in town this weekend-a, and

I've got a few things going on, but I think maybe late next-a week. Let-a me call you once I'm there. Okay?"

"No, sooner, Mista D. Let's talk Monday. I gotta see you this week."

He got out of the car and shook Luca's hand. "*Ciao*."

Before Luca could respond to Guillermo's initial message, he filled him in on the latest development. "We need to stabilize the fresco right now, before any more plaster fails."

Luca shrugged. "I don't have crew here right now, Guillermo. Just my brother, and me. We can grab a few tools and drive out now to see what we can do temporarily. But I can't commit to major repairs right now. I won't have guys free for another week, maybe two."

Guillermo sighed and closed his eyes. *Per favor, Signore. Give me something here. I need a little help.*

"*Bene. Grazie*, Luca. I appreciate whatever you can do today. I'll meet you back there?"

"Si, si."

On his way back to the villa, Guillermo called the large contractor he'd gotten to know on several of his big projects in Firenze. They'd become quite friendly over the years, and Guillermo trusted them. They did quality restoration work, and stayed on schedule and budget, so he made sure they were always short-listed during bids. They often won the contracts. They were expensive, but it was time to call in some favors. He made an appointment to meet with them early in the week to discuss the repairs.

How could all this chaos be happening in one moment in time? If the fear and tension didn't kill him now, it never would.

As he wound up the Cypress lined hillside back toward the villa, and wove between the rough golden limestone buildings of San Quirico d'Orcia, he felt for a moment as though time had stopped. Looking around him, it seemed the same as it had been when he was a boy. Summer heat radiated off of the old buildings, the image shimmering before his eyes. Old women sat on their benches surveying the street. Young people went about their business. Children raced. Laundry on balconies wafted in the summer breeze. Bougainvillea and oleander blossoms quivered against their trellises and fences, the shimmering blonde fields stretching out beyond the edges of town. Strangely, he felt a sweet sense of serenity seep through him like liquid honey, turning him golden warm inside and out.

It was as if the universe were trying to tell him something. Maybe this was the life he was meant to live. Maybe all of Nonno's teaching and love were meant to prepare him for this moment. It seemed to come naturally to him. Who was better qualified to be the steward for the estate, and for the family, than he was, with his profound respect and love of the villa, the land and its history?

Beyond the edges of the village, as he approached the gates of the villa, he glanced up. Soft summer sunlight illuminated the roof from behind, outlining the tower and portico in sharp relief, its outline perfectly proportioned. The image blurred as his eyes filled with tears, and he pulled the car to a stop.

The pale butteryellow limestone walls glowed, with contrasting red geranium blooms flashing at the verges, and tall twisting cypresses silhouetted against the bright cerulean blue of the Tuscan sky. So beautiful. So beautiful. This place where he learned what beauty meant. It was so much a part of him. The architect. The historian. The man.

He loved this villa so much it hurt. He couldn't possibly lose it. It was in his blood. No matter what happened with Jacopo next week. No matter what the bank said. He would find a way to keep it. He had to. A sob convulsed his throat.

Whatever he had to give up, he would. His apartment, his car, his bike. He would sell them all, and take out a mortgage, even if it meant he had to work his entire life to pay it off. What did any of it matter, compared to this, his true home?

THE ART OF ENCHANTMENT

"No, man, no. I mean, we gotta wrap this session, Mista D. I gave you extra time already, bro. Can't give you no mo'." Mad Richie sat across from Guillermo in his office, filling it like a telephone booth, scratching the ears of his smallest dog, Lil Peppa, who sat in his lap, resembling an unfortunate cross between a Pit Bull and a Bichon Frise. "I gotta get back to the States and get back to my own work."

Guillermo forced a generous smile and scraped a nervous hand across his beard. "I understand. If you can-a just wait another few days, I promise I will complete the–"

"I like you, Mista D, I do. We gotta connection, you an' me. But it's the principle of the thang. I see you doing great work here, yeah, and your rep is first rate. But yo can't con Masta Richie." He paused and shook his hand in an unconscious gesture to adjust the position of his Rolex, while Guillermo held his breath, feeling his heart thudding against his ribs. "It's like, you know what? I pickin' up the vibe that yo is hedgin' and there be somethin' goin' on you don't wanna confide. But I ain't nobody's stooge, bro. I gotta move on."

Guillermo fiddled with his fountain pen, scratching random marks on the tracing paper that lay across the drawings on his desk between them. He found it difficult to meet Richie's earnest gaze, staring instead at the first and feeblest of his three designs, knowing it was wrong on so many levels.

Despite the unusual circumstances, he'd never outright lied to a client before. He prided himself that he was an honest professional and maintained healthy trusting relationships with his clients. It was one of the secrets of his success. And Richie was right, the two of them had connected on some level and had enjoyed working together to set out Richie's wants and needs for the villa. He felt like a *pazzo*.

He sat back, crossed his arms over his chest and shook his head hoping he wasn't making a huge, unforgivable mistake. But he was determined to make this work, somehow. And this charade had gone on long enough. He chewed his lip, scowling. He never knew the English he'd learned in the States would be put to use right here at home. He hoped it adequate for the job, as he had a lot of explaining to do.

"You are right. I can't lie to you anymore, Richie. There is something I must tell to you."

Richie leaned forward, and the little dog let out a yelp of discomfort before a big black palm comforted it.

Guillermo pressed his lips together and cleared his throat. "There is really no easy way to tell you this. And…you must understand this had nothing to do with my family. Only me. But I have been leading you on with this design while I try to work out another option to save my family home."

Richie's eyes widened. This was clearly more than he'd anticipated. "Motha-fucka!" He sounded more astonished than angry, but Guillermo could see the mounting outrage glint in Richie's dark eyes as the realization of what he'd learned sunk in.

"The truth is, I don't want to sell it at all. And soon, very soon, I will know whether my plan to convert part of it to a non-profit historical foundation and art academy will be a success. That's why I need more time."

"Foundation?" Richie scowled. "Yo betta explain the whole thang before I do something I gonna regret, Mista D. I'm a reasonable man, but this sound like you trying to fuck wit me, and nobody fuck with Masta Richie."

Guillermo held up a palm. "Hold on. *Per favore*. Give me a chance to explain." Sweat bloomed all over his torso. He swiped a hand over his damp brow and over the back of his neck.

"I'm waitin'."

Guillermo filled Richie in on the plan and how he and Clio had been working hard since they first agreed to the sale of the villa.

He showed him the alternate plans for the research institute, conference facility and hostelry and gave him a brief overview of how it would work. And then, holding his breath, he pulled out the third set of drawings he'd been working on, his stomach rolling and his throat aching with dread.

"Now, before you comment on the fact that I've been doing all of this behind your back I want to show you one more thing."

He smoothed the roll of drawings out, pressing his hands against the desk top, trying to still their trembling. Everything rode on Guillermo's gut feelings, on his judgement of both Richie's character, the tenuous trust they had built, and his professional instinct about the design solution that would truly meet Richie's family's needs and make them all deliriously happy. Richie could cause them a load of trouble if he chose to be offended by Guillermo's gift, or if he just plain hated it. Guillermo steeled himself to expect the worst.

He started by opening the three-dimensional rendering on his laptop computer and wordlessly taking Richie on a flyover of the alternate property that Fitucci had found, followed by a virtual walk-through of the new villa design.

From time to time, he snuck a sidelong glance at Richie's face, gauging his reaction. His expression began with brooding anger and resistance, but Guillermo judged, as his features softened, that he was becoming intrigued.

"The advantages of this alternate scheme are many. Firstly, it's closer to the city airport. Much easier to come and go. Secondly, you don't have to assume the heavy responsibility for items of historic value that are of no particular interest to you, and instead can spend more on the features that are, such as recreational amenities and technology. And thirdly, without the financial burden of maintaining a historic structure, you are able to spend more of your funds on a truly spectacular high-end renovation—potentially award-winning, if I may be so immodest. With the assistance of a talented interior designer to help you with first rate finishes and furnishings, I believe this would be worthy of an Architectural Digest spread. That's good marketing for you, my friend." Guillermo refrained from mentioning the affect all this high-class potential might have on Richie's tremendous ego.

Guillermo at last raised his eyes to meet Richie's, praying that he'd have the vision to see that this was better for him. Meanwhile, Guillermo considered the consequences. He knew this would mean they had no safety net. He knew they didn't have everything they needed to make the foundation work, not yet, and save it from another turn on the auction block. It was a huge gamble. And still he had no choice but to believe everything would be alright. It had to be.

Richie sat very still, frowning at the computer screen, his eyes darting back and forth across the image frozen there. He glanced over the drawings between them, back at the computer, again at the drawings. His big bling-covered hand traced the lines on the paper as his eyes scanned the plans, jumping from room to room, label to label. Richie's signet ring was enormous - it had to be four or five carats - sparkling square-cut diamond embedded in it. For a long moment, Guillermo wondered if he had foolishly squandered Richie's considerable wealth, and the salvation it could have provided his family in exchange for an idealistic fantasy.

Guillermo waited, painfully aware of the passing minutes, listening to the murmur of voices in the studio beyond his closed office door, the quiet hum of machinery. He attempted to swallow, his mouth too dry, and he reached to take a sip of his cold *caffe*.

Richie seemed stunned, confused, dare he think pleased? Richie sat back, his eyes unfocused, and stroked his little dog absentmindedly. Blinking, he sucked his lip between his teeth.

Guillermo drew a breath, filling his too-tight chest, prepared to prompt him, or guide him through the new design, but he needed no assistance.

Richie released a long sigh, almost as though he had stolen the breath from Guillermo's lungs. "My man. My man. I am struggling to understand one thang."

Guillermo leaned forward, watching Richie's face for clues.

"Why?" Richie finally said. "That's what I want to know. Why did you do this?"

Guillermo sat back. He'd explained about the villa, the foundation, hadn't he? "My family home, it is very important to me. I thought–"

"No, no. I mean why this one? You didn't have to do this."

Guillermo glanced down at the drawings for the alternate villa. "But... of course I did. We had an understanding. My actions stole from you and your family, Richie. I could not live with myself if I did not compensate you in some way. If you are displeased–"

"This is mo than compensation, Mista D. This be a mastapiece of design."

Guillermo thought about that. Without surrendering his humility, he did understand what Richie meant.

"Perhaps I can explain this way." He cleared his throat. "Every project I undertake, comes with some fixed elements, *si*? A place, a user, a program of use, and usually a budget." He waved his hand. "Other minor things, technical and legal, for example. Less important." He searched for a way to explain. "For me to design the *perfetto* solution, these elements must come together in a way that is–ah..." Clicking his tongue, he struggled to find the words to describe his process. "Villa Cielo Incantato was not the right property for you, Richie. And I was not unbiased. So, therefore, I was unable to locate or *incanalato*...channel the... uh, the correct answers. You see?"

"I have only one word for you, Mista D."

Guillermo drew a breath, held it, listening to his heart beating in a slow cadence against his ribs.

"Genius, bro."

Guillermo released his breath, the tension draining from his neck and shoulders.

"If I understand what I'm seein' here, I love it. I dig it. I gotta take this back to my foxy lady and give her a chance to see it. Tha's only fair. An' we gotta talk and think it ova. But I have a good vibe about dis." He nodded. "Yeah, I do."

"Would you like to see the property?" Guillermo rolled up the drawings and slipped them into a small plastic tube.

"Hell, yeah. I'm gonna call up Fitucci right now. You gonna come?" Richie grabbed his little dog around the middle like a dumbbell and stood up. Guillermo handed him the tube of drawings.

Guillermo hesitated. He wanted to go, but there were just too many pressures on his time. Too much to do. Richie read his expression. "Don't worry about it. We're cool, bro. I'll call you soon."

Guillermo nodded and stood up.

Richie hesitated and then took a step forward, wrapping his free arm around Guillermo's shoulders, slapping him heavily on the back. He pulled back, his face somber. Then he broke into a radiant grin and planted a loud kiss on each of Guillermo's cheeks.

"An' I'm gonna pay you fo dis extra design work, don't you worry. I'll pay you for yo time to complete it and execute it."

Guillermo was deeply moved. On his first attempt to speak, the words stuck in his throat, burning. He cleared his throat. Nevertheless, his words came out rough and scratchy.

"No. I cannot allow you to do that, Richie. This is a thing I must do, for myself as much as for you. I feel much guilt for double-crossing you. I must-a do this. You don't owe me anything, *caro mio*."

Richie peered speculatively at him, his head bobbing slightly in a pensive manner. Then he turned and left, Lil Peppa tucked under one arm.

Guillermo couldn't feel his fingers or toes. A light, weightless feeling filled him, stealing the oxygen from his lungs, replacing it with helium. He might be deliriously happy, or he might be frozen with fear. Or perhaps a bit of both. He was so happy to be free of lies, but now, he was walking a tightrope without a safety net. And it was a long way down.

CHAPTER 30

Guillermo was back at Villa Cielo Incantato, finding himself drawn here. Too much was at stake. If only he were empowered to do more to guarantee the villa's safety. Though for now he could do nothing but worry.

Worry himself into wakefulness, despite his exhaustion. He paced the empty, echoing halls after Marcella and Martino retired for the night. Attempts to relax and distract himself with books offered no cure for his insomnia. *I need to get some sleep.*

A glass of warm milk might help.

Pulling his robe more snuggly around him to ward off the chill of the night, he shuffled downstairs in search of his sedative.

The pressure to save the villa and the family weighed heavily on him. He pressed the heel of a hand on his sternum, feeling the hard, hollow place that had plagued him and killed his appetite earlier in the evening, despite Marcella's delicious cooking.

Parliament assembled in two days. The bank remained unsatisfied with their financial *pro forma,* as they were still a hundred and thirty-five thousand Euros short of a balanced bottom line. Andreas Fitucci had called to say that Richie was in love with the new property. Fitucci had voided the original sales agreement and drafted a new one, despite his skepticism. The d'Aldobrandin's and Villa Cielo Incantato were free again. In a manner of speaking. If this scheme failed, the estate's bankruptcy would be on his head.

He went to the fridge, got out the milk and rummaged for a small saucepan to warm it.

"You cannot sleep?"

He jerked and spun, dropping the pot with a clatter. "Agh! Oh, Marcella."

"Shush. I startled you. Here, let me." She retrieved the pot and took the milk from his hand.

He sighed and perched on a stool, watching while she lit the stove and nursed the milk to the right temperature, then poured it into a mug.

"What's eating at you?" Marcella said as she handed it to him.

He shrugged. "I feel so powerless."

"You've done everything you can."

"Have I? Clio had the vision. I only helped her," he said, despondent. He blew on the warm milk and took a sip.

"She has a special spirit, that girl. A real passion."

"She does. I could not, would not, have done any of it without her. It's difficult to imagine a positive outcome without her inspiration and determination." He missed her enthusiasm, her support, her devotion. Even the prospect of victory paled without her to share it. The ache in his chest expanded.

Marcella peered at him. "You miss her."

"Mmm. I believed anything was possible when she was with me. Now, I'm not so confident." The ominous knowledge of Richie's withdrawal, the bank's demands, and Guillermo's reluctant reliance on the faint-hearted Jacopo, pressed in on him.

Strangely, this was a gift he wished he could give Clio, even more than his family. He longed to bask in the warmth of her approval. *Senza di te non sono niente.* Nothing.

How he wanted her back in his arms.

Clio. Senza di te non posso più vivere. How would he live without her? His eyes burned hot.

"Drink your milk, Memmo." Marcella stroked his arm. "She reminds me of Gemma."

"Mama? No."

"*Si*. When she first came here. She awoke in your papa the same passion. Your Nonno really liked her, too. He told me, she was just what this place needed. Clio is the same."

Maybe. Though he saw Mama as a bright, flighty butterfly, and Clio a little more like a caged colourful bird. If she were free, she would take flight, and shine. Perhaps she needed the villa as much as it needed her.

"Finish. Come," Marcella said and led the way out of the kitchen. He did as he was told and clicked off the light as he followed.

She stood in the hall, her arms across her middle, gazing at the portrait of Mama that hung on the stair landing above them.

He filled his lungs and released a deep sigh. Mama's portrait always gave him comfort and a powerful sense of belonging. Where would it hang if the villa were sold? Nothing would feel right again. In this portrait, made from a favourite photograph taken on their twenty-fifth wedding anniversary, she wore a beautiful ivory gown that complimented her lovely dark colouring. She was descending this very stair with a broad smile on her face, always elegant and gay. "Remember the sound of her laugh," he said now.

Marcella nodded. "She was such a solace to your serious papa."

And Papa, always working and worrying over finances, over management of the estate, seemed to be perpetually at his desk working. He seldom had time for Guillermo or the girls, drawing Jacopo aside for sober lectures. Only Mama could draw him out. An image flashed in his mind.

"Do you remember that other photo? The one of them together that night?"

"*Si, si.* It's in the red album. In the library."

"Go back to bed, *cara. Grazie* for the milk."

"Try to sleep, *carino.*" She stroked his arm and shuffled off toward her rooms.

He went in search of the album, determined to confirm an impression he had of his father that night. The way he looked at Mama, standing in the doorway of the study, looking up at her, admiration, chagrin and love in his eyes. Tonight, their absence affected him profoundly.

He stood in the doorway of the study, looking into the shadowy room. The memory of his father's hunched shoulders bent over papers on the large mahogany desk was burned into his mind. But again the image of his father's face uplifted, love shining in his eyes as he gazed at Mama, pushed itself forward. *Where is that photo album?*

In the library, he flicked on a desk lamp and searched the shelves until he found the red, leather-bound album Marcella had mentioned. He took it to the study and opened it on Father's desk, sitting and flipping the pages until he found the picture. *There. Just as he remembered.*

A folded sheet of paper fell out. He lifted it and opened it to see Father's familiar slanted handwriting.

Mia cara, mia innamorata.

Grazie per tutto quello che mi hai dato in questi ultimi venticinque anni. Mia vita non avrebbe alcun significato, nessuna gioia senza di te.

Sei tutto per me. Sei il grande amore della mia vita. Con te voglio invecchiare.

Tuo Gabriel

It was his love note to Mama on the evening of their anniversary. Guillermo caressed the parchment. He had said very similar things to Clio. Strangely, he never thought of his father as the type of man to express such romantic words, but here was the proof.

He realized that for Papa, it was all worth it. He may have been a quiet, dutiful man, uncomfortable with expressions of emotion or affection, but his heart was large and loving. And his love for Mama was so great that he did not mind at all the heavy load he bore.

Guillermo had always admired Nonno more. He was a man of energy and decisiveness, easily relatable for a lively, fiery boy, though ultimately no more successful at saving the family fortunes. On the surface there was more for him to respect and emulate. But now his chest swelled with pride in for his strong and quiet father. He no longer pitied him. What gave him his quiet strength was the love he shared with Mama.

Their love had sustained the family, and held everything together despite the challenges. It had given purpose and poignancy to their lives. Of course he knew nothing of that as a boy. But he knew what love looked like, and he felt a corresponding ache in his heart.

He closed the album, stroking its soft smooth cover.

Everything became clear. He could do anything, carry any burden, climb any mountain, if he could share his life and a love so deep, with a woman like that. If only he could have Clio by his side.

Mio Dio!

From the moment he'd met her, the evening of her crash, she'd stolen his heart. Unlike her namesake, Clio became so animated when she spoke of the arts, she was the antithesis of dull. She was an enigma. So brimming with passion, and so tightly buckled down. So afraid of her essential self, and yet it was that very essence that fired his blood. So bold, beautiful, intelligent. From their first kiss on the portico, when he and Clio had shared a tentative touch, the spark of passion awoke for each other.

The night of Clio's erotic dance of passion as she fell apart in his arms in the *Stanza Aqua*, he realized what an amazing, passionate woman she was.

No wonder he could not resist her.

He could still see the look in her wide, beautiful turquoise eyes. She wanted him, too. To save her, but also to surrender to her.

Fully. His heart hammered violently. That night he stood at a turning point and knew that a kind of annihilation awaited him just around the corner.

"Ah, Clio, *Bella*" he whispered to the night air. I am dying without you.

It frustrated him now, as it had then. What did she fear? What did she need? And how could he give it to her? Her essential makeup was defined by her family's notion of worth. She could never allow herself to just be. She had to accomplish something. Create something.

Whatever it was that made her so, he got it. Felt it in his gut. If he were truthful, although the circumstances of their upbringing were very different, they had that in common. His essential nature would be crushed by the need to conform to his family's expectations of what he should be. How he should be. Destroyed by it.

Except that he had spent his life rebelling. Rejecting all that they asked of him in order to hold on to his essential self. Whereas she… she had surrendered herself to please her family. Ironic. It sounded so simple now that he'd thought it through. But what was the answer?

He was compelled to get close to her. They were like mirrors to each other. They were both drawn and repelled by what they saw. Opportunity and risk. He wanted to help her, to heal her, but also to feed from the fiery core of her vibrancy and power.

She'd given herself to him eventually, and what a gift. So sensual, so passionate, as he knew she would be. But there still remained something of that restraint in her. As though she felt there would be some dire consequence of total surrender.

He stood and went into the library, where they had worked side by side for long hours, a dedicated team with a common purpose. His gaze fell on the polished wood tables, the book-lined shelves, and on the worn carpet at his feet. He remembered his surprise at Clio's playful seduction, her sudden transformation to a willing wanton woman. This was where they had first, at last, become lovers, right there on the floor. His body tightened with remembered desire, and his heart hammered rapidly as his blood responded to the sensations.

He was truly, deeply, madly in love with Clio. *But, how can I keep her without her respect and admiration?* He had shied away from accepting his responsibilities, but he couldn't do that anymore. It was his destiny. And he would do anything to keep Clio. Anything!

All of a sudden, he knew what to do. In order to win her respect, he must earn it, and for this he must respect himself. Even if it killed him. But then he remembered something she'd said. Something like, he was more alive when he was accepting challenges? It was clear, he was no more likely to die young running the villa than racing fast in his car. If he were meant to burn bright and die young, then so be it. He had been running away from his true self. If only he could convince her to stay with him, to be by his side, he could do all that he needed to do, and die a happy man.

He returned to his desk and opened his briefcase, withdrawing the folder of papers and forms Clio had left with him weeks before. He leafed through the pile until he found the form outlining the position of director of the foundation, which she'd already, bless her, filled in with his name and particulars. He picked up his pen, poised it over the signature line, then set down his name in ink.

CHAPTER 31

Clio hadn't left her apartment in several days, ever since she'd packed up all her belongings from her office at the university under Jonathan's dumbfounded stare.

"You've got to be bloody joking," was all he said.

She was running out of things to eat, but couldn't bear the thought of going out for something as mundane as shopping. Cash was short anyway, and rent would come due shortly. Determined to finish writing her thesis in the shortest time possible, nothing was going to get in her way, not even hunger.

Instead, she made pot after pot of *caffe*, nibbling on whatever scraps she found in her cupboards, rolled up her sleeves, and hunkered down to work. Completing her thesis, and finding someone who would sponsor her defense at a new university was her only hope.

At first Clio thought she could find some interim teaching position, or some other job to tide her over. But after browsing online, it was clear her best chances of employment depended on getting her degree. She was so close. If she could conquer it and write the thing to her own satisfaction, she could shop it around. There were people she knew at Perugia, Abruzzo or even Roma University who would gladly accept her and allow her to defend. It was good quality, original research anyone would be happy to have.

She worked around the clock, stopping only for a shower once a day. The harder she worked, the more she immersed herself in the material, the more sense it began to make. Little flashes of insight she'd had over the years, as she was collecting data, came back to her when she reviewed her photos, sketches and notes. Yet she was still missing something. A spark. When she reread her words, they were wooden and uninspired.

But time was short. She had to persevere.

With an aching back, a pinched neck, and eyes filled with sand, she sat at her computer hour after hour, through day and night. When her vision became bleary, she would get up and pace, make more coffee, splash cold water on her face. She didn't dare take a break, and she couldn't sleep. Through profound fatigue, her mind buzzed with worry and analysis. If she stopped, she'd lose momentum, and the critical thinking she had done would lose its shape and slip away. Then she'd have to begin again.

No. It was far better to keep going.

There was no one to see or care that she had fallen into a frenzy of work. Certainly her parents and Dr. Jovi would not be calling. They might never speak to her again. Even Jonathan, with whom she'd shared an office for three years, hadn't called to find out what she was doing, or if she was alright. No, no one.

There was no point in feeling sorry for herself. Everyone had their own agenda. Everyone was doing what they needed for themselves, and so must she. Even though terribly alone, unable to clearly see her future, she needed to take care of herself and begin to build an independent life of her own. She was finished tying herself in knots avoiding the displeasure of her parents, and trying to buy their love by jumping through hoops. Why did she need to please her parents and comply with their wishes at all? *I'm an adult. This is my life.* How had she become so malleable, so unwilling to assert her own will?

A huge yawn stretched her jaw, sending a shudder through her body. She rose from her desk and drifted to the window, gazing out onto the quiet night street. She knew the answer well enough.

Though she'd begun life feeling loved and valued by her parents, she believed there was something wrong with her. As she grew up, it became increasingly obvious that they were narcissistic and self-centered people. They were so absorbed in their own academic careers, their heads buried in the clouds, she wondered if they ever meant to have children, or thought about what that might require.

She shivered violently and pulled a blanket off of the back of her sofa, wrapping it over her shoulders like a shawl.

In any case, once she'd become a teenager, it was clear that her presence was more of an inconvenience than a pleasure. Mother was simply absent, both physically and emotionally, most of the time. Father, she supposed, did his best, forcing her into the mold he thought would be best, or at least something he could control. But he was inflexible, and he didn't seem to understand that she was a person with her own likes, potential and needs. There never was any room to expand into her own skin. The only time she had dared to explore, and found a group of carefree friends that summer in Greece, learned about both her own desires and discovered the possibility of love, well he'd shut her down and humiliated her. Rendering her that much easier to control. So effectively, she'd never recovered from it.

Not until Guillermo...

Another deep sigh escaped from her heavy, tight chest. Despite herself, Guillermo had broken through the barriers of her self-defense. From that first night, she'd not been the same. It wasn't only that he reminded her of Hektor, with his dark beauty and wild abandon. That alone was enough to unlock her desire. That was only the beginning. But also the way he looked at her. As though she were the most amazing, beautiful, sexy thing he'd ever seen. His admiration and desire elevated her.

"*Nei tuoi occhi c'è il cielo, cara.*"

She shivered at the memory of his words.

Guillermo had sensed the qualities in her that she had hidden because they were not acceptable to Father. Her natural energy and curiosity, her dreaminess and creativity, and her sensuality. Goosebumps rose on her skin, remembering how Guillermo's eyes, and his touch, and his murmurings of admiration, had awakened her. Unlocked her passion."*Ecciti i mei sensi, Bella.*"

He made her feel alive.

She touched her fingertips to her lips, gently stroking, remembering his kisses, and the divine molten state of her blood racing, her skin tingling, under his attentions. She blinked, loosening the tears that clung to her lashes.

The room swooped dangerously around her, darkening at the edges of her vision, her head as light as though full of spun glass. She closed her eyes, trying to steady her escalating heartbeat, and slow her rapid breathing.

"Guillermo."

Her heart leapt with a jolt of joy just saying his name. His absence haunted her like a fever, her breath catching in her throat, her head hot and her body chilled.

"*Bella.*" She heard his voice, soft and seductive, like a caress, and gave into the flood of memories that swamped her like a drug.

"*Ti desidero, Bella, Bella, Clio.*"

"Guillermo."

She laughed softly. As romances go, it was almost backwards. From his first approaches, tinged with arrogance and a bold, bright masculinity, and then more tentative, patient, watchful, and finally soft, vulnerable, childlike in his innocence and sincerity. His passion always there, but so much more tender and precious when tempered by his genuine emotions.

"*Bella, cara. Il mio cuore è solo tua. Ti voglio, ti voglio.*"

He had awoken her sleeping body, one caress and kiss at at time, stirring her blood and flaming her desire. By the time they had made love, she could no longer hold back, not just her need for the heat and power of his body, but her hunger to be closer to him, to mingle her breath and her heartbeat with his, to possess and be possessed by him.

She had felt truly loved and treasured.

She thought he felt the same way.

"Clio?"

She turned, confused. "Guillermo?"

He stood across the room, smiling, his eyes shining. Warmth flooded her body, driving her heart rate up, drumming in her chest. She was suddenly wide awake and energized. Hot tears inscribed a path across her tight skin. Guillermo! *Caro*.

She couldn't believe it. He was here! His image blurred until there were two of him, and she squeezed her eyes tight, opening them again, trying to focus. But he was gone.

Guillermo?

Her pulse thrummed.

He *wasn't* here. She shook her head, trying to clear it. The roiling in her stomach suddenly felt more like nausea. A cold sweat broke out all over her body. Her throat and stomach convulsed. If she eaten anything at all, she would have thrown it up.

Her knees wobbled, and she lurched, clutching at the back of the sofa to steady herself. "Perhaps I will rest just a little." Then the floor sprung up to meet her and blackness filled her vision like a falling curtain.

She came to gradually, and lay awhile with her cheek pressed to the cool floor, unsure where she was or why. Then all at once, like an epiphany, she knew. Of course. *This is what's been missing from my thesis.* This sense of possession and surrender. This feeling, this feeling that Guillermo and she had shared, was the closest thing to God that a man or woman could know with certainty.

All the questioning and theorizing about creation and meaning in their lives didn't matter. *We are ultimately limited by our earthly experiences.*

A conversation came back to her. The day Guillermo had come and dragged her, in his turmoil, to the Laurentian Library. It was almost as though he'd needed to find a church, a place of worship, and a confessor. He had his God, and yet he chose to commune with that God through the language of art, creativity and nature, and ultimately through the sensations of his body.

Extreme speed, beauty, pleasure, whether intellectualized as gifts of creation or not, were still experienced on a different plane from their pedestrian lives. Clio knew why Guillermo had been brought into her life. This was his gift to her, this insight, this clarity.

Ecstasy finally made sense. Not as something base or shameful or even primitive, as her parents made her believe, but as the ultimate expression of oneness in being. And just like they'd spoken that day of different ways of experiencing bliss, the art she'd been studying was a natural extension and form of expression of something universal, divine and cosmic.

She had intuited an abstract idea, but it took hedonistic, dangerous, mercurial, passionate Guillermo to show her the truth of it. To share it with her and make her feel it in her skin and bones, her blood, and her heart.

She pulled herself up, squeezed her eyes to clear and focus them, and stumbled back to her desk. Dropping into her chair, she began to type. And type. And type.

She wrote and edited like a madwoman, without stopping, for untold hours. She did not stop. And could not stop, until it was done.

At last she stopped typing. For a long moment, she stayed frozen in that position, staring at the last line of her conclusion. Her hands cramped in claws over the keys, her neck stiff and aching with tension from the long, unbroken hours. Her eyes fell closed, heavy as lead.

Then she opened them as the first rays of morning sun reached in to illuminate her room, its fingers of warmth touching her face.

She straightened her back, cracking and creaking, and stretched her shoulders, feeling fatigue in every cell of her body. She was utterly empty.

Pushing out of her chair, she went to the window and watched bright golden rays of lights cut through thin gaps between buildings, flaring off of windows in dazzling radiant sparks, and slicing the dawn into shreds of dark and golden light.

"Now what?"

Before she collapsed, she had to do something. She rubbed her temples, thinking. She didn't have the patience to start the process of calling various colleagues. The notion made her furiously angry and frustrated.

She turned back to her desk, flipped on the printer, and sat down to send the document to print. That alone would take a half hour.

Clio paced into her kitchen, banging open bare cupboards, searching fruitlessly in the empty fridge. She reached for the coffee pot, and noticed her hands were shaking violently. More coffee was a terrible idea. She grabbed a glass and ran the tap, filling and drinking glass after glass of water, until her shrunken stomach felt bloated.

She slammed the glass down on the counter and returned to the printer, sighing that it should take so long, now that she was finally done. She sat on the arm of the sofa, hypnotized by the pages jerkily emerging from the printer one by one. Come on, come on!

"What to do? What to do? What to do?" she chanted in time with the printer cartridge's path back and forth across the pages.

By the time the last page slid out into the tray, she knew. She bundled her hundreds of pages together, thumping them on the table into a neat block, and found a large envelope to shove them into.

Then she threw on a sweat shirt, grabbed her cell phone and bag, and raced across the city to Dr Jovi's house. She would submit it first to her old advisor for approval. He might reject her right to defend, but it wouldn't be because she'd abandoned it. Or that it wasn't worthy.

∼

T*Hump! THump! THump!*
Clio paused, her fist in the air, listening to shuffling bumps and shouts and murmurings through Dr. Jovi's door.

"*Bene. Cosa diavolo?* I'm coming. *Chi l'inferno? IO vengo!*"

The door swung open.

Dr. Jovi stood across from her in a blue satin bathrobe, the thin grey hair at his temples sticking out like antennae, trying to adjust his glasses on his reddened face. He was puffing. She'd never seen a scowl so dark.

"Clio? *Mio Dio. Che cosa stai facendo qui?*"

"Dr. Jovi. Thank God you're here. I brought my thesis. It's done. It's finally done!" She pushed past him, entering his sitting room. "I'm so sorry for everything. But you have to give me another chance, you have to read it. I finally got it. I got it! *Per favor.*"

She yanked the envelope out of her bag and shoved it into his hands. He stood with his mouth open, and his brows pulled together like he'd seen a ghost. Then his face fell, and he shook his head sadly, his watery eyes filled with pity.

"*Per favor*, Dr. Jovi, *per favor.*" Clio mumbled, and collapsed onto his sofa. "Just read it. Please read it."

"*Caspita, bambina. Straordinario.* What have you done?"

Despite her exhaustion, she bounced, excited to see his reaction. "You won't be sorry."

"I couldn't possibly do it today. I already have committments."

"Not later. Now! Please read it right now," she begged.

"*Ora? Incredibile.* How can I deny you?" He went to his kitchen, and soon the aroma of fresh *caffe* and something sweet teased her nose.

She fought burning, scratchy eyes, but she mustn't sleep. She had to know how he reacted.

He returned a few minutes later with a tray of coffee and pastries, and she dived on them, filling her mouth. Heaven.

"*Dio*," Jovi muttered, and settled in across from her with a cup of coffee, her stack of pages in his lap, and adjusted his reading glasses on his nose.

When she'd had her fill of pastry and cheese, and a second cup of coffee, she sighed and leaned forward to watch his face as he read. His expression hardly changed, except from time to time, a slight lift of his eyebrow, a small nod of his head. It was excruciating. He read a page, set it aside, read another, and she watched for any clue as to his opinion.

"Do you have any questions?" she asked. "Can I expl–"

"Shh."

The minutes ticked past, and her eyes grew heavier.

She lay a moment, trying to remember where she was. All of sudden, she recalled what she was trying to do, and shot upright.

"Dr. Jovi?"

"*Si, si*. Relax. I'm right here."

Where was here? She recognized his living room, his house. What? She frowned.

"Don't you remember paying me an unexpected visit at five o'clock this morning?"

She remained silent, piecing together her last hours at her apartment. Slowly, she nodded, her gut clenching in trepidation. Was he furious?

"Have some fresh *caffe*, some more breakfast. You look like hell, Clio." He waved a hand at the low table between them. Her stomach growled.

She smoothed her wild hair back. *I must be a wreck.* Tentatively, she reached forward and poured a cup of coffee, added some hot milk from a silver pitcher. Her hands were steady but weak, and it was an effort lifting the cup to her lips. But the hot liquid passing her lips, her tongue, her parched throat, were delicious and immediately revived her, zinging through her veins. The coffee she drank earlier hadn't been enough to stave off her exhaustion.

Then, suddenly, she was ravenous again. She took a small plate and loaded it up with bread, cheese, and fruit. Her heart squeezed. He'd done all this for her? The food flew into her mouth as quickly as she could lift it, chew it and swallow, and she reached for more.

Dr. Jovi sat across from her, sipping his *caffe*, shaking his head with a puzzled expression.

At last, sated, she sat back and lifted her gaze to meet his.

Well? Was this a sympathy meal?

Slowly, very slowly, his old wrinkled face cracked and stretched into a smile. Coy at first, but as she realized what it meant, and her own face showed her shock, her joy, his smile grew into a wide grin full of crooked yellow teeth.

"Really?" She sat back, rubbing her eyes, which were crusty with sleep.

"I knew you could do it, Clio. It's excellent. I'm very proud of you."

"I can't believe it. I can't believe it," she gasped.

Clio's moment of shock and delirious happiness was interrupted by the muffled ringing of her phone. She blinked, then looked around for her bag. It was there on the floor beside the sofa. She grabbed it and rummaged, pulling out the phone, and pushed the button on the fourth ring.

"*Si?*"

"Clio! There you are. I've been calling for days! Where have you been?"

"Pia?" She'd been calling? *Why didn't I hear–?*

"*Si*, it's me. Listen what are you doing tomorrow night?"

Clio shook her head. Tomorrow? "Uhh...?"

"Never mind. Cancel it. You have to join us for dinner tomorrow. We're... well we're not exactly celebrating, but we might be. Can you come?"

Clio's brain was too foggy to figure out what Pia was talking about. "I uh... I don't know. I–"

"You have to be here, *cara*. Say you'll come."

"Oh-uh-o-kay. I guess."

"*Bene*. It's Jacopo. He speaks in the house at seven tomorrow night. Come at six for drinks." Clio heard a click, and Pia was gone.

Jacopo in the house? Parliament? What the hell was Guillermo up to now? She brought her fingertips to her brow and rubbed, scowling. A sudden hollow ache pulled at her chest, weighing her down, as though she had left something immeasurably precious behind, or lost her way. Why did she feel such an intense longing? *I'm sure they're all handling it well. I'm sure Guillermo has the whole thing well in hand.* They didn't need her help anymore. It's only that she'd been so involved, so intensely, for so long.

"Clio?"

She looked up, jerked back to reality.

"So." Dr. Jovi cleared his throat. "I checked the schedule..."

Her voice broke on her reply. "Y-es?"

"When can you defend?"

"Tomorrow?" Really, now that it was written, she only wanted to get it over with. To be free.

He chuckled. "How about in a couple of weeks. Is that soon enough?"

She felt her chest fill with air and light, like champagne bubbles, lifting her up. She wanted to laugh hysterically. "That would be just fine. *Grazie*, Dr. Jovi."

She leaned toward the old man and kissed his cheeks, one after the other, embracing him. She was right to trust him. He'd come through for her in the end.

Her eyes burned and filled with tears. She had done it, she had really done it.

And then Clio realized that her thesis meant nothing except as a means to an end. A ticket to forge a new life for herself. Of course she was happy it was done, proud of herself. Her pulse kicked up, and her gaze turned inward. With sudden clarity, she knew she wanted her Ph.D. so she could apply for the Villa Cielo Incantato directorship position with Cornell more than anything. There wasn't another job in the world she'd rather have, if it were still there to be had. It seemed tomorrow night would decide it.

While she loved her thesis topic, teaching at a Renaissance research institute was exactly the kind of work and life she would love, even if it were not as prestigious as a tenure track position at Princeton or some other stuffy Ivy League University. And she also realized two other things: she wanted to remain in Italy. She loved it and it was her true home. And she couldn't imagine being happy without Guillermo.

She loved him. She felt a stronger sense of connection and belonging with him and his family than she had ever felt with her own.

She would stay at the institute and help Guillermo, even if he wouldn't ask her for himself. She knew she loved him. But she also wanted to live her own life, away from the influence of her parents. What they valued was not what she cared about. She knew what would make her happy. And there was no shame in knowing your own heart, and acting on it.

CHAPTER 32

Clio arrived at Pia and Paulo's place the following night at six. Intense memories of the first night she met Guillermo after her car crash flooded back. Each step, each sight, each sound reminded her of Guillermo. The thought of seeing him again tied her stomach in knots.

"*Buona sera*, Clio." Paulo, wearing a kind and friendly smile, flanked by his excitable dogs, answered the door, and she was immediately swallowed up in the warmth and affection of their home, and surrounded by delicious smells of cooking food, and a buzz of sociable sounds.

Clio and Paulo exchanged polite kisses, and she took his hands. He was such a lovely, quiet man. So different from the bold and demonstrative d'Aldobrandins. A charming counterpoint.

Entering the green salon, she searched for the sight of Guillermo's familiar face and form. *He's not here.* If he'd been there, she would have sensed him.

She exhaled, slowly and controlled. It would be easier this way. He must be in the city, coaching Jacopo or something. Or perhaps celebrating with a friend. Some new woman.

She found Pia and Bibi sitting with drinks, chatting excitedly with another woman she didn't know, with her dark hair pulled tightly back. "Clio, *cara*! You came." They both squealed with delight and rose to kiss and embrace her. She hadn't seen either of them since the last day she'd seen Guillermo. They must know what had happened but felt only their warm welcome.

They introduced her to the woman, who it turned out was Valentina, Jacopo's wife. She had a thin face, and seemed withdrawn, and aloof. They shook hands politely but her dark eyes slid past, maintaining a wall of detachment between them.

Pia explained what they were waiting for, what Jacopo was attempting to do. They had reason to be excited and nervous. All their work would be lost, and their home too, if he did not succeed in pulling a rabbit out of a hat tonight. Valentina appeared tense. But Clio's future hung in the balance too. Her newfound thesis success would be irrelevant and useless to her if Jacopo failed. She would be cut loose, and have to begin again.

Paulo brought a glass of his red wine and set it beside her, and she slid down into a corner chair, straightening the folds of her skirt, wrapping her arms around her middle. It was different now. She was neither a co-conspirator, madly engrossed in a passionate project, nor was she a pseudo-family member, involved romantically with their brother. Really she hardly knew any of them. Without Guillermo, she didn't belong.

She shouldn't have come. What was she thinking? Why did they even invite her?

∼

Guillermo pulled into Pia's driveway in his Alpha Romeo and crunched to a stop on the gravel. He was late, but he was so tense, he couldn't imagine sitting around sipping wine and chatting while waiting for the Parliamentary broadcast to begin. This was their final chance for heritage designation. The villa's salvation rested on Jacopo's success or failure tonight.

Come on Lapo, Guillermo prayed. *We're depending on you now.*

He let himself in, and immediately greeted and calmed the barking dogs. Paulo met him in the archway of the green salon, and they kissed and shook hands, their eyes meeting with a knowing look. "*Fratello.*" Paulo knew what this meant to Guillermo, perhaps more than anyone. He understood what is was to hold onto your family's estate and heritage by a thread, and be willing to risk everything to restore it.

Guillermo stepped through the archway into the salon, rolling his shoulders. He clenched his fists, trying to control the familiar tingle that signaled an urge to move and let off steam.

Then he saw Clio. He swallowed, his throat suddenly dry and tight. Pia didn't tell him she'd be here. He forced himself to smile at his sisters and Valentina to avoid staring at her like a *pazzo*, and embarrassing them both. But her image stayed with him. She wore her hair down, tamed into a silky, curling mane of fire. For him? His pulse leapt. Her magical turquoise eyes were wide and scared, as though she were shocked to see him too, and perhaps alarmed.

He approached his three sisters, kissing each one in turn. Then, finally, he turned to greet her. The evening just took on even more significance.

"Clio," he said.

She stood up jerkily, her eyes cast down, smoothing her skirt. "H-hello Guillermo."

He reached for her hand, taking it in his. It was papery dry and smooth and cool. He squeezed her hand, smiling, and searched her face. *Come on, Bella. Look at me.* He kept his gaze on her face as he kissed her hand. At last she looked up, and their eyes met, fraught with emotion. Leaning toward her slowly, he pressed his lips to her silken cheek, once, twice, three times, closing his eyes and inhaling her divine floral scent. His heart skipped and raced, and her breathing accelerated too, her delicious breasts rising and falling rapidly like a frightened bird.

It took everything he had to step back and release her hand, instead of grabbing and devouring her the way every cell in his body screamed at him to do.

"It's time," Paulo announced. "Everyone come into the den. I have my large computer screen set up and tuned in to the *Camera dei deputati* Web TV. They are starting now." He led the way. "Please find a seat." The room was small, and the makeshift assortment of chairs were squeezed closely together. Guillermo hung back, waiting for Clio, so he could find a chair next to her. But she was so tentative, moving so slowly. He went to get a drink before rejoining them, and found her sitting next to Bibi near the back of the room, but the chair on her other side was free. He stalled a moment by Paulo, who fiddled with his computer, adjusting the volume, deflecting attention from his entrance.

"There shouldn't be much lag," Paulo said.

Guillermo dimmed the lights, and slid into the chair beside Clio, his pulse racing.

Clio fidgeted, smoothing her hair, but keeping her eyes averted, facing forward. It was as though ions leapt from one skin surface to the other in a wild reunion, crashing and casting sparks in the air between them, her nearness was that tangible.

Conversations continued, murmured and hushed, while the Speaker opened the session, and outlined the agenda. Guillermo gripping one fist in the other, squeezing tightly, and prayed. *Coraggio, Lapo. Per favor, Lapo. You can do it, fratello.* Jacopo had to find his moment. He had to use the normal way of things to take the stage and hold it. There was no knowing when or how it might happen.

Guillermo could hardly breathe. The odds were against them. Jacopo's speech would be unconventional, even unprecedented. Filibustering was unheard of these days. It might even be received with hostility or ridicule. Anything was possible.

∼

THE ART OF ENCHANTMENT

The session marched on, one mundane topic after another. Minor bills being passed. Various MPs ranting about their favorite causes and pet peeves. They all listened in silence. It was difficult to concentrate with Guillermo sitting beside her. She sat on pins. Her ears buzzed, and her skin tingled with the thrill of his nearness. Her shoulders were pinched with cramps from holding still, hardly breathing, yet she kept her gaze trained on the computer screen.

"There he is, there he is!" Pia said, and everyone's murmured conversations died as they all leaned in to the monitor. Paulo nudged the volume up a bit more.

On the screen, Jacopo stood rigidly at his podium, gripping a sheaf of papers in front of him, eyes downcast. After saluting the Speaker of the house and its members, he began his speech.

"*I doubt you will pity me, though I am pitiable. But I ask you to listen to my explanation and request. After today, if you wish me to resign my position, I will do so graciously.*"

In the chamber, a confused murmur rose up among the MPs like a wave.

"*Detailed* documentazione *have been distributed to every member, and to the press, and I trust you will all take an opportunity to familiarize yourselves with them.*

This latest series of events, in all honesty, was not my doing."

Jacopo placed a palm against his chest, and Clio flinched as Guillermo's hand came down on top of hers, gripping it tightly. She gasped, held her breath again, waiting. But he kept it there. With difficulty, Clio forced herself to pay attention to Jacopo, studying his polished, confident manner. What he was doing was very hard, but he was stronger than she'd thought. More like Guillermo than her first impression of him.

Jacopo continued talking... "*–found out about it after my esteemed colleague, Senior Brunello and the press already knew.*" There was a soft roar. He held up a hand. "*Hear me out. I understand that seems implausible. I find it all rather hard to believe myself.*

As you know, my family's legacy is long and honorable. And through the generations, my ancestors have attempted–"

"We have to talk," Guillermo whispered.

She glanced at him at last, to find him staring at her intently, his blue eyes shining in the dim light. "Now? But–"

"Now. Come." He rose and tugged gently on her hand, and they slipped quietly out the door to the hallway.

"We should be listening."

He nodded but continued to the adjacent green salon, where they could speak without being heard. "The outcome will not be altered by our listening. But much else is at stake."

She peered closely at him. His eyes shone with... tears?

Guillermo grabbed her other hand, and raised them both to his lips, pressing a kiss against her knuckles. "*Bella.*"

"What is it?"

"I'm so sorry. You were right. I should have listened to you."

"About?"

"The directorship. I know I have to do it."

She shook her head. "You can't do it if... if it makes you unhappy. I understand that."

"I could do it. There is a way I could–"

"Hey, you two. Come back. You have to hear this." Bibi leaned out of the den door and hissed at them, beckoning. "*Vieni!*"

Their eyes met and Clio burned with intense questions. With a sigh Guillermo led them back to their seats.

∼

Guillermo listened to his brother's speech with only half his mind. He had to tell Clio how he felt before the opportunity was lost. He took her hand.

"—expect us to continue on as before, providing focus and consequence to their towns and villages.

This responsibility pertains primarily to the ownership and stewardship of our historic properties. And while these are a legacy of our great privilege, they also have always been and continue to be a legacy of our great responsibilities—"

Guillermo turned to Clio and leaned in, pressing his lips close to her silky hair. "I'm excited about it. About the directorship. This is what I'm meant to do. You said it yourself. This is a challenge that I must face."

Clio's eyes darted toward him, and then back at the screen.

"—deeply regretful for these mistakes—"

He persisted. "Even if this doesn't work tonight, I'm willing to do what I need to do to keep the villa. I'll become a farmer if I need to. Take tenants. Whatever."

That brought her piercing gaze back to his face, her brows pinched together. "Are you serious?"

"Perfectly. Clio, *Bella*. There's just one thing that I need."

"Shhhh," came several voices from the room.

"I'm proud of you, Guillermo," she whispered, barely audible.

He swallowed the lump that formed in his throat. Jacopo's speech was important, but he had to make Clio understand how much he needed her. She couldn't leave here without knowing how much his happiness depended upon her.

"—this government, on behalf of our citizens, for whom I work. I hold this post as a continuation of the role that my ancestors played as leaders and caretakers of the people, our culture and the land. And I take this role very seriously.

Last year's unfortunate events in my personal affairs are, ironically, not unconnected with my role. I will speak freely, since I no longer have any secrets from you. In the first instance, in an attempt to save the very villa—"

Clio leaned closer, whispering against his ear, her breath raising gooseflesh on his neck. "I'm not going to take the job in Ohio."

What?

"I've fallen out with my parents."

His attention shifted fully to her, their eyes meeting. *What happened?* He couldn't ask now with Jacopo building his argument. He squeezed her hand.

"*–offer for sale the historic estate that I and my family hold so dear, and that last year I was attempting to hold onto. I believed it was necessary, and that it was concluded, and that my family supported this decision. This, you can imagine, has caused members of my immediate family great heartache. I cannot begin to express the heartache it has caused me personally.*" Jacopo's chin wobbled. He paused, dipped his head, and pressed his thumb and fingers into the corners of his eyes, pinching the bridge of his nose.

The room was silent. Her throat thickened with tears, and she peeked at Guillermo. He stared at the screen, his jaw tight. His hand came up to smooth his brow, and he cleared his throat.

Drawing an audible breath, Jacopo continued.

"What's he saying?" Clio asked. "Is he withdrawing our ap–"

"Sh. Just wait."

"*Without my knowledge, difficult as that may be to believe, members of my family have been working on a plan to save our villa, to keep it, not just for our family, but for all Tuscans, for all Italians, for all the citizens of the world who treasure its history and legacy. It is these recent efforts that Minister Brunello has discovered, and exposed as yet another example of my alleged* corruzione *and lack of respect for our laws.*"

He paused. "*Nothing could be further from the truth.*"

"*This I lay at your feet. My brother, the esteemed and talented Florentine architect, Guillermo d' Aldobrandin, along with my sisters and the assistance of an expert in Renaissance art, have put together a scheme to–*"

Clio gasped.

Guillermo's warm hand came over hers again. "This is it."

"Is he referring to me?"

"Yes, that's you." He squeezed. "Without you, Clio, none of this would be happening. The villa would be sold and lost forever." Guillermo lifted a hand and pushed back her hair, caressing the back of her neck with his fingertips. She shivered, her mouth opening slightly, and he laid his arm across the back of her chair, gently rubbing her shoulder. His touch filled her with warmth, and her heart fluttered and filled like a balloon, lifting her, giving her a glimmer of hope.

Clio listened to Jacopo explain their scheme to parliament, but Guillermo's warm fingers on her skin, the familiar scent of him, drew her focus away.

"–and preservation of Renaissance art and architecture. As are the wishes of the people, the programs and funds are available to make this possible, and are open to anyone who qualifies, and cares to do the work and apply. It's a complicated business, as the documentazione before you attests. At least as complicated as running the estate and farm were several hundred years ago. They have been working without my knowledge to –"

"These are your ideas, *Bella*. This is your work."

"No. I only made suggestions. You are the one–"

"I could not have done this without you. I cannot– Clio, I can't do this without you. I want you to stay–"

Clio turned to him, a tingling sensation racing across her skin like a brush fire. He wanted her to stay?

She drew in a breath and held it, her chest tight as a drum from the pressure, the need to shout and laugh. Guillermo *wanted* her to stay. He needed her help. "I have decided to stay in Italy, Guillermo. To work here."

"Work where?"

"I am going to apply for the position of academic director, if I can. I already spoke to Dr. Bensen today. He seemed agreeable–"

"How? What about your thesis?"

"I completed it."

"You did it?" He pulled her closer, squeezing her. Then he planted a kiss on her cheek. "Beautiful. My clever Clio."

She nodded, smiling.

"*Mio Dio, Bella.* What about the defense?"

"It's all good. Dr. Jovi has arranged it."

"We will work together," Guillermo said, his voice breathy. "Of course you will get the job. You are perfect for it."

The room had gone silent, and so was the parliamentary chamber on the screen. He squeezed her shoulder again and turned to watch. Praying silently, she listened to Jacopo's closing statement.

"–humbled by their efforts. Had I been as creative, as diligent and as committed as they have been, perhaps I would have thought to do something like this years ago, using the tools that rested in my hands, instead of my feeble and failed attempts at raising funds through business investments. It does a greater honor to my family legacy, and to the office that I hold, and I am ashamed I did not think of it myself. I am so very proud of them.

Now, however, their ambitious plans are at risk because of my behavior in the past."

Jacopo slowly shook his head. "*It doesn't seem right or fair. But it is no longer in my power to judge. I give this power to you. I ask you, individually and collectively, to review the materials in their application, and to vote according to your conscience, in favor of or opposed to the heritage designation for my family villa and estate, affectionately and appropriately known as Villa Cielo Incantato, which will enable the establishment of this foundation and academic institute.*"

Jacopo stood silently for a full minute, casting his gaze around the chamber, undoubtedly catching the eye of various colleagues who knew him well, either friend or foe. Then he sat down.

The chamber erupted into a thunder of muffled shouts and murmured conversations. The cameras captured heads bent and turned this way and that as the members conferred with each other.

Despite the hope that soared in Clio's chest, she couldn't go on without understanding. She wouldn't wait to find out that Guillermo meant that he *only* wanted to work together, and have her heart break like a fool. Better to be sure, so she could go into it with a strong spine, and her head held high.

CHAPTER 33

"Memmo?"

He turned to her. "*Si, Bella?*"

Clio bit her lip, casting her eyes down, plucking at the pleats of her skirt. Her voice trembled. "I want you to understand…"

He dipped his head closer to hear her better.

"There's no need for us to go back to… the way we were. It's alright. I understand if–"

Her quiet voice couldn't compete with the sudden hubbub in the room. Everyone talked at once. Pia, Bibi, Paulo, milled about restlessly, hugging. Pia sobbed, and Paulo wrapped her in his arms. Valentina cried softly, too, as she approached Guillermo. He sighed, apologizing to Clio with a glance, and turned toward Valentina, soothing her, patting and rubbing her back. She drifted away at last to speak to the others.

"I'm sorry, Bella. What are you saying?"

"I… I just want to work together, to do the things we planned. That we both care about. I'll be okay if–

"*Bella.*" She had it all wrong.

Her chin trembled, and she drew her lips between her teeth.

"You misunderstand me, Clio. I meant what I said. *Sei tutto per me.* I can't do it without you. I can't do anything without you anymore. *Senza di te la vita non ha più senso, Bella.*"

She peered up at him, her eyes widened in understanding, shining with tears.

Could she doubt his intentions? "Let me be perfectly clear. I want us to work together, *si*, you directing the institute, me the foundation. But... *Bella*, I want more than that. Even if Jacopo fails, I want us..." He gestured between them. "I want us to be together. I need you, *cara*."

He pulled her close, feathering kisses over her face, burying his face into the crook of her neck. "*Per favore.*"

She nodded, her hair brushing against his face, and made a small sobbing sound.

"Does that mean yes?"

She nodded again, and he pulled back to look at her, flushed now with a rosy hue, a wide smile stretching her face. "*Si*. That's what I want. What I was afraid to want." Tears coursed down her cheeks, and her eyes shone with happiness.

He laughed and threw his arms around her, held her tightly and lifted her off the ground. "*Ti amo! Ti amo, mi cara.*"

He lowered his mouth to hers, and her lips parted and met his in a kiss that answered all his dreams. He swore on the grave of his parents to keep her and protect her, to nurture her brilliance and love her till the day he died. No matter what happened. She was his. He fell into their kiss, home at last.

A loud cheer broke out among his family, and he pulled back, embarrassed. This conversation should have occurred somewhere more private. They parted and looked up, giggling, but no one was looking at them. Everyone else stared at the monitor, their arms in the air or hugging each other, as the cheering continued.

What? The vote came in so quickly? They had won?

The cheer in the room drowned out the dull roar of cheering and thumping applause that echoed through the parliamentary chamber, even louder than the roar of blood in his ears. Most of the MPs were standing. They were giving Jacopo a standing ovation. Unbelievable! A few angry members jostled and it even looked like a skirmish would break out, but they were pulled apart.

They had won!

~

To celebrate, everyone ate a late meal together, Clio seated close beside him, his family gathered around Pia's table, laden with the delicious banquet she had prepared in advance. The family toasted Jacopo's courage and success, and all the hard work that had come, at last, to fruition. They toasted Guillermo's leadership, and Clio's vision and ingenuity. His family's knowing smiles and glowing looks told him what they thought of his reunion with Clio. They loved her, too, and that intensified his own happiness a hundredfold.

Guillermo kept a hand on her at all times, squeezing and caressing her shoulder, her thigh, touching her hair, leaning in to kiss her. She was his again. How could he bear such joy?

Could all of this be happening? It was too good to be true.

A trilling ring interrupted their festivities. He dug his cell phone out of his pocket and glared at the screen.

"Who is calling me at this hour?"

"It's after nine o'clock," Pia said.

"Maybe it's Jacopo!"

"Jacopo, Jacopo!" someone cheered.

"Shh." Guillermo hissed and rose from the table, his palm held out for silence. "*Si, si*, this is he? How can I help you?" He hurried from the room into the hall for a measure of privacy and quiet.

"*Senior d'Aldobrandin. This is Senior Belloggi, from the Banco Nationale. Your loans officer?*"

What the hell? "*Si.* Of course. *Buena sera*, Senior. How can I help you."

"Well. I'm afraid I have bad news."

His heart lurched. Everything with the bank should be fine. All they needed was the heritage designation and the numbers would work. "What is it?"

"*Unfortunately, there was some, er... I understand your brother made a speech tonight in parliament about your villa, which went in your favor?*"

"*Si*. We are very happy. Our application for heritage designation was approved."

"Uh... I don't know how to explain it. I didn't see it myself. Apparently some of the members took offense. Someone with influence. In any case, one of the departments that had approved a grant for your project has withdrawn its support. I'm terribly sorry."

"Withdrawn? Which one? How much?"

"It's the Director General of Enhancement of Cultural Heritage. Your trust is now one hundred and fifty thousand Euros short. We won't be able to approve your loan."

CHAPTER 34

Before they slept, Clio sat down with the d'Aldobrandin siblings, less Jacopo of course, for an emergency meeting. It seemed clear that someone in a position of power in the office of the Director General of Enhancement of Cultural Heritage was either a crony or a pawn of Brunello. Someone had pulled strings. And someone else had pulled out money.

There was no time to worry about it, and no opportunity to turn it around. Clio and Guillermo needed to plead their case to the bank.

In the morning, woozy after an amazing, breathtaking, passionate night of lovemaking, during which they'd shared much laughter and tears, Clio drove with Guillermo to meet Senior Belloggi at the bank. Both she and Guillermo had completed and signed the final paperwork committing to their respective roles as directors, and had gone over their pro forma once more.

Clio had wanted Pia, Bianca, and even Jacopo to come with them, to express their commitment and beg. They were all stakeholders, after all. Guillermo disagreed. In the end it was deemed a bit desperate to drag the entire family along, so they went alone. Guillermo seemed determined to try to persuade Belloggi to approve their loan anyway, on the strength of the funds that were committed, as well as their passion for the project. His enthusiasm and commitment left no doubt in her mind, or in her heart. Hopefully Belloggi agreed.

A revision to the proposal had been hastily drafted outlining a phased approach, which would give them additional time to drum up support. It would be harder, it would be tight, but they could make a case.

"*Buon giorno*, Senior Belloggi," Guillermo said, striding into the man's office. "Allow me to introduce my colleague, Signorina Clio Sinclair McBeal."

The loans officer greeted them warmly. Clio shook the man's hand, and they sat. Guillermo took the lead, since he was familiar with the banker. He seemed a gentle, jolly man, and so she remained optimistic he would be sympathetic.

Guillermo pulled a stack of papers from his briefcase and pitched their argument. Disconcertingly, Senior Belloggi sat back, his small eyes blinking rapidly, and rummaged amongst the papers on his desk. He didn't seem to be paying attention to Guillermo's words.

Not finding what he wanted Senior Belloggi opened a desk drawer and shuffled through his files there, at last pulling out a sheaf of paper.

When Guillermo paused, Senior Belloggi said, "I am very sorry for the confusion, Senior d'Aldobrandin. Seniorina Sinclair McBeal." He coughed and scratched his thinning pate. "It seems you are missing some information?"

Guillermo attempted to jump in and clarify what they were asking for, but Belloggi put up a hand to stop him.

"No, no. Please. Wait." He lifted his papers and shook them. "You are not aware of this?"

Clio squinted at him, then looked to Guillermo, who was shaking his head, obviously as confused as she was. *What is he talking about?*

"You called me last night, to tell me–" Guillermo began.

"No, no, no, no." Belloggi shook his head. "This was awaiting me when I arrived at my office this morning. You don't know what it is?"

They stared at him, confused.

Belloggi laughed. "Oh, my." He chuckled. "Oh, this is delightful. This…" He waved the papers before them, but all they could do was wait for his explanation. "This is a new donation, from… he peered at the paperwork. "From a donor by the name of Senior Cleveland R. Richmond." Belloggi's brows lifted, and he leaned forward, regarding them expectantly.

Clio frowned and glanced at Guillermo. He appeared just as baffled. They shook their heads, muttering their incomprehension.

"You were not expecting this?"

Tell us already. How much is it?

"This is a cash donation to your trust of three hundred thousand dollars. American," he added, his face splitting in a wide grin. "All I need is your signature, Senior d'Aldobrandin, and we can accept the transfer of these funds, and, *ecco!*"

Still, it didn't make sense. How could they receive a donation from a private individual that they didn't even know. "Is he the manager of some foundation we forgot about?" Clio said.

Belloggi frowned and squinted at the letter. "I don't believe so. If you like, I can telephone the agent. *Uno momento.*" Belloggi picked up his phone and dialed a number, waiting.

"Ah, *si*, hello, senior." He introduced himself and explained that he had Guillermo and Clio in his office, and they were looking for an explanation for the donation. He listened a moment, nodding, then pushed the phone receiver toward Guillermo.

He took it, scowling and put it to his ear. "*Buon giorno, Guillermo d'Aldobrandin.*" Then he listened for a moment, running a hand through his hair. "What? Wh–?" He shook his head with an incredulous expression, and burst out laughing.

A quick, light fluttering in the pit her stomach left her dizzy and shivering. What was this all about? Something good, apparently. She leaned closer, trying to catch Guillermo's eye, and tried to ask the question with her expression.

"Yes, I will. Tell him *grazie mille, grazie infinite,* from all of us. This means the world to us. You have no idea... *si.* Good bye." He handed the phone back to Belloggi, his expression stunned.

Guillermo turned to Clio, his face split with a wide grin, his eyes sparkling with laughter and joy. "That was QTip. It turns out Senior Cleveland R. Richmond is Mad Richie's real name. He has found a way to pay me for his new villa design after all."

EPILOGUE

An atmosphere of celebration filled the warm night air. His family gathered for an *al fresco* dinner on the large terrace at *Villa Cielo Incantato*. Everyone who was important to Guillermo was present: Jacopo and Valentina, who had reconciled, and their children. Pia and Paulo and their children. Bibi, Marcella and Martino. And of course, his Clio. His heart swelled with happiness, overflowed with a sense of joy and contentment.

They had plenty to celebrate.

The bank loan had been approved, the heritage designation finalized, the trust assembled and set up, the foundation established. It was a bit slower getting the *Instituto di Arte I Architetturi di Rinascimento d'Aldobrandin* going, but it was well underway. Clio had been officially hired by Cornell to run it, and the program was in development.

In any case, the first order of business was the renovation itself, which Guillermo closely supervised. First the public rooms gently restored and upgraded with new electrical and data communication systems, under a healthy new roof membrane. The first bank of guest rooms with new ensuite bathrooms for visiting faculty and students were underway. And more ambitious, a new stainless steel commercial kitchen, about which Pia and even Marcella, after some reluctance to change, were ecstatic.

Sated from their extravagant meal and ample wine, everyone sat back, satisfied smiles on their faces, quiet conversations murmured up and down the long table. The children had long ago slipped away from the table to race up and down the stairs, squealing and laughing.

He had only one note of tension to sour his stomach. One yet-to-be-determined detail that prevented him from relaxing completely. And that involved Clio. He stole a glance at her, reveling in her glowing pre-Raphaelite beauty. She wore her vibrant fiery curls down around her shoulders, and relaxed in a simple, light floral sundress that bared her golden freckled shoulders to his hungry gaze.

His groin tightened in a familiar longing. Ah, *Bella*. He smiled, feeling warmth suffuse his core, and seep outward through his limbs, like a banked fire, waiting to be stoked into life. But that was for later. Now, it was family time.

Guillermo had passed around small floor plans, showing everyone his new layout for the family suites. One wing of the second and third floor had been set aside to accommodate the family, and would be maintained as private quarters. There was a large, luxurious apartment with private sitting room, terrace and kitchen, and several bedrooms, as well as a few separate bedroom suites. This way, Guillermo, or whoever took his place as director in the future, would have a complete and comfortable residence, and other family members could continue to come and go as they wished. All this, separate from the workings of the foundation and institute.

These were accommodated in another wing, with adequate offices for Guillermo, Clio, faculty and any support staff they might hire over time. Downstairs, there were seminar and meeting rooms, with state of the art presentation technology planned.

Later, once this work was complete and operations underway,

perhaps in another year or so, work would begin on upgrades to a series of crofts and barns across the home farm, to accommodate holiday rentals.

Under the veil of excited chatter that followed his brief presentation to the family, Guillermo dipped his head close to Clio for a private word, his stomach clenching. How would she respond? He was so afraid of scaring her away with his ardor.

"Come with me a moment, *Bella*?"

Her brows pulled together gently, curious. "Hm?"

He rose, slipped his hand into hers, and pulled her away from the table. He led her under the canopy of the sheltering chestnut tree, down the staircase, between oleander and olive leaves that shimmered black and white in the moonlight, to the grotto below. The burbling sound of the fountain masked the hum of voices from the terrace above, and the foliage screened them from view, creating a bubble of privacy.

Guillermo led Clio to the edge of the fountain, where the geometric stone wall inscribed its formal edge. Light from the moon, its image fractured into jewels, danced on the surface as the stream of water fell, splashing softly. Urging her to sit, he settled beside her, their backs to the three muses at the fountain's centre, and gazed out at the darkened gardens and fields below.

"I imagine you are wondering about your own accommodations," he said.

Her shoulder rose and fell. Of course she would be curious, perhaps even worried. But she wouldn't complain, trusting him to sort it out.

"I have not forgotten you, *cara*. As institute director, you will of course want to be here at the villa most of the time. But then..." he hesitated, "...sometimes you will need to be in Firenze, for meetings and perhaps research. *Si*?"

Clio nodded. "That... seems... reasonable." She spoke tentatively, as though she anticipated some catch.

He smiled to himself in the dark. His dinner rolled over in his stomach. He swallowed through the tightness in his throat, and dragged a hand through his hair and across the back of his neck.

"I imagined that I would stay here, also, as I said before." He cleared his throat. "Em. I would live in the largest suite, of course. It would be my principal residence. But I would keep my apartment in the city. It would be necessary for me to be in town a few days a week, to keep my architectural practice going. To meet with clients. Um."

He felt her turn toward him. She set her hand on his arm, squeezing gently, and he felt the heat of her seep through his sleeve, into his skin. "What is it, Memmo? What's troubling you?"

Stronzo. He was behaving like a school boy. "Clio, I... I don't want to assume... uh. I'm asking if you would be willing, interested, in living with me. Both here, and in Firenze. We could make a home together, *Bella.*" He stole a glance at her face, uncertain.

"Guillermo. Of course I would. I love you. I want to be with you. Haven't we already talked about this?"

"*Si.* But, um." He turned to her and took both her hands in his. "I want...*Resta sempre con me!*"

Clio smiled. "We don't have to make those kinds of decisions now, Guillermo. This is already a big step for both of us. Don't feel–"

"No!" She misunderstood. She thought he was uncomfortable with their commitment, but it was the opposite. He wanted more. He wanted her to be his.

"It won't bother you, being around my large noisy family? You are not used to it. Perhaps–"

"Absolutely not. I adore your family. I always wanted a family just like yours, Guillermo. I feel almost as though your family is my family now. We have been through so much together, and we are going forward together, so invested in a common future."

"*Si!*" Guillermo filled his lungs and released a long, quivering breath. Be a man. Come on. He slowly slid down to the ground onto one knee, feeling the gravel dig into his flesh through his trouser leg. It awakened his senses, fortifying him, anchoring him.

Clio drew in a short breath, staring at him. "Memmo?"

"*Bella.*" His voice was choked, and came out as a whisper. He cleared his throat again. "I want to share more than apartments and work with you. *Con te voglio passare la mia vita.* My whole life, *cara*. I can't imagine my life without you in it. Would you, Clio, stay with me, and make a large boisterous Italian family of our own?" He drew a shuddering breath, feeling his heart beating wildly in his chest.

Above the trickle of the fountain, the murmur of conversation from the terrace above rose and fell in waves. There was a child's squeal, and a muffled shout.

Clio hadn't responded. He looked intently into her eyes, glinting with reflections of moonlight in the dimness, shining with tears.

"Stay with me here, at *Villa Cielo Incantato*, forever. Be my wife, be the mother of my children. *Con te voglio invecchiare, se Dio vuole.* With you beside me Clio I can do anything. Will you be my muse?"

He watched her smile grow wide. "*Si.* Yes, I will. *Ti amo*, Guillermo d'Aldobrandin. You are my family. You are my home."

Guillermo reached up and took her face between his hands. He pulled her closer and pressed his mouth tenderly to hers.

She pulled away, and whispered words of devotion against his lips, their breath mingling. "*Ti voglio. Il mio cuore è solo tuo.* My heart is yours alone and always." Her arms slipped around his shoulders, and her fingers threaded into his hair.

He pulled her into a tight embrace and kissed her again, hot and hard and possessive.

Suddenly there was applause and cheering. Gasping, they broke apart and looked up. His family stood on the steps peering between the shrubbery, moonlight illuminating their smiling faces. This time, there was no mistaking the reason. The family was cheering for them.

∼

Thank you for reading The Art of Enchantment. If you liked this book, please leave a review where you purchased the book! Turn the pages for a sample of A Forged Affair, next in the Life is a Journey series.

THANK YOU

WANT TO READ THE FIRST BOOK IN THE HAVING IT ALL SERIES?
BUY ON AMAZON *ASIN:* B01KP7IMUC

WANT TO CONNECT WITH ME?
www.maryannclarkescott.com
maryann@maryannclarkescott.com

If you enjoy reading this book, please rate it and leave a review on Amazon HERE. Your opinion can make or break an author's success, and it means the world to me.
Go here to leave a review: https://www.amazon.com/review/create-review/ref=cm_cr_dp_d_wr_but_top?ie=UTF8&channel=glance-detail&asin=B06XFX4B7C

Thank you as always to the Mountain Mavens, Michele, Donna & Joanna, who have supported me and championed my career, and who critiqued sections of this book when it was still a rough NaNoWriMo draft. I'd also like to acknowledge the NaNoWriMo organization and all its volunteers, for creating a supportive and fun environment that allowed me to blitz this manuscript and several others in a high energy event that helps keep me productive and creative. Thank you to Kyla who patiently beta read an early version, and provided honest and helpful feedback when I needed it most, to beta-reader Holly who cheered me on, and to the many RWA chapter contest judges who volunteered their time to comment and critique early drafts. Also, a heartfelt thanks to Deborah, a fellow RWA-GVC member who beta-read the nearly-there manuscript, pointed out the million exclamation marks (!), and taught me something so important about my writing that I was finally ready to hear. Finally, thank you to Gabrielle Prendergast for designing a beautiful cover for Clio and Guillermo's story. As always, to my family, who continue to indulge my passion– Thank you.

My apologies to Renaissance Italian history and anyone who's particular about it for any liberties taken for my story.

XO, MA

ABOUT THE AUTHOR

MaryAnn Clarke is a Chatelaine Grand Prize winner and Next Generation Indie Book Award finalist for The Art of Enchantment, first in the Life is a Journey series about young women on journeys abroad who discover themselves and fall in love while getting embroiled in someone else's problems. Her Having it All series is about professional women struggling to balance the challenge and fulfillment of their careers with their search for identity, love, family and home.

Always eager to fill blank pages and empty canvases with ideas swirling in her head, MaryAnn set out to write emotionally engaging stories that walk a tight rope between intelligent Women's Fiction and heart-warming Romance.

A polymath who studied Fine Arts, Urbanism, Architecture and Gerontology at university on both coasts of Canada, she turned to her first love, writing stories, when she realized she could have more fun with fewer rules to follow as an author, than working in an office as an architect, or in a university as a researcher. When not writing, she meditates while hiking wooded mountain trails, does yoga and Pilates to fend off decrepitude, reads eclectically, contemplates wormholes, experiments with painting abstract expressionism, kills plants and tries not to burn dinner while solving her next plot problem. Now that her chick has flown the coop, Clarke lives on beautiful Vancouver Island, Canada with her husband and cats. Although she knows she lives in Paradise, she still loves traveling the world in search of romance, art, good food and new story ideas.

You can read more about MaryAnn, her books and ideas that strike her fancy at www.maryannclarkescott.com. Join her mailing list to receive a free novel. You'll get instant access to cover releases, chapter previews, bonus content and exclusive offers!

WANT TO READ THE FIRST BOOK IN THE HAVING IT ALL SERIES?
BUY IT TODAY : books2read.com/beminethistime

WANT TO CONNECT WITH ME?
www.maryannclarkescott.com
maryann@maryannclarkescott.com

If you enjoy reading this book, please rate it and leave a review on Amazon HERE. Your opinion can make or break an author's success, and it means the world to me.
Go here to leave a review: https://www.amazon.com/review/create-review/ref=cm_cr_dp_d_wr_but_top?ie=UTF8&channel=glance-detail&asin=B06XFX4B7C

Subscribe & Follow MACS!
www.maryannclarkescott.com
Question? Fan mail? Sure, you can reach me here.

ALSO BY MARYANN CLARKE

To read a sneak preview of Book 2 in the Life is a Journey series, turn the page…

A FORGED AFFAIR SNEAK PREVIEW

As Niki Ballantyne had told herself many time before, risk was something to manage, not fear.

She squatted on the wooden platform, firmly gripping the zipline handle in her gloved hands, hoping for a moment of exhilaration. High in the tall pine forest of Aquitaine, in the south of France, she waited for the all-clear signal from Paul, *Parc-en-Ciel*'s owner, before launching.

Paul's assistant Aziz, an agile youth with skin the same rich blue-brown tone as the bark of the pine trees where they perched like tree sprites, mumbled in French and touched his headset. "All set, Niki?" His English wasn't half bad, though strongly accented with his native Moroccan French. Anything was better than her broken French, they'd quickly learned.

Lifting her face, she filled her lungs with the fresh tangy air of the evergreen forest. Not quite as majestic as her own North Shore Mountains in British Columbia, it was still a cool refreshing break from the hot sun and dust of the winding country roads she'd been cycling this past month.

She sought out *Parc-en-Ciel* because she'd heard about the

extreme zipline runs, but it had taken a bit of convincing to persuade Paul that she was up to it. It was the extreme height, speed and relative risk, however, that she found appealing.

Once Paul had seen her search and rescue credentials, and her IRATA rope access certification, and she'd signed the release of liability waiver, she was finally good to go. She could ride and climb and jump circles around most people, but her petite build and girlish features threw them off. She nodded, winking, and pushed the play button on her iPod, releasing a blast of EDM into her earbuds. "You bet, Aziz."

He grinned, his white teeth flashing brilliantly against his skin. "*Trois, deux, un, ALLEZ!*"

She gripped the rope tighter and leapt from the platform into the trees, shutting her eyes and drawing cool forest air through her teeth for the first few moments, feeling the breeze whipping against her face and throat. Her pulse quickened as her speed built, the canopy of green whizzing by in a fifty-five kilometer per hour blur, the high-pitched whine of the hardware hummed in her ears as much as into her hands and arms.

Part of the risk involved stopping unassisted at two intermediate platforms high in the trees and re-hooking her gear from one line to the next. In the two-and-a-half minutes or so that it took her to reach the final platform, she had time to acknowledge that, however invigorating a good zipline run was, the cheap thrills were wearing thin. It fell far below her threshold for true excitement.

As the ride came to an end, she prepared for her landing. She twisted her body to align with Paul, who braced himself to catch her. Landing with the agility of a flying squirrel, she laughed and gave Paul a kiss on the cheek as he unhooked her harness from the line, and then from her body.

"*Merci* buckets, *mon ami*." Laughing, she let the harness drop to the platform and spun away from Paul, crouching and springing off the edge of the deck into a double back flip, landing on the soft thick layer of needles at its base.

"*Mon Dieu!*" Paul's voice echoed through the forest. "Niki! You could have killed yourself!"

She cussed in French and faced him, grinning, craning her neck to look up the fifteen feet or so to where he crouched and peered down at her. "Admit it. You're impressed."

His wry expression told her she'd done it again.

"What?"

"'Shit of the bull?' You can't keep translating English expressions literally."

She shrugged. "You knew what I meant, right?"

Paul shook is head. "I told you no monkey business on my gear, you crazy girl," he said.

She laughed. "I thought you were in the monkey business."

"It's a good thing you have ten times the training that I do."

"I'm not on your gear anymore, Paul. I'm on Mother Earth and she gave me a nice soft landing, thank you. And anyway, if you'd fainted you know I'd revive you."

"You give me hives. Cure that!" He liked to put on a grumpy face, but she knew he was teasing.

Aziz drifted to a stop beside her on his ATV with a spray of dirt and pine needles. Paul snorted and scampered down the ladder to her side. "That's it. No more rides for you. You're trouble." Belying his stern words, his grin stretched wide.

Aziz did a poor job of hiding his amusement, too.

"S'okay, Paul. I gotta go anyway." She'd already spent the better part of the day climbing and riding all over Parc-en-Ciel with these guys. She threw her arms around each of them in a quick hug and hoisted her pack onto her shoulders. "Hey, can you tell me the closest village where I can find a bed tonight?"

Paul made a face. "Le Village de Petit Bergeron is a few kilometres to the West, but I don't think you'll find a vacant room. The Medieval Festival starts tonight."

"Thanks, guys. That's where I'm headed then. See you!" she shouted as she leapt onto her bike and careened down the path toward the road, waving with one hand.

"*Adieu* Niki!" called Aziz.

"Good riddance!" she heard Paul tease as she pumped hard on her pedals, riding into the low rays of late afternoon sun. The further west she got, the sooner she'd be home.

She missed the sense of purpose, urgency and involvement that her usual rope access and search and rescue work both provided. The challenge and unpredictability of dealing with real high elevation rope work, and especially HETS rescues, were the only thing that made her feel truly alive, and could drive the darkest thoughts from her head. Both chief, who'd started all this, and her boss, would be happy that she was well-rested, at least. Thankfully she was almost at the end of this enforced break, and would fly home from Bordeaux in another couple of weeks.

"*Alors.* We'll see you around six for dinner then?" Charles, who had just arrived home from his workday in Toulouse, turned away to pull his briefcase from the trunk of his Renault and slammed it shut.

"*Oui,*" Luc, astride his bike, replied. "I'll ride into town, help with a bit more set up and meet you after I change." He hesitated, not certain he wanted to raise the subject. "Adèle will make it in time?"

Charles nodded. "*Bien sûr.* She'd never miss the start of festival." His eyes narrowed as he peered closely at Luc.

"What?" He sometimes wished Charles didn't know him so well. It made his intentions so much more awkward. It was difficult enough proposing marriage to your best friend's sister, someone you'd known since childhood, and considered an old friend. Never mind that Luc and Adèle had managed to hook up these past few summers, however casually. Charles still thought that was weird. But it's what Luc had decided to do.

Charles shook his head slowly, his thoughts obvious enough. "Never mind. See you later."

"*Salut!*" Luc pushed off and rode out of the driveway and onto the narrow paved road heading toward Petit Bergeron. Charles and France's house, his home away from home, was a mere twenty-five minutes ride outside of the Beaux Village he'd visited every summer since he was twelve years old. At first, with his parents and sisters, spending a month each summer with his father's old university friend and his family, and then, as they grew up, on his own. When his own, and then Charles' parents both passed away several years back, Luc continued to come, though his sisters no longer did.

It was strange indeed to contemplate the prospect of a permanent move to France. He'd thought about it long and hard. And despite his reluctance to leave the teaching job he loved at home in Vancouver, and his sisters and their families, it's what would be necessary. Adèle owned a couple of prosperous fashion boutiques in Toulouse and Bordeaux, and he wouldn't think of asking her to give them up and move to Canada to be with him. They'd known each other here, on her *territiore*, after all, most of their lives. Anyway, he figured she'd be able to support them while he got settled and found teaching work here.

Luc had not yet told Charles of his plan. First, he needed to talk to Adèle and make sure she would actually go along with it. He felt strongly that she would. She'd made enough broad hints. But still. One needed to ask the lady first and make it official. And it's not like he needed permission or a blessing from Charles. It's only that he wasn't as sure of Charles approval as he was of Adèle's.

Though he'd never thought of Adèle as the family type, and she certainly wasn't the love of his life, she'd been unsubtle in her hints that he should settle in France. Maybe she even wanted him to be a stay-at-home father so she could carry on with the career that she loved. The French were very pragmatic about marriage.

It might not be precisely the dream of idyllic family life he so badly wanted. That he'd been dreaming of since... well since his mother, then his father had died too young, and ripped away the supportive, loving atmosphere he'd grown up with and craved so much. Both his older sisters had married and had kids, and Charles had married Frànce. They all had kids now, and were each in their own way recreating the perfect family that they'd all shared growing up. Except for Luc.

Mentally he shrugged. He loved France. He loved kids. He was a teacher, after all. As he prepared for his thirtieth birthday, he was more than ready. And he wanted a family of his own, even if it meant moving to France, leaving his job and his family, and settling down with a woman who was, in the end, merely a good friend.

The village on the mound turned out to have a steep approach, so by the time Niki pedalled partway up, to the outside edge of the ancient town walls of Petite Bergeron, she was breathing hard.

Now she understood what Paul had been saying as she left. It was like arriving in the midst of a circus or passing through a time portal. Or both. A bigger production than she'd expected, makeshift stone piers and a wooden gate and portcullis had been built from plywood and expertly painted, creating a sense of arriving in a Medieval town. Beyond the fake gate though, and the knight in full shiny tin armour being photographed with throngs of tourists, the town was real enough, and Medieval enough, that no further enhancements were needed. Colourful banners with coats of arms hung from the golden limestone buildings, and yellow and blue pennants flew, competing with the riot of red geraniums that tumbled from window boxes. Dozens, maybe hundreds, of people hiked up the steep cobbled avenue beyond the gate. A sense of building anticipation filled the air. She'd seen many French cities and towns so far this summer, but this was by far the prettiest.

She pushed on up the ramp that wrapped the village walls, following the music. Even as she'd approached the walls, she began to pass people in costumes. Now that she was entering the town, there were more people dressed in Medieval clothing than modern.

Soon, smells joined the sounds, drawing her onward and upward. Winding up a long cobbled street that bent around the walls, between the curving facades of two and three story stone houses and a wide limestone baluster overlooking the countryside below, were rows of small white tents and market stalls. She pumped her bicycle over the cobbles, past farm produce, averting her eyes from a pile of oranges gleaming under lanterns lit to enhance the sinking sun. Instead she admired small smelly cheeses and withered *saucisson sec*, as well as displays of clothing, toys, leatherwork and armour. To her left, narrow twisting cobbled streets lead uphill. A ghost image of the oranges lingered in her mind, but she pushed it away. There was no point in wishing that Sam were here, sharing this adventure with her. But he surely would have loved this Medieval fair. He always was fascinated by history, and circuses, and this felt like a marriage of the two.

Everything had been more fun with Sam. Like a perpetual child, his excitement, had fed her desire to maximize the joy he felt every day and had measurably enhanced her own experience. Despite the hard times, they'd had the best of times together. That old familiar heaviness in her chest hit her. She missed him as much now as ever, and felt a hollow sorrow every time she wished she could share something new with him, and see his sweet face light up.

The best part of doing anything with Sam was that he always had wanted to share. He always cared as much about how she felt as he did for his own pleasure. No one else had ever replaced him in this way.

She paused at the entrance to an even narrower lane that led uphill, past a few shops selling *jambon-beure* sandwiches and ice cream cones, wondering if the town square were up there somewhere. The path teemed with people, some obviously tourists, others locals who were as much a part of the spectacle as participants in it. She'd need to save enough leg strength to hike up there and see what was happening.

Winded, she nearly stopped to dismount when another cyclist surged past from behind her, shredded, cut legs driving forward, his lean butt raised from his seat, waggling in the air. Except for the padded crotch of his cycling shorts, he held no secrets. Here was a heart-stopping, beautiful specimen of manhood. And she wasn't about to cack out in view of him, so she pushed up on her own pedals and strove to keep pace.

Thankfully, in another dozen strokes he stopped and dismounted just ahead of her, so she followed suit, breathing hard, her heart pounding with the extra effort. He tugged off his helmet to reveal short dark hair mussed and spiked with perspiration, and scratched his scalp roughly with a gloved hand. She knew that feeling, how itchy her head got, after a few hours of cycling, especially in this heat.

She should have pushed her bike past him. She should at least have pretended to ignore him. Instead her eyes raked the man's lean, ropey cyclist's body, right down past his lycra-clad hard-as-rocks buttocks to his sinewy calves. This was without a doubt one of the perks of cycling, and her pulse quickened at the thought of tangling between the sheets with someone as hard and fit and energetic as she was herself, liquid heat pooling in her belly. He was a good match for her, and she was even ripe for a little dalliance after weeks on the road. Not that she got any regular action back home. But this was a holiday, after all.

His head turned in her direction, and their eyes caught. She quickly looked away, but he'd seen her checking him out, and his sexy mouth had quirked in amusement, his bright eyes flicking up and down her body in reply. Her already overheated face flushed hotter. Damn. She turned away, and angled her bike toward the narrow uphill street to escape his knowing stare.

"Are you just arriving in Petit Bergeron?" His voice was as sexy as the rest of him, his caramel-toned tenor wrapping around the French syllables like a magic spell, drawing her in.

She groaned inwardly, stopped and turned. "I'm passaging through."

He seemed taken aback. "Where're you from?" He switched to unaccented English, surprising her. There'd been no hint in his French that he wasn't a native speaker. Not that she was qualified to judge.

"Canada. You?"

"Same. Vancouver." He opened his fanny pack and pulled out an orange.

So *not* Quebec. "No shit. Me too. Small world." She rolled her eyes at the inane cliché, mentally tripping over the orange. *Don't open it. Please don't open it.* But he did. Of course he did, spoiling the moment.

A brilliant white grin split the handsome taut planes of his beard-shadowed face, and his intelligent blue eyes conveyed all kinds of naughty, flirtatious thoughts that made her stumble on the rough cobblestones beneath her feet. His teasing smile told her he could read her thoughts. Though perhaps not all of them.

She swallowed, watching his strong tanned fingers puncture the pitted skin of the orange, breaking the brittle flesh. Frost vaporized into the hot afternoon air and dissipated, carrying the strong scent of citrus to her nose. Her stomach pinched and her head felt light and buzzy.

She recoiled, averting her gaze, suddenly needing to escape. "Uh– can you tell me where the town square is?"

"The *Place des Arcades* is straight up there." A toss of his chin indicated the narrow street while he pocketed the peel from the orange and slipped a section into his mouth. He even chewed sexily.

Her throat worked, unable to swallow again, and she cleared her throat. "Why put the town square on the top of a hill? Kind of inconvenient, isn't it?"

He nodded. "That was the idea. To make it difficult for the enemy to get to. These small fortified towns were built during the Hundred Years War, close to six hundred years ago."

"You sound like a teacher."

He lifted one shoulder. "Maybe I am." He offered her a chunk of his orange.

"Hmph." She shook her head, no, and blinked at him. She wanted to enjoy a pleasant conversation in English, after a month of struggling in French, but she fidgeted, needing to move on. "Good for you."

His bark of laughter surprised her. "Do you want a hand getting your bike up the hill?"

Her smile faltered. "No. Thank you."

He pointed at her loaded bike. "But… It's no trouble."

"I've got it." She put up her hand, palm out, and moved ahead, shouldering her bike, saddle bags and all, and trudging up the steep slope, her quads burning with every step.

"Alright then. See you 'round."

She tossed one last glance over her shoulder, shaking her head and smiling at his attempted chivalry. Too bad. Delicious as he was, it was a good thing she was moving on so soon. The last thing she needed was a stupid fling with a guy from home, however tempting. She could run into him somewhere, and wouldn't that be awkward? She pushed on, feeling his sharp eyes following her

A FORGED AFFAIR SNEAK PREVIEW

progress up the hill, painfully conscious of her own lycra-wrapped butt.

~End of Sample~
Read A Forged Affair today! books2read.com/ForgedAffair

Join my VIP Readers list to stay informed about my latest releases.

www.ingramcontent.com/pod-product-compliance
Lightning Source LLC
Chambersburg PA
CBHW020514080526
44583CB00013B/598